Language and Politics

The research and teaching of language and politics has mainly been carried out in the fields of critical discourse analysis and sociolinguistics. This groundbreaking book provides a concise introduction to the field from the perspective of cross-cultural pragmatics. It introduces a strictly language-based, bottom-up and comprehensive model for analysing political data, which allows the reader to examine political and socio-political data without pre-held convictions and prejudices, avoiding many pitfalls that have lurked for a long time in the study of political language use. It is illustrated with a wealth of data and case studies drawn from many linguacultures, including Anglophone ones, China, Japan, Germany and the former Yugoslavia, and from different contexts of political language use, such as diplomacy, activism, public communication and news articles. It includes handy further reading lists, discussion points and a comprehensive glossary, making it ideal for anyone keen to know how language interacts with politics.

JULIANE HOUSE is Professor Emerita at University of Hamburg and Professor at the HUN-REN Hungarian Research Centre for Linguistics. She is also Distinguished University Professor at Hellenic American University and an Ordinary Member of Academia Europaea (M.A.E.).

DÁNIEL Z. KÁDÁR is Chair Professor at Dalian University of Foreign Languages, Research Professor at the HUN-REN Hungarian Research Centre for Linguistics, and Professor at the University of Maribor. He is Ordinary Member of Academia Europaea (M.A.E.).

Language and Politics
A Cross-cultural Pragmatic Perspective

Juliane House
*University of Hamburg/HUN-REN Hungarian Research Centre for Linguistics/
Hellenic American University*

Dániel Z. Kádár
*Dalian University of Foreign Languages/HUN-REN Hungarian Research Centre for
Linguistics/University of Maribor*

Shaftesbury Road, Cambridge CB2 8EA, United Kingdom

One Liberty Plaza, 20th Floor, New York, NY 10006, USA

477 Williamstown Road, Port Melbourne, VIC 3207, Australia

314–321, 3rd Floor, Plot 3, Splendor Forum, Jasola District Centre, New Delhi – 110025, India

103 Penang Road, #05–06/07, Visioncrest Commercial, Singapore 238467

Cambridge University Press is part of Cambridge University Press & Assessment, a department of the University of Cambridge.

We share the University's mission to contribute to society through the pursuit of education, learning and research at the highest international levels of excellence.

www.cambridge.org
Information on this title: www.cambridge.org/9781316515136

DOI: 10.1017/9781009092180

© Juliane House and Dániel Z. Kádár 2025

This publication is in copyright. Subject to statutory exception and to the provisions of relevant collective licensing agreements, no reproduction of any part may take place without the written permission of Cambridge University Press & Assessment.

When citing this work, please include a reference to the DOI 10.1017/9781009092180

First published 2025

A catalogue record for this publication is available from the British Library.

Library of Congress Cataloging-in-Publication Data
Names: House, Juliane, author. | Kádár, Dániel Z., 1979- author.
Title: Language and politics : a cross-cultural pragmatic perspective / Juliane House, Dániel Z. Kádár.
Description: New York, NY : Cambridge University Press, 2025. | Includes bibliographical references and index.
Identifiers: LCCN 2024042268 | ISBN 9781316515136 (hardback) | ISBN 9781009095129 (paperback) | ISBN 9781009092180 (ebook)
Subjects: LCSH: Communication in politics – Cross-cultural studies. | Rhetoric – Political aspects. – Cross-cultural studies. | Pragmatics – Cross-cultural studies. | Linguistic analysis (Linguistics)
Classification: LCC JA85 .H685 2025 | DDC 320.1/4– dc23/eng/20241205
LC record available at https://lccn.loc.gov/2024042268

ISBN 978-1-316-51513-6 Hardback
ISBN 978-1-009-09512-9 Paperback

Cambridge University Press & Assessment has no responsibility for the persistence or accuracy of URLs for external or third-party internet websites referred to in this publication and does not guarantee that any content on such websites is, or will remain, accurate or appropriate.

Contents

List of Figures	*page* vii
List of Tables	viii
Acknowledgements	x

1	**Introduction**	**1**
	1.1 Situating Our Approach	3
	1.2 Contents	7
	1.3 Conventions	11
	1.4 Recommended Readings	11

Part One: Methodological Issues		**13**
2	**Framework**	**15**
	2.1 Pitfalls in Language and Politics	15
	2.2 Our Approach	17
	2.3 Data Types in the Study of Language and Politics	27
	2.4 Recommended Readings	29
3	**Pitfall 1: Following an Ethnocentric View When Studying Politically Relevant Data**	**31**
	3.1 Introduction	31
	3.2 Methodological Approach	32
	3.3 Case Study	33
	3.4 Reflections	48
	3.5 Recommended Readings	48
4	**Pitfall 2: Associating Values with Political Actors and Entities at the Very Outset**	**50**
	4.1 Introduction	50
	4.2 Methodological Approach	51
	4.3 Case Study	52
	4.4 Recommended Readings	70

v

vi Contents

5 Pitfall 3: Using One's Research to Demonstrate a Pre-held Conviction   72
  5.1 Introduction   72
  5.2 Methodological Approach   73
  5.3 Case Study   74
  5.4 Reflections   89
  5.5 Recommended Readings   90

Part Two: Key Topics   93

6 Research Involving Sensitive Topics   95
  6.1 Introduction   95
  6.2 Our Case Study   98
  6.3 Recommended Readings   117

7 Communicative Strategies in News Reports   120
  7.1 Introduction   120
  7.2 Case Study   123
  7.3 Recommended Readings   130

8 Ideological Convictions and Language Use   133
  8.1 Introduction   133
  8.2 Case Study   135
  8.3 Recommended Readings   151

9 Aggression in Political Institutions   153
  9.1 Introduction   153
  9.2 Case Study   155
  9.3 Recommended Readings   172

10 Politics and Translation   175
  10.1 Introduction   175
  10.2 Case Study   177
  10.3 Recommended Readings   196

11 Conclusion   198
  11.1 Retrospect   198
  11.2 Prospect   199

References   201
Glossary   223
Index   230

Figures

2.1	Our framework	*page* 18
2.2	Our speech act typology	20
2.3	Types of discourse	23
3.1	Our analytic approach to avoiding Pitfall 1	33
4.1	Our analytic approach to avoiding Pitfall 2	52
4.2	Our speech act typology	57
4.3	Outcomes of our analysis	69
5.1	Our analytic approach to resolving Pitfall 3	74
6.1	*Der Kniefall*	113
6.2	Contrastive differences between the pragmatic dynamics of Japanese and German war apologies	116
9.1	Types of heckling	164
9.2	The camera's focus on the speaker and the heckler	165
9.3	A heckling sign for a hockey referee	169
10.1	House's system of comparative text analysis and evaluation	180
10.2	Our methodological procedure	183

Tables

3.1	Number of pre-1949 and post-1949 occurrences of *M/minzu-zhuyi* and *nationalism* in the political-speeches corpus	*page* 37
3.2	Number of occurrences of *M/minzu-zhuyi* and *nationalism* in the media corpus	37
3.3	Number of occurrences of *M/minzu-zhuyi* and *nationalism* in the political speeches and media corpora with numbers of qualifying adjectives	37
3.4	Chinese and American interviews on *minzu-zhuyi/nationalism*	46
4.1	Speech acts in our first data set	58
4.2	Allocation and realisation types of Requests in our first data set	61
4.3	Allocation of Willings in our first data set	63
4.4	Types of speech act in our second data set	65
5.1	Our corpus	79
5.2	Quantitative features of aggression realisation in Cushing's diplomatic notes	87
5.3	Quantitative features of aggression realisation in Ching's diplomatic notes	89
6.1	Apology components in the Japanese corpus	104
6.2	Apology components in the German data	110
7.1	Expressions in the case study which gain deferential meaning in the ritual context	127
8.1	Speech act sequences in the first part of our data	142
8.2	Ratio of non-aligned to aligned responses in our main corpus	149
8.3	Ratio of non-aligned to aligned responses in our ancillary corpus	150
10.1	Our corpus of media texts (Chinese texts only)	184
10.2	Annotation categories for *civilised* and their frequency in our sample of 200 examples (BNC)	185
10.3	Characteristics of the uses of *civilised* (in order of frequency)	186
10.4	Frequency and annotation categories for *wenming* in our sample of 200 examples (BCC)	187

10.5	Characteristics of the uses of *wenming* (in order of frequency)	189
10.6	Similarities and differences between the uses of *civilised* and *wenming*	190
10.7	Translations of *wenming*	191
10.8	Translations of *wenming* by Chinese translators	194

Acknowledgements

As with our previous work, the manuscript of this book came into existence as we laughed together and shouted at each other madly for very many hours, both in person and digitally. Our families kindly tolerated our crazy noises – and all the many hours we spent writing this book – and so we should express our gratitude to them before anyone else. Juliane would like to say thank you to Miriam, Wissem, Emilia, Patrick, Tessa, Eva, Mailin, Lucia and Joe, as well as Bobby, for bearing with her while she was working overly long hours with Dániel. Dániel would like to say a huge thank you to Keiko, Naoka and Zita, Eszter and András, and of course Koma, for all their patience and care. Eszter is now in heaven, together with Koma, and it was her unfailing love and wisdom which inspired and continue to inspire Dániel in his academic work. Along with Eszter, we would like to express our ongoing gratitude to Willis, Juliane's late husband, who greatly inspired our joint work. Eszter has now joined Willis in heaven, and we are sure that both of them are proud of us.

We would also like to say thank you to many colleagues who greatly supported us. In China, Emily Fengguang Liu has provided continuous support for our work, both personally and institutionally, and here we would like to express our gratitude to her. Other colleagues in China whom we would like to say thank you to include Dan Han, Yulong Song and Sen Zhang. We also owe a big thank you to our colleagues in Slovenia, at the University of Maribor, who helped us to collect and analyse data from the former Yugoslavia. These colleagues include David Hazemali, Tomaž Onič, Tadej Todorović and Katja Plemenitas. A special thank you to Tomaž for helping to organise projects, which led to obtaining amazing data for our research. We would also like to express our gratitude to those expert speakers – kept anonymous to protect their privacy – who have contributed to our research as informants.

Our big thank you goes to Helen Barton, the most caring editor one can ever wish for. Thank you, Helen, for bearing with us while we were swearing and shouting at one another when discussing our book plans with you in Brussels! We also owe a thank you to Isabelle Collins for all her support and care. We are also indebted to the five anonymous referees involved in the review process, as well as our clearance reader.

Finally, on the institutional level, we would like to acknowledge the funding we received from the National Excellence Programme, National Research Subprogramme, sponsored by the National Research, Development and Innovation Office of Hungary (TKP2021-NKTA-02), hosted by the HUN–REN Hungarian Research Centre for Linguistics.

1 Introduction

In this book, we study political language from a cross-cultural pragmatic point of view. By **political language** we mean the language use of professional politicians inside and outside institutions, mediated descriptions of political-language use such as those appearing in news articles, and the language used in sociopolitically relevant situations centring on burning issues such as the welfare of children or animals. Our definition of **politically relevant data** also includes public discourse with potential political consequences: due to the effect of social media, public discourse and political discourse cannot be neatly separated any longer, and indeed we interpret politically relevant public discourse as a form of political discourse in this book. The approach we use in this book is **strictly linguistic**. By this we mean that through studying the language of politics we are looking at politically relevant data without any previously held political conviction at the outset of our investigation. Rather, we attempt to examine politically situated data with the cold eye of the linguist.

Why is having such a strictly linguistic viewpoint crucial? The field of language and politics tends to be an emotively and ideologically loaded area, and in particular when one analyses how politicians speak it may be tempting to set out to prove, in an uncritical and moralising way, what the researcher already knows. For example, many academic articles have been devoted to controversial statements made by Donald Trump at some point in his career, in order to prove his negative effect on US American political language use. For instance, Körner et al. (2022: 631), in their study of the language used by Trump and Joe Biden, argue as follows: 'Whereas Biden emphasizes dignity, respect, and social responsibility, Trump uses derogation and celebrates egocentrism.' This claim is produced at the very beginning of Körner et al.'s work, only to be proven later, and one may indeed wonder what the merit is of proving something that one knows from the very beginning! Further, by attempting to validate a pre-held conviction through academic argumentation, one ultimately associates preconceived values with political actors, which unavoidably determines the way in which one looks at the language use of these actors. Having a strictly linguistic approach to political language use allows the analyst to leave behind – as far as possible – personal sympathies and antipathies, ideological presumptions, convictions and prejudices, which are all lurking in many accounts of language and politics. We believe that a fruitful way to do this is to adopt a bottom-up approach to language and politics anchored in the field of pragmatics.

Pragmatics is a key area in linguistics which originates in the philosophy of language. Until the 1960s, linguistics had been dominated by concerns about the way sentences are formed, as well as the truth conditions of the meaning of sentences, while the way in which linguistic structures such as sentences are used by human beings was backgrounded. The language philosopher John Austin – whose work was published posthumously in 1962 – and his student John Searle (1969; 1979) famously challenged this view, by introducing the concept of **speech act**, which is also a key concept in this book. As Austin (1962: 20) argues, 'The more we consider a statement not as a sentence (or proposition) but as an act of speech ... the more we are studying the whole thing as an act.'

Pragmatics later developed into a field in which scholars examine **contextually embedded** language use in different **units of analysis**. As we will point out in Chapter 2, the most important units of analysis in the field include **expressions**, speech acts and **discourse** (see also House and Kádár 2021b). Since, in the study of language and politics, the notion of context is of primary importance, discourse is naturally the central unit of analysis in this book. Discourse, however, often needs to be broken down into replicable components, particularly when we take a contrastive view of discourse (see more below), and so we prefer treating discourse as inseparable from the other two units – expressions and speech acts.

From the perspective of language and politics, the salient features of pragmatics are the following:

1 *Linguistic anchor.* Pragmatics operates ideally with linguistically based concepts and methodologies, reflecting an endeavour to avoid using cultural and psychological concepts, such as 'values', 'attitudes' and 'identity'.
2 *Bottom-up approach.* Pragmatics, as we interpret it in the present book, follows a typically Popperian bottom-up view of language use. The philosopher Karl Popper argued that in any respectable empirical research one should aim to *disprove* rather than *confirm* one's hypothesis.
3 *Pursuit of replicability.* In pragmatic analysis one is advised to exclude idiosyncratic behaviour from the scope of one's inquiry, considering that one can only capture and contrast conventionalised patterns of language use by looking at replicable pragmatic patterns. This focus on conventionalised language use can be best done through the empirical study of **corpora**. Corpora encompass collections of machine-readable oral or written texts of varying size and nature.

4 *Geographical, social and temporal variation and/or more than one language.* It is also recommended to take a contrastive view of the analyst's data because such a view allows the analyst to distance himself from his object of analysis and put political language use in perspective.

We discussed the foundations outlined above of pragmatic research first in House and Kádár (2021b), arguing that the pragmatic approach we are proposing here represents contrastive **cross-cultural pragmatics**. In this book, we will attempt to overview *methodological issues* and *key topics* in language and politics by relying on the four features of pragmatics outlined above.

1.1   Situating Our Approach

Let us discuss previous accounts of language and politics here, in order to position the present book. John Joseph (2006) provided a broad overview of the field of language and politics, describing many key issues well beyond the realm of politics in a narrower sense, such as the relationship between 'linguistic correctness' and social politics. Joseph's broad interpretation also motivated us: for example, following Joseph, in this book we venture beyond the study of language use of professional politicians. Similarly, in his now classic study, Geis (1987) provided a broad overview of the relationship between language and politics, describing issues such as the use of tense and aspect in mediated political speeches. Geis's study also influenced our thinking because he draws attention to the importance of foregrounding language rather than other phenomena such as culture in the study of politics. This is a fundamental point also in this book. Another important source for our work is the now widely used textbook of Beard (2000), who overviewed the main issues of analysing English political data, providing insight into many phenomena, such as how various political actors take stances in interaction. Similar to Beard, we have an interest in a wide variety of linguistic phenomena. Finally, Chilton (2004) offered a thought-provoking overview of language and politics, describing language use in various political arenas, such as parliamentary interaction. Similarly to Chilton, in this book we also feature a variety of politically relevant contexts.

To the best of our knowledge, no book has taken a strictly language-anchored and contrastive cross-cultural pragmatic view of language and politics. By a contrastive cross-cultural pragmatic view, we mean different but potentially interrelated analytic procedures:

1 *Using multilingual data.* In attempting to study language and politics from a pragmatic angle, we prioritise data from different linguacultures. An advantage of such a multilingual and cross-cultural approach is that it allows us to avoid relying on **ethnocentric** views, and also helps us to relativise our own analytic stances. While we do not think that any of the aforementioned

books are actually ethnocentric, they mainly used English as their data, and we believe that it is more productive at present to study language and politics by focusing on other linguacultures as well, such as Chinese, and comparing them with anglophone data. An advantage of this approach is that it helps us to avoid certain pre-held assumptions which seem to be unavoidable if one uses English as one's exclusive data source. For example, in Chapter 8 of this book, we will demonstrate that many politically relevant notions are difficult to translate; nevertheless their English version is often used in academic research as the 'gold standard'. This practice is clearly misleading because it tends to lead to the irretrievable loss of finer nuances of the linguaculturally embedded meanings and uses of such notions. Further, we will argue in Chapter 2 that ethnocentrism manifests itself not only in foregrounding certain languages and the terminological repertoire expressed in these languages, but also by exoticising certain political linguacultures. Such exoticisation is very common in inquiries which pit 'Eastern' and 'Western' political linguacultures against one another in a dichotomic way. For example, Bull (2017) compared the language use of US, British and Japanese politicians, arguing that speakers from anglophone countries are from 'individualistic' cultures, while the Japanese represent a 'collectivistic' culture. According to Bull, this cultural background automatically influences the pragmatic behaviour of politicians belonging to different national groups. We decidedly distance ourselves from such an essentialist view: we intend to pursue a more linguaculturally diverse approach to language and politics without ever exoticising our data.

2 *Approaching political language in comparison with 'ordinary' language use.* We will also consider how the language of politics *differs* from the way in which social members who are not professional politicians communicate in settings outside politics. For example, we will examine how political convictions change the language of arguments in politically relevant settings in comparison to arguments in 'ordinary-life' scenarios.

3 *Comparing the language of politicians in different participation roles.* It is rewarding to consider how the phenomenon of **participation framework** (Goffman 1981) influences the ways in which politicians speak, by comparing their language use in different participation roles. For instance, when a political actor is speaking in his institutionally **ratified role**, he is in a very different position from cases where he takes up the role of an animator; that is, 'the talking machine, the body engaged in acoustic activity' (Goffman 1981: 144). We will compare realisations of language use produced in such different roles with one another. For example, Chapter 4 of this book features a case study in which participants in a **political negotiation** – where they were essentially powerless – report to other politicians on the outcomes of the previous negotiation during a debriefing. It is fruitful to compare the

language use of these politicians during and after the negotiation because such a comparison allows us to capture issues such as how the lack of power in diplomacy manifests itself in the pragmatic behaviour of the politicians involved.

Apart from these contrastive viewpoints, we believe that it is also rewarding to engage in other forms of contrasting because any comparative viewpoint helps us to move one step towards having a more objective view on politically relevant data.

The pragmatic approach to language and politics that we propose here is different from **critical discourse analytic (CDA)** inquiries, in particular the area of political discourse analysis (PDA) in CDA (see e.g. Dunmire 2012; Fairclough and Fairclough 2012). PDA represents a body of CDA-grounded research which deals especially with the reproduction of political power, power abuse or domination through political discourse. In this book, we will use CDA as a collective term for both CDA and PDA inquiries. Our approach is different from CDA for the following reasons.

A particular agenda of CDA has been critiquing 'the dominant discourses and genres that effect inequalities, injustices and oppression in contemporary society' (Van Leeuwen 2009: 278). Further, as Meyer (2001: 15) argued,

The assumptions of CDA [are] that all discourses are historical and can therefore be only understood with reference to their context. In accordance with this CDA refers to such extralinguistic factors as culture, society, and ideology. In any case, the notion of context is crucial for CDA, since this explicitly includes social-psychological, political and ideological components and thereby postulates an interdisciplinary procedure.

Although pragmatics and CDA have various commonalities when it comes to the study of political language use (see e.g. Blommaert and Verschueren 1991; Wodak 2007), unlike CDA scholars, in this book we do not pursue an underlying agenda to identify social injustices. Rather, our aim is to stick to the subject of language use and its relation to politics, without considering social woes and attempting to resolve them in any way. In line with Joseph (2006: 130), we do not intend to criticise CDA in this book, particularly not on the basis of the fact that 'CDA has its own strong political commitments, i.e. it does not provide any "objective" analysis of texts, but a politically interested analysis.' As Joseph rightly states, a politically motivated analytic focus by itself does not necessarily invalidate the power of CDA analysis. Rather, in our opinion, pragmatics provides an important conceptual and methodological *alternative* for mainstream CDA, in particular if pragmatic analysis is conducted in a strictly language-anchored and bottom-up way, as promoted in this book. As we will point out in various parts of the present book, CDA and our pragmatics-anchored framework have many common interests, with the main difference between these two approaches being that we radically foreground language over any other phenomenon. This practice of foregrounding language over social injustices allows us to look at politically relevant data from an alternative angle. For example, when it comes to a particular social injustice, we will concentrate on patterns through which this injustice is talked into being and whether these patterns are recurrent in other linguacultures as well, instead of considering whether linguistic pragmatics can help resolve this injustice.

Let us consider, for example, ideology. As CDA experts like Van Dijk (1998) and Krzyżanowski and Tucker (2018) point out, language is a carrier of political ideologies. An important goal of CDA analysis is to uncover and challenge hidden political ideologies which negatively influence the lives of certain members of societies. True, in our methodological framework, we also consider how ideology can be pinned down from a pragmatic point of view. However, where we substantially differ from CDA is that we have little interest in ideology per se as a phenomenon to be unmasked and challenged. Rather, we try to unmask exactly how ideology gives rise to ethnocentric views of language and politics, and also how ideology manifests itself in political language use through the expression of individual convictions in actual politically relevant interactions. Thus, even if we do not agree with an ideology, for us it is simply a factor which needs to be taken into account in order to understand why and how language use is realised in a particular politically relevant context. CDA scholars like Krzyżanowski and Tucker (2018), on the other hand, are more interested in how language builds up and conserves ideologies.

Another important difference between CDA and cross-cultural pragmatics as we interpret these fields is the following: while many CDA scholars pursue their analysis with the agenda of contributing to the cause of the political left, we believe that this is somewhat problematic in pragmatic research, particularly in cross-cultural pragmatics. Aligning cross-cultural research with any side of the political palette would only compromise our strictly bottom-up view of language use. To illustrate this difference between CDA and our own framework, let us cite here a section from the work of the renowned CDA scholar Norman Fairclough (2003: 26–27), who described the politically relevant notion of 'political correctness' in his study as follows:

There is clearly a need for a better theoretical understanding of the 'PC' [political correctness] controversy on, broadly, the left. Discourse analysts and sociolinguists can contribute through researching and theorizing the 'PC' controversy, and seeking ways to bring their perspectives into the political debates. What is missing on the left is a general understanding of the significance and nature of cultural and linguistic interventions in the transformations of contemporary social life. We need a balanced view of the importance of language in social change and politics, which avoids a linguistic vanguardism as well as dismissing questions about language as trivial, and an incorporation of a politics of language within political strategies and tactics.

Clearly, Fairclough, like many CDA experts, is interested here in contributing to the cause of left-wing politics – this is why he talks about the problem that a more appropriate use of 'political correctness' 'is missing on the left'. While no scholar of language and politics might be entirely free from political predispositions, in this book we try to distance ourselves from any predisposition.

Finally, as already mentioned above, we aim to keep our analysis strictly linguistic. This is another key difference from CDA research which is conventionally multidisciplinary due to its extralinguistic interest. As Dunmire (2012: 735) argues,

PDA comprises inter- and multi-disciplinary research that focuses on the linguistic and discursive dimensions of political text and talk and on the political nature of discursive practice. This research is interdisciplinary in that it recognizes that discourse analysis can not operate solely within a linguistic and discursive framework and must draw upon methods, frameworks, and contents of other disciplines to adequately analyze its object of study. It is multidisciplinary in that it brings together multiple disciplines to investigate socio-political issues and phenomena pertinent to various areas of scholarship.

While in the cross-cultural pragmatic study of language and politics we also need to draw on the outcome of research on areas such as diplomacy studies, as far as methodology is concerned our analysis is strictly anchored in language-based approaches.

What we propose in this book is not unheard of in pragmatics: a number of scholars have approached language and politics from a clearly pragmatic point of view outside the CDA paradigm (see e.g. Obeng 1997; Ilie 2003; Ihalainen 2006; Bull et al. 2020). However, we believe that there is a need for a book-sized pragmatics-anchored framework to be devoted to language and politics. While Chilton and Schäffner (2002), Fetzer and Lauerbach (2007), Fetzer (2013) and other scholars edited volumes dedicated to the pragmatics of language and politics, these edited volumes naturally did not follow a single coherent framework.

1.2 Contents

In the following, we summarise the contents of the present book.

Part One presents our methodology and illustrates its use by discussing how it helps us to avoid several frequent pitfalls in the study of language and politics. In Chapter 2 we first discuss what we regard as three major pitfalls in the field: (1) following an ethnocentric view of one's data, (2) uncritically associating values with political actors and entities and (3) using one's research to prove a pre-held conviction. We argue that these analytic traps are interrelated and reflect a typically **top-down** view of political language use. Second, we discuss the three key pragmatic units of expressions, speech acts and discourse in detail. In studying political language use with the aid of these units, it is recommended to look at conventional pragmatic patterns, which allow us to conduct replicable analyses. Further, we argue that political language use can be effectively interpreted if we look at its **ritual** manifestations. Ritualised political language use imposes a **frame** on the participants; that is, in many political contexts the rights and obligations of the participants are preset and language tends to be generally used according to such rights and obligations. We finally discuss how our analytic units can be brought together with a contrastive view of language and politics.

In Chapters 3, 4 and 5 we discuss what we believe are the major pitfall types in the field. Furthermore, in each chapter we use case studies both to illustrate these pitfalls and to show how they can be overcome. In these case studies, we focus on various units of analysis: in our first case study we consider the use of politically relevant expressions, whereas in the other two case studies we break down discourse into speech acts. Furthermore, in each case study we engage in a contrastive procedure using different data. The second and third case studies will also illustrate how and why the concept of ritual frame becomes important in the study of language and politics. We will point out that many aspects of political interaction, such as diplomatic language use in our third case study, can be best interpreted if one considers the ritual rights and obligations influencing the behaviour of the participants.

First, in Chapter 3 we discuss the pitfall of following an ethnocentric view in the study of politically relevant data. We argue that it is not fruitful either to associate a particular positive or negative value with a particular country or area, or to attribute a political notion or an actor with a positive or negative value. Here we critically consider the universal validity of notions such as 'egalitarianism' and 'nationalism', which may appear at first as clearly positive or negative and as such non-controversial from a Western viewpoint. We will refer to cases in which members of non-Western linguacultures conventionally interpret these notions differently from how they are conventionally seen in the West and how they are often used in academic inquiries in a seemingly 'neutral' way. We argue that it is ethnocentric to dismiss linguaculturally embedded standard interpretations of such notions as 'undemocratic', 'unenlightened' and 'autocratic' because, through such a dismissive attitude, one is led to automatically associate a particular positive or negative value with a specific country or area.

Second, in Chapter 4 we discuss the pitfall of associating positive and negative values with political actors, including both individuals such as Trump or Biden, and political entities such as the US and the EU. In our view, such an association is problematic and dangerous because it precludes approaching language and politics in a more neutral way. As a case study, we analyse the transcript of an unofficial tape recording in which representatives of the EU – an entity which is often regarded as a democratic organisation – attempted to prevent the newly established Slovenian and Croatian states from declaring independence following plebiscites in the 1990s. We use strictly linguistic evidence to illustrate the rather undemocratic procedure through which representatives of the EU – who were supposed to be the upholders of democracy – aggressively persuaded Slovenians and Croatians to temporally suspend declaring independence, hence opposing the results of valid plebiscites.

Finally, in Chapter 5 we present the pitfall of using one's research to prove a pre-held conviction. As a case study, we present a historical diplomatic correspondence between representatives of China and the US at the time of colonialism. We argue that it is not productive to attempt to demonstrate how evil colonialism was, which is a frequent research goal in spite of the fact that the devastating nature of colonialism is an accepted truth. Rather, we believe that it is more productive to look at exactly how the coloniser used language in order to coerce representatives of the colonised country to fulfil their exploitative demands.

Part Two of the book discusses key topics in the pragmatic study of language and politics. In Chapter 6 we turn to the difficulty of studying sensitive data. In studying politically relevant issues, one may unavoidably encounter phenomena which are sensitive to talk about because they are painful for many. We point out that such data can be best studied if we distance ourselves from the object of our inquiry, by taking a contrastive look at our data. As a case study, we examine political apologies realised after the Second World War by representatives of the Japanese and German states, following war crimes perpetrated by their respective countries. Japanese and German war apologies are highly controversial and have often been described with sweeping overgeneralisations. We believe that it is important to venture beyond such overgeneralisations, and examine in a bottom-up contrastive way exactly how representatives of these countries realised their apologies.

In Chapter 7 we discuss how mediated political monologues can be optimally studied from a pragmatic point of view. Considering that news and other forms of media often present political events, it is important to investigate them in the field of language and politics, and for the pragmatician a key issue is how to tease out the interactional dynamics of such monologues, hence making them pragmatically relevant. We believe that it is particularly important to consider how such monologues gain an interactional effect with members of the public because gaining such an interactional effect is the very goal of these monologues. Thus we focus on textual features through which a monologue covertly interconnects the readers with politicians and political entities. Here we will rely on the concept of alignment, proposed by the renowned sociologist

Erving Goffman (1981). We will argue that many seemingly 'innocent' phenomena in political monologues aim to trigger the alignment of the public with politicians or political entities represented by the monologue. As a case study, we examine a corpus of political monologues published in Chinese newspapers in the wake of a national crisis. Following our cross-cultural pragmatic contrastive view, we will compare political monologues of various types in order to tease out the interactional dynamics through which they trigger the alignment of their readers.

In Chapter 8, we consider how sociopolitical ideological convictions impact on how social members, such as political activists, use language outside political institutions. Due to the global popularity of social media, such non-institutionalised language use is becoming important and needs to be studied on a par with institutionalised political language use. Jonathan Haidt (2012) insightfully argued that sociopolitical ideologies manifested through political conviction divide social members worldwide, and we believe that it is an important task for the pragmatician to capture this global dividing effect with the aid of strictly linguistic evidence. We examine a clash, featured in social media, between a radical animal rights protester and the organisers of a children's party. We show that the organisers of the party and the protester put moral oughts representing sociopolitical ideological convictions against one another in an irreconcilable way. Due to this irreconcilability, their interactions completely lack alignment with one another. In this case study, we also follow a contrastive view, considering how clashes driven by sociopolitical convictions differ from more 'mundane' clashes.

In Chapter 9 we look at how one can capture the interactional dynamics of seemingly confusing cases of aggression in mediated political settings. In mediated scenes of politics, conflict may evolve in a seemingly ad hoc way, and in order to be able to analyse such settings it is necessary to linguistically analyse exactly what is happening in them. As a case study, we present a corpus of heckling incidents, including cases such as when the former US first lady Michelle Obama was heckled in public. We argue that the disorderly manifestations of **heckling** incidents can be categorised into major types, imposing different ritual frames on the public speaker being heckled. Following this view, our analysis shows that heckling represents a standard situation in which the participants actually follow conventional forms of behaviour.

In Chapter 10 we revisit the problem that certain politically relevant, culturally embedded notions are very difficult, if not impossible, to translate. A key issue that such a difficulty of translating causes is the following. Often, when we talk about a politically relevant issue in two linguacultures by using English as an academic lingua franca, we may be comparing apples with pears. Such a comparison leads to the previously mentioned problem of ethnocentrism, and so it is important to consider how to resolve it by merging research on language and politics with translation studies. As a case study, we examine the problem of translating the sociopolitically relevant Chinese expression *wenming* ('civilised') into English. Following House's (2024) translation framework, we argue that untranslatability can be overcome by her notion of 'cultural filtering'.

In Chapter 11 we summarise the contents of the book and propose vistas for future inquiries. This conclusion is followed by a glossary, which provides a summary of technical terms used in this book for early-career readers.

1.3   Conventions

The present volume addresses both advanced scholars and students. For the benefit of this latter audience, the book has the following textbook features. Firstly, all chapters include a section of recommended readings, consisting of excerpts drawn from sources representing key research in the area discussed in the given chapter. Second, as the present chapter has already illustrated, we highlight keywords in bold. All the keywords are included in the glossary. Third, whenever we present a transcript of an interaction, we use simple, reader-friendly transcription conventions.

We freely alternate male and female references in this book. After we introduce our typology of speech acts in Chapter 2, we indicate speech acts in capital (e.g. 'Apologise' instead of 'apology'). We also capitalise broader speech act categories (e.g. 'Informative').

1.4   Recommended Readings

Paul Chilton. 2004. *Analysing Political Discourse: Theory and Practice.* London: Routledge.

Chilton's book is one of the best-known summaries of language and politics, which we highly recommend to our readers. In the section quoted below, Chilton discusses speech acts, which play a central role in our book:

Only in and through language can one issue commands and threats, ask questions, make offers and promises – provided one has convinced one's interlocutors that one has the requisite resources to make the speech act credible. And only through language tied into social and political institutions can one declare war, declare guilty or not guilty, prorogue parliaments, or raise or lower taxes. Speech acts have been treated by 'ordinary language' philosophers and some pragmaticists within linguistics as a largely technical problem. It is clear, however, that the non-logical parts of meaning-making cannot be easily separated from social and political interaction, its conventions and institutions ...

Classical speech act theory as proposed by Austin (1962) and developed by Searle (1969) sought to make generalisations about the conditions under which speech acts would 'fire' or 'misfire', or 'come off' or not, be 'felicitous' or not ... Without pursuing all possible avenues of explication and critique here, it is relevant to note two points that apply to many if not all speech acts, particularly when viewed within a social and political perspective. First, several of these 'felicity conditions' depend on assumptions about the utterer's intentions and abilities, and about the wants of the recipient. Second, viewing these matters within a political framework, as distinct from the decontextualised framework of ordinary language philosophy, it is impossible to avoid far-reaching questions about the political notion of credibility, the notion of utilities or wants and the notion of power and distribution of resources. (Chilton 2004: 30–31)

Patricia L. Dunmire. 2012. Political discourse analysis: Exploring the language of politics and the politics of language. *Language and Linguistics Compass* 6(11): 735–751. https://doi.org.10.1002/lnc3.365.

In the present chapter, we have outlined how our pragmatic approach relates to CDA and PDA. Readers with interest in a concise overview of these areas are advised to consult the work of Dunmire. In the following excerpt, Dunmire outlines the relationship between CDA and PDA:

The critical study of political discourse closely aligns with the discourse analytic approach of CDA. Aligning PDA and CDA assumes that political discourse is (and ought to be) carried out through a critical lens and that CDA is, at its core, a political endeavor. In his argument for a 'more critical reading of the label' PDA, van Dijk ... contends that this domain of research should be understood as encompassing the analysis of political discourse and a political approach to discourse analysis. Moreover, he insists that to be 'studied most interestingly', political discourse analysts should assume a critical vantage. This 'critical-political discourse analysis' examines the means by which 'political power, power abuse or domination' manifest in and are enacted through discourse structures and practices.

Depending on how inclusively or exclusively one defines political discourse, most CDA research could be characterized as PDA or only that which focuses specifically on the discourse of formal political institutions and actors would be so considered. I adopt an inclusive definition of political discourse which recognizes both the key role language plays in struggles over power, meaning, and material resources and in acts of cooperation and resistance and the political nature of discursive practice ... Furthermore, I adopt Luke's ... characterization of CDA as an 'explicitly political inquiry into social, economic, and cultural power'.

Fairclough ... and van Dijk ... offer the earliest articulations of CDA. Fairclough urged discourse analysts to attend to the broader macro-level social and political conditions that give rise to micro-level interactions and behaviors. Such critical analysis, he argued, should focus on the distribution and exercise of power in social institutions and social formations. Moreover, 'critical discourse analysis' should examine and clarify the means by which ideology is naturalized ... through discursive practices and structures and, relatedly, should make more apparent the social determination and effects of discourse typically invisible to discourse participants. (Dunmire 2012: 738–739, references elided)

Part One

Methodological Issues

2 Framework

In this chapter, we present our analytic framework. First, we describe what can be regarded as the three major pitfalls in the field of language and politics. Second, we present our methodology, through which these pitfalls can be avoided. In this methodology we approach politically relevant data by contrastively examining language use in different units of analysis. We also point out that it is important to focus on conventionalised and ritual aspects of political language use. Finally, we discuss issues surrounding data types in the field.

2.1 Pitfalls in Language and Politics

As noted in Chapter 1, in language and politics we advise that the following three pitfalls be avoided:
- Pitfall 1: Following an ethnocentric view in the study of one's data.
- Pitfall 2: Uncritically associating values with political actors and entities.
- Pitfall 3: Using one's research to demonstrate a pre-held conviction.

Such pitfalls often occur together. To illustrate this tendency, let us consider the following extract from an article of the political-discourse analyst Shi-Xu (2012: 168):

> The discourse of Asian, African and Latin American and their diasporic peoples are characterised by a shared past and present of colonialism, cold war and imperialism since at least the 19th century, in which they were (and continue to be) dominated, exploited and excluded from social, political, economic, scientific and various other spheres. Under these historical circumstances, the Eastern communities face common problems and challenges and have their similar concerns and aspirations ... Very importantly, but far too often ignored or misunderstood, Eastern cultures have their own norms and values, in terms of age, kinship, gender, the state, etc., for human life in general and linguistic communication in particular. For instance, some Eastern societies take humane and communal consciousness and harmony with others and with nature to be the highest principle of conduct and communication, in contrast to Western values of individual reason and control.

This quote starts from an ethnocentric view (Pitfall 1) and it sets out to prove a claim which the author accepts as valid at the outset, confirming the author's conviction (Pitfall 3): the author argues that 'Eastern communities' and 'Eastern cultures' are different from their 'Western' counterparts and associates the behaviour of these major social groups with ideological notions such as 'shared past and present of colonialism'. The quote also pursues a clear ideological agenda, which is to be proven by the arguments. It would be just one more step for the author to associate certain 'Eastern' and 'Western' values with political actors (Pitfall 2), even though this particular pitfall does not occur in the above quote. We believe that the reason why these pitfalls tend to occur in accounts like Shi-Xu's (2012) is that they follow a typically top-down train of thought in the study of language and politics.

The problem with such top-down approaches becomes clear as soon as we consider their accuracy. For example, in Shi-Xu's argument above one is faced with the following fundamental problems:

1. Individuals are treated as cultural robots with no independent agency. For example, Shi-Xu (2012) subordinates individual behaviour to values such as 'harmony' and 'individual reason', which are overgeneralising and **orientalist** (for an overview see Said 1978). When using overgeneralising notions such as 'harmony', it may be impossible to take a neutral view on the language use of an 'Eastern' political decision maker as a strong and individual actor because any of her utterances may ultimately be associated with deep-seated overgeneralising cultural values.

2. Notions such as 'Eastern' and 'Western' cultures are difficult to apply (see Mills and Kádár 2011; House and Kádár 2021b) in any serious linguistic analysis of political language use. Clearly, both the pragmatic conventions and political systems of so-called 'Eastern and Western cultures' often significantly vary within such macro-groups, and many linguists, such as Leech (2007) in his renowned work, have pointed out that the infamous 'East–West dichotomy' cannot be rigorously applied in pragmatic analysis. For example, the value of 'harmony' – which is attributed to 'Eastern' political cultures in the account of Shi-Xu (2012) – has long been associated with various East Asian countries, including Japan (e.g. Ide 1989; Hirata and Warschauer 2014). Such an association is, however, problematic because, unlike countries such as China and Korea, Japan has never been a victim of 'colonialism' and other ills mentioned in the text above.

3. The argument that so-called 'Eastern cultures' are 'too often ignored or misunderstood' raises two fundamental problems. First, these cultures are all but understudied: disciplines such as Sinology, Japanology and so on have several centuries of history, and so any expert in Asian studies may rightly argue that the above claim conveniently ignores a huge body of existent academic inquiries. Asian studies cannot be dismissed as 'Western' or 'colonialist', even though early East Asian studies indeed had a colonialist element (e.g. Gu 2012): China, Japan and other East Asian

countries are now at the forefront of East Asian studies! Second, the argument that East Asian languages and cultures are somehow 'misunderstood' not only is exoticising, but also shuts the door on the contrastive study of data drawn from these linguacultures (House and Kádár 2021b).

It is tempting to dismiss accounts like Shi-Xu's (2012) as too vague and non-linguistic in scope for the linguist to consider in the study of politically relevant data. However, such top-down views have had a significant influence on the linguistic study of political discourse. For example, Shi-Xu's account cited above represents an entire area which is called **cultural discourse analysis** (e.g. Carbaugh 2007), where politically relevant data are often discussed in such culturally biased top-down ways. Similar overgeneralisations of language and politics also occur in other areas. For instance, pragmaticians like Laszlo (2013), Ledoux and Bull (2017) and Rahmani (2022) applied overgeneralising concepts like 'collectivism' in their work, while scholars of political communication such as Richey (2009), Wang and Chen (2010) and Kim and Kwak (2022) described how generalising concepts like 'hierarchy' influence the behaviour of entire political linguacultures. The following extract from Richey (2009: 137) illustrates this point:

Chiefly, cultures that emphasize subservience to social superiors may have deleterious effects on the goal of bringing about increased political comprehension through informal discussion. Obedience to hierarchical superiors will limit one's ability to engage in open, frank discussions that increase political knowledge. Considering the impact of cultural norms on unstructured informal discussion, we must scrutinize whether political discussion can help people make wise decisions.

Further, in the subsequent chapters we will show that many such arguments – which denigrate 'Eastern' politicians and other actors as 'collectivist' – are orientalist in nature. We will also point out that the pitfall types outlined in this chapter are lurking in many forms in the study of language and politics, well beyond linguacultural overgeneralisations.

2.2   Our Approach

As we argued in Chapter 1, our framework operates with the four features of *linguistic anchor*, *bottom-up* approach to language use, pursuit of *replicability* and a *contrastive view* underlying any analysis. 'Linguistic anchor' refers to a terminological and conceptual choice. Simply put, in this book we attempt to use an exclusively pragmatic inventory of concepts. For example, the reader might have noted that at various points we have used the term **'linguaculture'** instead of 'culture' because we are interested in culturally embedded language use, rather than (national) cultures per se. As regards our bottom-up view, as we argued in Chapter 1, we follow Karl Popper's experimental paradigm (see also Edmondson and House 2011 for an overview).

18   Language and Politics

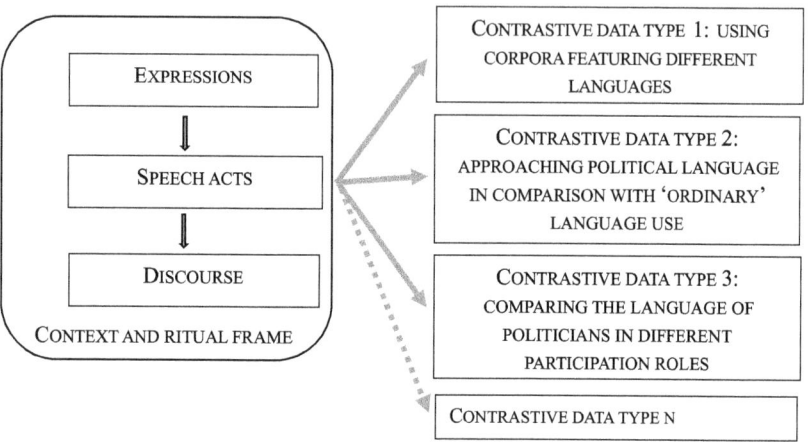

Figure 2.1 Our framework

Unlike our linguistic anchor and bottom-up approach, replicability and a contrastive view need to be discussed in more detail as part of our framework. Figure 2.1 summarises the essential elements of our framework.

Our pragmatic approach departs from the tenet that, in order to analyse politically relevant data in a rigorous and replicable way, it is necessary to look at and compare such data with the aid of different units of analysis. In our view, the most important units of analysis include the three categories of expressions, speech acts and discourse. The right-hand side of Figure 2.1 features types of contrastive cross-cultural pragmatic data, which influence the way in which we look at our units of analysis in the study of political language use.

2.2.1   Expressions

Expressions in the pragmatic study of language and politics include lexical items which are politically relevant, such as 'nationalism' and 'democracy', as well as expressions which become important in a particular political context, such as ones through which speech acts like apology are realised in political interaction.[1] A related category of politically relevant expressions includes political metaphors, which have been widely studied in the field

---

[1] Such expressions were defined as 'illocutionary force indicating devices' (IFIDs) in Blum-Kulka et al. (1989). In this book, we do not use this term because we look not only at the speech act-indicating function of pragmatically important expressions, but also at the way in which they indicate the broader ritual frame in which a politically relevant interaction unfolds.

(e.g. Lakoff 1995; Fauconnier and Turner 2008; Musolff 2021). In our model, the phenomenon of 'expression' also covers conventionalised multi-word sequences. Many such expressions indicate a specific speech act or an interactional move. In the realm of language and politics, many expressions are **formulaic**, with strongly conventionalised pragmatic use (see Coulmas 1979). Such expressions often indicate the participants' awareness of the broader ritual frame holding for a particular political situation. Because of this, in House and Kádár (2021a) we defined them as **'ritual frame indicating expressions' (RFIEs)**. For example, as Bull et al. (2020) pointed out, the expression 'Mr Speaker' addressed towards the Speaker of the House in the British Parliament indicates awareness of ritual rights and obligations in a situation in which a politician can only make an attack on another Member of the House by addressing the Speaker of the House (see more in Chapter 9).

Among the expression types outlined above, the study of the category of politically relevant expressions such as 'nationalism' can be particularly challenging. This is because, in the study of such expressions, one or more of the pitfalls outlined above are prone to influence one's analysis. For example, in her study of the notion of 'Bulgarian-ness', Sotirova (2021) used an East–West dichotomy-like analysis to study issues such as why 'Bulgarian-ness' triggers negative emotions like anger and frustration. A key problem with an analysis like Sotirova's relates to the previously mentioned issue that the outcome of the analysis is decided before the analysis itself is conducted: while Sotirova uses interesting data to prove her point, her study ignores the possibility that, for many individuals, the politically relevant notion of 'Bulgarian-ness' may actually be positive.

2.2.2 Speech Acts

When it comes to the study of speech acts in politically relevant data, we rely on a finite and minimalist speech act typology (Edmondson and House 1981; Edmondson et al. 2023), illustrated by Figure 2.2.

Having a finite typology of speech acts allows us to rigorously analyse and compare speech acts through which politicians and other actors in politics interact with one another. It also allows us to capture the interactional patterns and broader pragmatic conventions holding for any pragmatically relevant situation under investigation. Further, in written political language use, the above typology also allows us to break down written messages into speech acts. An advantage of a finite speech act typology like the present one is that it precludes inventing 'political speech acts' *ad libitum* (see more below). Another key advantage of relying on such a finite system of speech acts is that it also allows us to break down discourse into components.

20 Language and Politics

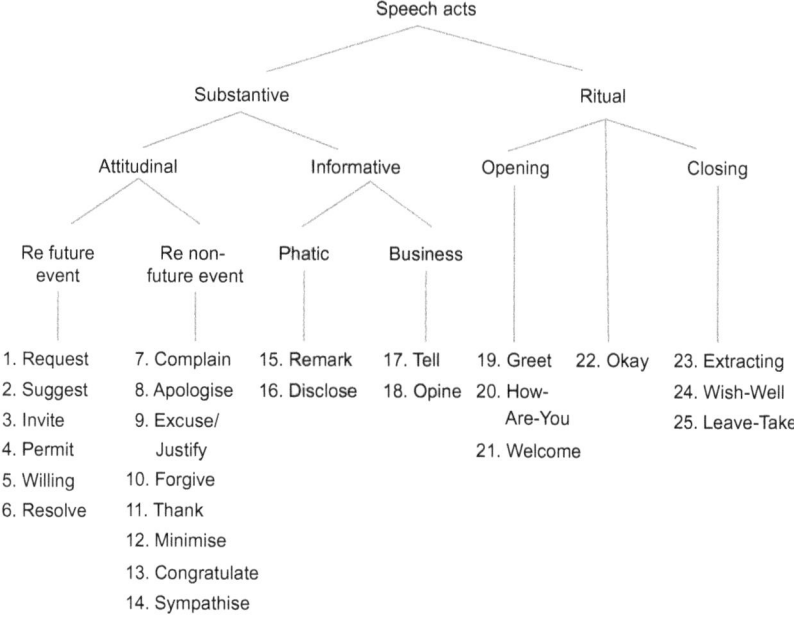

Figure 2.2 Our speech act typology
Source: Edmondson and House 1981; Edmondson et al. 2023

Ever since Austin and Searle, the idea that speech act categories need to be finite has been present in pragmatics (Habermas 1979; Vanderveken 1990; Kissine 2013; Levinson 2017). The idea of finiteness precludes 'discovering' new and context-specific speech acts, such as 'the speech act of persuasion' in politics (e.g. Natsheh and Atawneh 2021), and the more general notion of so-called 'political speech acts' (see e.g. Hepple 2003; Bolsover 2018). Operating with speech act categories embedded in the realm of politics shuts the door on the replicability of our research (see House and Kádár 2021b). For example, while scholars like Saito (2015) distinguished the speech act of 'political apology', we believe that applying such a category is not useful because it precludes studying Apologise realisations in the political arena on a par with other apologies – a train of thought which we will elaborate in Chapter 6.

The speech acts we propose are such simple and basic constituents of linguistic behaviour that they can easily be replicated in the study of interaction across languages and data types (see a detailed discussion in House and Kádár 2023). In annotating our data in terms of speech acts, we rely on the standard speech act–analytic procedure of inter-rater coding.

Framework

Following our bottom-up approach, we naturally do not assume that a particular political phenomenon is realised by one particular speech act. For example, in Chapter 4 we examine the political ritual of diplomatic mediation. While one could assume that – in the context of a diplomatic conflict which requires the involvement of a mediator – future-related Attitudinal speech acts like Request are frequented, we do not set out to investigate such an assumption. Instead of zeroing in on any speech act, we first examine frequent speech acts in our data and then interpret the outcomes of the analysis. When it comes to quantifying our data in speech act analyses, we annotate our corpus or corpora manually.

In the study of speech acts in freely co-constructed interaction, like in Chapter 8 where we analyse ideologically loaded clashes in public spaces, we break down interaction into moves and examine how speech acts in moves relate to one another, as **Initiating, Satisfying, Countering** and **Contra-ing** moves (see Edmondson 1981).[2] 'Initiating' refers to speech acts through which an exchange is started; 'Satisfying' includes speech acts through which an Initiating speech act is satisfied; 'Countering' points to speech acts through which an initiation is countered – that is, objected to but not entirely rejected; whereas if an utterance is turned down entirely it would be 'contra-ed' in our terminology. Let us explain how these categories can be operationalised with a simple example. In a politically relevant conflict like a clash between a protester and a public figure, a speech act through which a morally loaded verbal attack is initiated by the protester may be either 'contra-ed' with another speech act, or responded in an unrelated manner, which we will define as the lack of alignment below. In such a case, the responding speech act operates as a 're-Initiation'.

With the aid of our interactionally interpreted set of minimal speech act categories, which are formulated on the basis of corpus-based interaction projects (see Edmondson et al. 2023), we are able to distinguish interactional moves from speech acts. For example, we do not interpret 'refusal' as a speech act because we combine speech acts with interactional moves like 'counter', and so we are able to break down more complex interactional phenomena such as refusal into speech acts through which a Countering or Contra-ing move is realised.

Using our typology implies that, for us, speech acts represent utterance-level phenomena which do not span different turns in face-to-face interaction. Further, in written or scripted data such as the case of Apologise in political settings (see Chapter 6), we break down the phenomena under investigation into different speech acts.

---

[2] We hyphenate 'contra' as 'contra-ed' and 'contra-ing' because this is not a term which appears in dictionaries as a verb.

An advantage of defining speech acts on the utterance level and approaching discourse by examining the relationship between speech acts is that this procedure allows us also to examine how an interactional goal is achieved through speech acts in subsequent moves. For example, in Vladimirou et al. (2021) we examined a social protest on Twitter through the lens of realisations of speech acts, in particular Complain. Examining the relationship between speech acts in Tweets allowed us to consider how the interactional behaviour of complaining escalated as the participants in the protest reflected on others' Complains in their own Complain realisations.

As noted in Chapter 1, in the present book we capitalise all speech acts; for example, we use 'Apologise' instead of 'apology'. When we talk about an interactional phenomenon like 'complaining' (versus the speech act Complain) we do not use capitals.

2.2.3 Discourse

Discourse is the highest unit in our analytic framework. The importance of discourse in the study of language and politics relates to the fact that our ultimate goal is to understand political language use as a discourse process, and we often apply smaller units of analysis like speech acts and expressions to break down this process into replicable components. Our definition of discourse is linguistic; that is, we interpret discourse as a unit larger than a sentence or an utterance. This is different from how 'discourse' is used in social theory and in many CDA inquiries, in which discourses – often in the plural – describe social engagement and language use unified by a certain goal or set of characteristics (e.g. Wodak 2011). As Jaworski and Coupland (1999: 6) argue,

> If we ask what is the purpose of doing discourse analysis, the answer from critical discourse analysts would go well beyond the description of language in use. Discourse analysis offers a means of exposing or deconstructing the social practices which constitute 'social structure' and what we might call the conventional meaning structures of social life.

Following the renowned debate between Widdowson (1995) and Fairclough (1996), we do not argue that discourse is simply synonymous with 'text' because it is a product of interaction often involving a complex participation framework in language and politics. For us, discourse is therefore a unit of analysis which can be best studied if we break it down into contextually embedded components and first analyse the contextually embedded use of these components, and then consider whether such uses reflect broader pragmatic conventions or not. It is also possible to have a systematic look at discourse by categorising context and role types in a corpus of discourse data (see e.g. Chapter 9).

It is also necessary here to consider **types of discourse** through which one can reflect on the nature of a politically relevant data type under investigation. Figure 2.3 overviews our system of types of discourse.

Discourse in pragmatics always interrelates with a specific medium. In language and politics, medium is particularly relevant to the way in which a message is formulated. As an example, let us here refer to Tweets, which have played a significant role in recent political events worldwide (see, among many others, Breeze 2020; Scott 2021). Furthermore, many key topics in the field of language and politics – which are to be covered in Part Two of this book – need to be considered through the medium of discourse (see the right-hand side of Figure 2.3). A particular issue which one is advised always to consider is whether a piece of political data is spontaneous or not. '[–marked]' in Figure 2.3 refers to the fact that spoken data are non-premeditated due to their real-time synchronous nature, whereas '[+marked]' indicates that many types of asynchronous written interaction are premeditated. The line pointing from 'spoken' to '[+marked]' shows that some types of spoken data, such as institutional ritual interaction, often lack ad hoc character, at least to some degree, and are of a premeditated nature. Computer-mediated communication (CMC) represents an 'in-between' category, as some types of CMC are of a synchronous nature whereas others are of an asynchronous nature (an excellent overview is Susan Herring's work, e.g. the edited volume Herring 1996). As studies such as Smith et al. (2013) have shown, the (a)synchronous nature of politically relevant data has a significant influence on the dynamics of such data. What we define as 'examples' in Figure 2.3 represents discourse types.

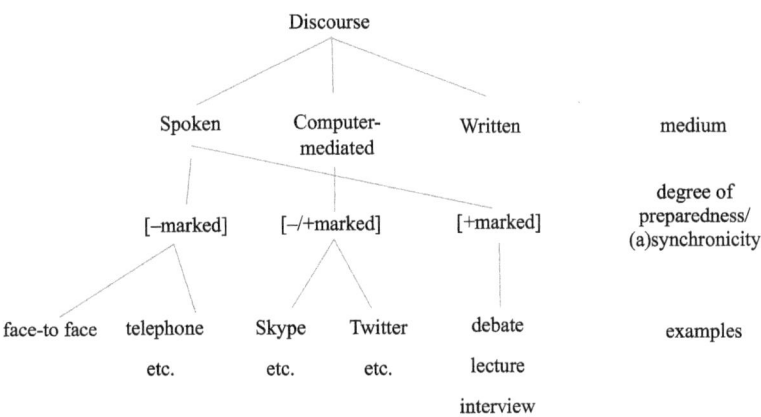

Figure 2.3 Types of discourse
Source: taken from House 1986: 179

As we have shown thus far, Figure 2.3 presents a basic typology of discourse types based on the pragmatic dynamics of the (a)synchronous nature and the related degree of premeditatedness of a data type. Another distinction we need to consider when it comes to the study of discourse in language and politics is whether a particular instance of discourse is created by a single producer or multiple producers (multiple producers of a single-source discourse like an anonymous news item may be invisible). This is different from the standard terminology in various areas of the humanities and social sciences like literature where a frequently used binary pair through which types of discourse are analysed is 'dialogue' and 'monologue' (see also studies like Musolff 2011 in the field of language and politics). We propose to use another terminology, to align with the strictly linguistic scope of our inquiry, namely **single-source and multiple-source discourse**. As House (1986: 179, 180, references elided) argues,

Multiple-source discourse arises whenever more than one participant is overtly involved in purposefully creating linguistic structures, and single-source is a type of discourse where there is only one participant overtly involved. Compare the following diagram:

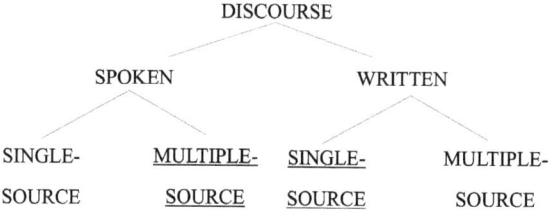

... As has been stressed by Sinclair ... and Widdowson ... written discourse is, in fact, more closely related to spoken discourse than has traditionally been assumed, and both single-source spoken and single-source written discourse may be considered to be derived from the primary mode of communication: multiple-source spoken discourse, in which meanings are negotiated by a constant shift of perspectives in the on-going interaction.

In using the three analytic units outlined above, it is important to bear in mind what we have already emphasised: *they are distinct but always interrelated*. For example, as already noted, in order to analyse discourse from both qualitative and quantitative points of view, it is preferable for the pragmatician to break manifestations of discourse down into expressions and speech acts, and also to consider expressions through which, for example, the broader ritual frame of an institutionalised political interaction is indicated. Expressions often indicate speech acts as well, they are discursively embedded, and they also have an intrinsic relationship with the context of the interaction. Finally, speech acts are never 'stand-alone' or isolated phenomena: similar to expressions, they are discursively embedded, and they are often realised through conventionalised formulae.

2.2.4 Context

As Figure 2.1 shows, we interpret our units of analysis in **context**, which often imposes a ritual frame onto the participants in the realm of language and politics.

In the tradition of pragmatics, conceptualisations of context have played such an important role that the very definition of pragmatics is often bound up with the notion of context. Thus Stalnaker (1999: 43) writes, 'Syntax studies sentences, semantics studies propositions. Pragmatics is the study of linguistic acts and the contexts in which they are performed.' And we might even say, with Levinson (1983: 32), that pragmatics is 'a theory of language understanding that takes context into account'. The underlying assumption here is that in order to arrive at an adequate theory of the relation between linguistic units and what they express, one must consider the context in which these units are realised. In pragmatics, attention is given to how the interaction of context and content can be represented, and how the linguistic realisations used relate to context. The relationship between content and context is, however, never a one-way street: content expressed also influences context; that is, linguistic actions influence the context in which they are performed. The effects of this dependency are omnipresent and decisive for the construction and recovery of meaning. But context also plays a role in the overall organisation of language, affecting its syntactic, semantic, lexical and phonological structure to the point that, as Ochs (1979: 5) puts it, 'we could say that a universal design feature of language is that it is context-sensitive'. Any pragmatic framework of language and politics, then, needs to include a general representation of contextual features that determine the values of our pragmatic units, with context being represented by a body of information presumed to be available to the participants in the interactional situation.

Studying context in the realm of language and politics implies that the researcher needs to consider as much information about the historical events and the participants as possible. For example, in Chapter 5 we examine a corpus of colonial-era documents. For us, these documents represent the unit of discourse, and in order to analyse their contents by breaking them down to sequences of speech acts, we consider as much contextual information as possible, including information on the participants, the diplomatic event which brought these documents alive, and so on. Such information not only helps us to consider patterns of language use in our data, but also allows us to draw inferences regarding the replicable pragmatic features of our results, for example by considering how the pragmatic patterns emerging from our data represent the aggressive language use of the coloniser. We do not, however, assume at the very outset that the data we study constitute a particular historically embedded genre or discourse(s). This latter approach is preferred in CDA, in particular in its discourse-historical approach (for a summary see Reisigl and Wodak 2001). The discourse-historical approach argues that a text always belongs to something much broader, and this broader phenomenon defines the features of discourse(s) in an intertextual and interdiscursive way. As Flowerdew (2018: 166, original emphasis) argues,

A particular type of contextual relation that has received a lot of attention in . . . [CDA] is that of intertextuality . . . the process whereby textual features of one text reappear in another. This means that an individual text may not be analysed without considering other prior texts with which it may relate . . . Fairclough (1992) breaks intertextuality down into *manifest* intertextuality and *constitutive* intertextuality: the former refers to overt uses of citation, quotation and paraphrase, while the latter refers to generic features that do not leave an obvious trace . . . Constitutive intertextuality is sometimes referred to as *interdiscursivity.*

Studying **intertextuality** and interdiscursivity allows the CDA scholar to capture broader social discourses, which influence the formation of a particular text. For instance, Flowerdew (2018) illustrates the use of context by interpreting particular features of a data set he studies through abstract intertextual and interdiscursive notions, such as 'Western conceptions of democracy' (Flowerdew 2018: 172). However, in a language-anchored pragmatic investigation like ours it is problematic to interpret features of a particular data set through a pre-existing extratextual notion like 'Western conceptions of democracy' without conducting a data-driven contrastive analysis of relevant discourse corpora. Intertextuality therefore may only be used in our analysis if it evidently emerges from individual discourse units in our corpus, while we do not consider interdiscursivity at all because it assumes that an inquiry operates with corpus-external phenomena. Context in our pragmatic framework therefore only includes historical information relating to the particular interaction under investigation, which helps us to interpret what is said in our data in the here and now.

2.2.5 Ritual Frame

Along with context, the frame in Figure 2.1 also includes the notion 'ritual frame'. 'Ritual frame' refers to the fact that many instances of political language use, in particular institutionalised ones, are ritual in nature (see more in Chapter 9). Following Goffman (1967) and Kádár's (2017; 2024) pragmatic adaptation of Goffman's view, we argue that political language tends to represent a form of interaction ritual where pragmatic conventions follow underlying rights and obligations, indicate an invisible ritual frame, are often ostensible in nature and embody a **moral order**. Furthermore, political language use is also ritual in a more ceremonial sense in settings such as parliaments, where ritual in the very literal sense of the word is frequent. The more institutionalised a political interaction is, the more visible the ritual frame becomes; for example, in a televised presidential debate the pragmatic rights and obligations of the participants are regulated by rules and by a mediator who can enforce such rules. While in less institutionalised political settings the ritual rights and obligations are not set in stone, and political actors often have means to follow strategic agendas, any form of strategic behaviour often needs to be hidden under a veneer of ritual conventions (see e.g. Chapter 5).

Unlike intertextuality and interdiscursivity, the features of a ritual frame cannot be taken for granted but should rather be examined in a bottom-up way across data types. Let us take diplomatic mediation as an example, which is to be studied in Chapter 4. While we assume that a frame is in place in diplomatic mediatory situations right at the outset of our research, we have no way to know how it actually influences discursive behaviour before conducting a bottom-up examination of our data.

The term 'frame', which we use in the context of the ritual nature of political language use, is also frequently used in linguistics, as witnessed by high-impact cognitive research such as Schank and Abelson (1977), Tannen (1979), Fillmore (1982), Barsalou (1992), Chafe (1994), Bednarek (2005) and so on. What distinguishes our use of the term 'ritual frame' from other interpretations of 'frame' is our predominantly bottom-up focus, which traces a path from linguaculturally embedded units of analysis to the underlying cognitive frame. This path is rarely discussed outside pragmatic inquiries. Using the concept of frame implies that we look at conventionalised and ritual aspects of language use and we exclude idiosyncratic behaviour from the scope of our analysis.

2.2.6 *The Right-Hand Side of Figure 2.1*

In Figure 2.1, the right-hand side includes contrastive approaches (see also Chapter 1). As already noted, these contrastive views are rooted in cross-cultural pragmatic research. Contrasting can be done in many different ways, and what we advocate in this book only represents certain types of contrasting, without the claim of being comprehensive.

2.3 **Data Types in the Study of Language and Politics**

Many scholars in pragmatics have considered whether naturally occurring data are more 'valuable' than elicited and constructed data (see e.g. Eelen 2001; Bednarek 2011). Such discussions are not relevant for the study of language and politics, where **spontaneous data** are rare, even though they exist and are worth studying (e.g. in Chapter 4 we examine a closed-door emergency meeting which is spontaneous in nature). This is why, in the field of language and politics, it is more fruitful to consider which type of discourse a particular data set represents, instead of speculating about whether a piece of data is more or less 'natural'.

Following our approach, we recommend using corpora in the study of language and politics whenever possible. As already noted, the term 'corpus' refers to a searchable collection of machine-readable texts of varying size. Using corpora does not mean that we dismiss the value of rigorously conducted **case studies**, provided that such case studies are carefully designed. It is also advisable to combine corpus studies with case studies. A case study is often used to further investigate what was initially observed in a corpus. In all endeavours of collecting and analysing pragmatic data, we are faced with a fundamental conflict between the goal of pragmatic analysis and the means of reaching this goal. On the one hand, we want to recognise, understand, describe and explain systematic, generalisable linguacultural tendencies of political language use. On the other hand, every single interaction is a separate linguistic action. The renowned linguist Wallace Chafe (1994: 10) captures this brilliantly: 'Understanding of whatever kind is the ability, through imagination, to relate limited, particular, concrete observations to larger, more encompassing, more stable schemas within which the particular experiences fit.'

As the corpus linguist Partington argues, in language and politics the two perhaps most important data types include the language use of political actors and the media. As Partington (2012) points out,

In both types of study, researchers will typically need to compile their own data set, very generally by downloading texts from the Internet, rather than exclusively accessing large pre-existing so-called 'general language' corpora such as the Bank of English or the British National Corpus. A number of political institutions make available a good number and variety of political texts, for example, the White House Library, the UK government Web site and the Web sites of political parties. Several countries make available transcripts of their parliamentary discussions, though this raises the vexed question of authenticity. UK Hansard reports, for example, are frequently altered after the actual speeches have been delivered.

This argument is important for the present book due to our contrastive and multilingual view of language and politics. We often compare data drawn from linguacultures like anglophone ones, where corpora are readily available, with data from linguacultures where no comparably large corpora of political texts are available. An additional problem that is worth mentioning here is that, for example in the case of Chinese, certain digitalised politically relevant corpora such as the Hong Kong Newspaper Archive[3] consist of scans which can only be

---

[3] See https://mmis.hkpl.gov.hk/web/guest.

used as images, and so if one wants to use them one needs to manually input every utterance into one's analysis.

In this chapter, we have outlined elements of our framework, including our units of analysis, the way in which we look at data, and data types in the field of language and politics. In the following, we move on to study the pitfall types presented in Chapter 1.

2.4 Recommended Readings

Noam Chomsky. 1988. *Language and Politics.* Oxford: AK Press.

Chomsky interprets the concept of 'politics' in a broad sense, and this interpretation may be useful to readers with interest in how politics can be pinned down. In the following section, Chomsky discusses the problematics of relying on data to draw generalisations about language use, which we also discussed in the present chapter:

If you go back to the time of Galileo and look at the array of phenomena that had to be accounted for, it seemed prima facie obvious that the Galilean theory, the Copernican theory, could not be supported. That is, there were just masses of unexplained, or even apparently refuting, data. Galileo plowed his way through this, putting much of the data aside, redefining what was relevant and what was not relevant, formulating questions in such a way that what appeared to be refuting data were no longer so, and in fact very often just disregarded data that would have refuted the system. This was not done simply with reckless abandon, but out of a recognition that explanatory principles were being discovered that have insight into at least some of the phenomena. Now, a willingness to move towards explanatory principles that give insight into some of the phenomena at the cost of not being able to handle all of the phenomena: that I think was one of the most striking intellectual achievements of the great scientific revolution. (Chomsky 1988: 211)

Michal Krzyżanowski and Joshua Tucker. 2018. Re/constructing politics through social & online media: Discourses, ideologies, and mediated political practices. *Journal of Language and Politics* 17(6): 1–14.

The work of Krzyżanowski and Tucker is relevant for readers with interest in issues of data in the field of language and politics. The study of language and politics not only involves clearly 'political' data such as reports on political news, but also many seemingly 'non-political' manifestations of language use, such as social media uses. Krzyżanowski and Tucker describe this phenomenon as follows:

Thus, we build on the premise that whether within 'elite' or 'mass' politics, or at the intersection of the former and the latter, the role of language as a carrier of political ideologies and practices remains central. It hence requires us to build on the key language-related 'turns' in interdisciplinary research accelerated by the ascent of the political use of online and social media. Accordingly, we set off from a very peculiar 'linguistic turn' in the broad field of political research – including the traditional political science but also political sociology, democracy studies, electoral studies, analysis of new social movements, international relations, etc. – and argue that social media have recently very effectively put language – whether seen as 'discourse' or 'data' – at a central point of political analysis. Although political communication research has since the arrival of methods of content analysis paid attention to the 'contents' or to the 'language' of political messages, the arrival of online media has very significantly deepened that trend. It has also shown that the political-scientific explorations of, in particular, social media language require new approaches to dealing with the quantity as well as quality of mediated political messages.

On the other hand, looking from the perspective of language and discourse analysis as well as of the wider communication research, we also draw from a 'political' turn that, spawned by the development of online and social media, has very significantly deepened linguistic, discourse-analytic and communication-scientific interest in the increasingly political character of mediated communication. We recognise, however, that the new character of communication on online media – including brevity of social media texts, huge quantity and volume of messages, irregularity of language use, etc. – have all posed very significant challenges to many language- and discourse-oriented theories and methodologies. (Krzyżanowski and Tucker 2018: 5)

3 Pitfall 1
Following an Ethnocentric View When Studying Politically Relevant Data

3.1 Introduction

In the present chapter, we examine the first of the pitfall types outlined in Chapter 2 – the problem of following an ethnocentric view when studying politically relevant data. Here, and in Chapters 4 and 5, we will discuss how to avoid these pitfalls, and we will also provide case studies where we put our methodology into practice.

As the political scientist Hooghe (2008: 11) argues,

> Ethnocentrism is a basic attitude expressing the belief that one's own ethnic group or one's own culture is superior to other ethnic groups or cultures, and that one's cultural standards can be applied in a universal manner. The term was first used by the American sociologist William Graham Sumner (1840–1910) to describe the view that one's own culture can be considered central, while other cultures or religious traditions are reduced to a less prominent role. Ethnocentrism is closely related to other attitudinal indicators for racism, xenophobia, prejudice, mental closure, and, more generally, an authoritarian personality structure. Ethnocentrism is widely used in research on social and political attitudes because it proves to be a very powerful and easily identifiable attitude that can be measured in a valid manner with a limited number of variables.

Clearly, ethnocentrism is an important phenomenon to be studied for its own sake in language and politics (for an overview see Cunningham et al. 2004). However, we aim to investigate a very different manifestation of ethnocentrism, namely the way in which ethnocentric conceptions influence researchers themselves.

Ethnocentric views emerge in the study of language and politics if politically relevant notions are used in an uncritical way, without taking potential variation in their meanings across linguacultures into consideration. A representative example is the notion of 'democracy'. As Schaffer (1997; 2000; 2012; Schaffer and Gagnon 2023) has shown in many studies, the word 'democracy' is subject to significant linguacultural variation and because of this it simply cannot be used in a neutral way without considering what it means in different linguacultures. Yet various scholars used 'democracy' and other concepts as grand notions, reflecting their own understandings of these notions. As an example, let us refer to the following excerpt from the study of Kirsch and Welzel (2019: 59):

> An intriguing phenomenon consists in the fact that widespread support for democracy coexists in many countries with the persistent absence of democracy itself. Addressing this phenomenon, we show that in most places where it exists people understand democracy in ambiguous ways, such that 'authoritarian' notions of what democracy means mix with – and even overshadow – liberal notions, in spite of the contradiction between these two notions. Underlining this contradiction, our evidence shows that authoritarian notions of democracy question the authenticity of liberal notions when both are endorsed conjointly. Worse, the evidence further suggests that authoritarian notions reverse the whole meaning of support for democracy, indeed indicating support for autocracy instead ... In a nutshell, the prospects of democracy are bleak where emancipative values remain weak.

This is a heavily ethnocentric argument in which certain nations are conveniently dismissed as less 'emancipated' than others – an error which also paves the way to Pitfall 2, namely the association of values with certain actors or entities at the outset. While it is possible to academically measure the degree of democracy across countries and political systems, even though any such measures need to be handled with some caution (for an overview see Boese 2019), the argument that there is only one appropriate and generally accepted understanding of the concept 'democracy' is clearly ethnocentric and **colonial** in nature. As we will show below, a serious danger of claiming ownership of notions like 'democracy' is that these notions can be self-righteously used as interactional resources (see Thornborrow 2002) not only by non-liberal actors like the ones mentioned by Kirsch and Welzel above, but also by the very actors who associate themselves and are associated with liberal political systems.

3.2 Methodological Approach

Following the contrastive approach pursued in this book, we now propose an analytic procedure through which it is possible to systematically compare politically relevant notions across different linguacultures. This contrastive take involves the following three methodological steps outlined in Figure 3.1.

As Figure 3.1 shows, the first and second steps in our approach allow us to examine and compare the ways in which political actors and the media use particular politically relevant expressions, hence teasing out contrastive similarities and differences between their use with the aid of different corpora. While these steps involve a diachronic analysis, they are different from the discourse-historical approach discussed in Chapter 2. In the third step in Figure 3.1, we propose relying on an **ancillary methodology**, by means of which the contrastive outcomes of the first two steps can be tested. Here we

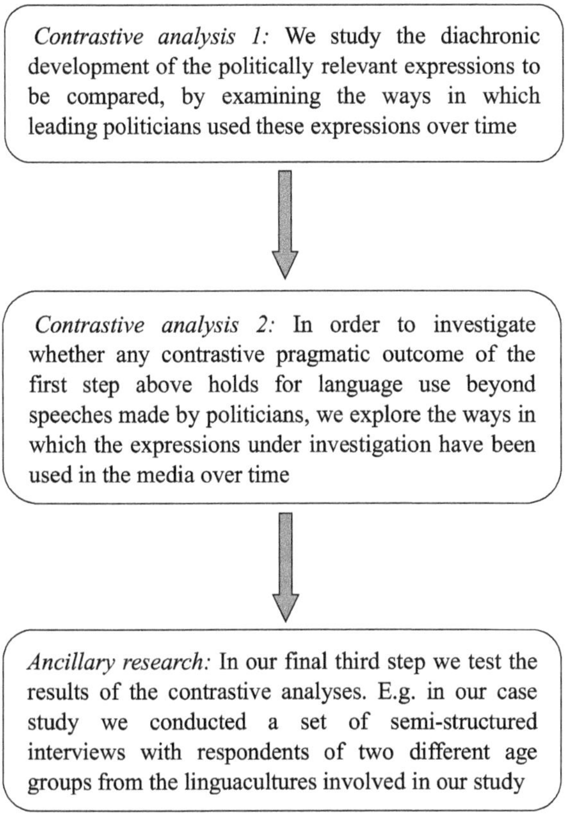

Contrastive analysis 1: We study the diachronic development of the politically relevant expressions to be compared, by examining the ways in which leading politicians used these expressions over time

Contrastive analysis 2: In order to investigate whether any contrastive pragmatic outcome of the first step above holds for language use beyond speeches made by politicians, we explore the ways in which the expressions under investigation have been used in the media over time

Ancillary research: In our final third step we test the results of the contrastive analyses. E.g. in our case study we conducted a set of semi-structured interviews with respondents of two different age groups from the linguacultures involved in our study

Figure 3.1 Our analytic approach to avoiding Pitfall 1

follow a broader contrastive procedure suggested in House and Kádár (2021b), where we argued that involving an ancillary step is a good practice in contrastive pragmatic analysis.

3.3 Case Study

In this study we investigate uses of the expression *M/minzu-zhuyi* 民族主义 in the Chinese linguaculture and the expression *nationalism* in the US linguaculture. Our case study will not only show that *M/minzu-zhuyi* differs significantly from *nationalism*, but also that in the Chinese linguaculture *M/minzu-zhuyi* is used in two essentially different ways: in a positive 'native' and a negative 'foreign' sense. This fits into a major lexical pattern that one can often observe in Chinese language and politics. As Kádár and Ran (2015) have highlighted, in the context of early twentieth-century politics, the Chinese borrowed a number of expressions, and at the same time began to use various of their own 'native' terms alongside these borrowed expressions. Thus a set of dual expressions emerged in Chinese language and politics, which often only had a single English (or other Western) translation. In summary, in Chinese *M/minzuzhuyi* has a very different meaning and diachronic trajectory than *nationalism* in English, and **'nationalism'** as a macro-sense technical term may not be suitable to account for such cross-cultural differences.

In terms of the general methodology outlined in Chapter 2, in this case study focusing on politically relevant expressions our key unit of analysis is expressions, and we engage in a contrastive procedure whereby we compare corpora drawn from different languages and different data types.

3.3.1   'Nationalism' in CDA Research

In order to position our case study, let us briefly summarise previous CDA research involving the concept of *nationalism*. In a body of such inquiries, cross-cultural research has been used to validate dominant 'Western' conceptualisations of 'nationalism' as an exclusively negative phenomenon. For instance, KhosraviNik and Zia (2014) adopted a CDA approach to study how a form of Iranian national(ist) identity is constructed and presented on the popular Facebook page 'Persian Gulf'. While KhosraviNik and Zia used Persian data, they interpreted Iranian 'nationalism' without considering native conceptualisations of this notion. Others, such as Setiyadi et al. (2018), examined linguacultural equivalents of the term 'nationalism', and they approached these equivalents in a top-down manner, assuming that 'nationalism' is an essentially negative phenomenon in the linguacultures studied. By so doing, they unavoidably fell into Pitfall 1: notwithstanding whether or not a scholar is a linguacultural insider of Persian or other linguacultures involved in the inquiries outlined above, the uncritical use of a Western definition of 'nationalism' shuts the door on any objective study of this subject.

The work of Ruth Wodak and her colleagues deserves particular attention here. Wodak (2017) defined 'nationalism' using cultural and ethnic criteria, by proposing a discourse-historical approach to this notion (see also Chapter 2). Further, Wodak and Boukala (2015) explored the diachronic patterns in the emergence of 'nationalism' across various European countries, providing a model for the historical development of nationalism. While we agree with Wodak that examining the historical development of *nationalism* (and its equivalents) provides a key to understanding 'nationalism' as a concept, our approach is very different from it because we do not start from the assumption that equivalents of *nationalism* always have a negative default connotation across different linguacultures.

3.3.2 Methodology and Data

Following the tripartite design proposed in Figure 3.1, in our case study we proceed as follows:

1 *Contrastive analysis 1.* We study the diachronic development of *M/minzu-zhuyi* and *nationalism* in China and the US respectively, by examining the ways in which politicians used these expressions over time. This research revealed major cross-cultural contrastive pragmatic differences between the use of *M/minzu-zhuyi* and *nationalism*. The results also revealed a certain rupture which followed the end of early modern Chinese politics, coinciding with the founding of the People's Republic of China in 1949.
2 *Contrastive analysis 2.* In order to investigate whether this rupture holds for language use beyond speeches made by politicians, we explore the ways in which *M/minzu-zhuyi* and *nationalism* have been used in the Chinese and US print media between 1949 and the present day.
3 *Testing the results of the contrastive analyses.* We conduct a set of semi-structured interviews with Chinese and US respondents of two different age groups in order to measure – at least in a modest way – how present-day language users in China and the US perceive the meanings of *M/minzu-zhuyi* and *nationalism*.

Adopting this approach, we examined the following three corpora:

1 *Corpus for contrastive analysis 1.* Transcripts of speeches made by politicians between the 1920s and 2019. The Chinese corpus consists of 951,887 Chinese characters, while the US corpus has 978,768 words. The Chinese corpus was collected from twelve Chinese websites. The US corpus was retrieved from millercenter.org/the-presidency/presidential-speeches.
2 *Corpus for contrastive analysis 2.* Newspaper articles published between 1949 and 2019. The Chinese corpus of newspaper articles consists of approximately 630,000 characters, while the US corpus has 205,500 words. The Chinese newspapers studied include *China Daily* and *Global Times*, while the US newspapers include the *Washington Post* and the *New York Times*. We studied data drawn from these newspapers because, internationally, they are among the best-known newspapers published in the two countries involved in our case study.
3 *Testing the results of the contrastive analyses – interviews.* Our interview corpus includes two lots of thirty interviews with Chinese and US respondents from two different age groups: under and over thirty-five years. We chose thirty-five years in a relatively arbitrary manner, arguing that by reaching this age people have usually settled down, and so after this age interviewees may have a different view on politics than younger respondents. We assumed that the age factor is a crucial determinant when it comes to evaluations of the expressions *M/minzu-zhuyi* and *nationalism*. Due to the effect of globalisation

and related exposure to international media, younger people have a different view of *M/minzu-zhuyi* and *nationalism* than members of the older generation. This assumption was based on previous research on the pragmatics of globalisation, such as Sifianou (2013) and House and Kádár (2020).

When constructing our corpora, we used the computer software AntConc v. 3.5.8 to search for occurrences of *M/minzu-zhuyi* and *nationalism*. We examined not only occurrences of these expressions, but also their collocations with adjectives: up to three words before and after the occurrence of *nationalism* and, similarly, up to three words before but not after the occurrence of *M/minzu-zhuyi* because Chinese adjectives only occur before nouns. We examined adjectives to determine whether they tended to have a positive, negative or neutral meaning in the linguacultures being contrasted. As part of this analysis we also examined the broader contextual use of each example, to determine whether the expressions under investigation were used positively or negatively in a particular text. Typical examples of positive and negative adjectives modifying *M/minzu-zhuyi* in our Chinese corpus are the following: *fandiguo-de-Minzu-zhuyi* 反帝国主义的民族主义 ('anti-imperialist *Minzu-zhuyi*') [positive meaning] and *youyi-de-minzu-zhuyi* 右翼的民族主义 ('right-wing *minzu-zhuyi*') [negative meaning]. In the case of our US corpus, while we could not identify positive adjectives modifying *nationalism*, we found various adjectives such as *economic*, which we initially classified as 'neutral'. However, as our more detailed analysis later revealed, in many cases such semantically neutral adjectives also gain a negative meaning in US political language use. A typical adjective negatively modifying *nationalism* is *nastiest*.

In our semi-structured interviews, we asked three questions in English and Chinese (see more below). When selecting our respondents, we included people with a university education background who said 'yes' to our question whether they are interested in politics and frequently read or watch different media. The interviews were conducted via email and Skype or WeChat in two steps. First, we provided our respondents with the interview questions by email or WeChat and then arranged the Skype or WeChat interviews. The average interview lasted approximately ten minutes. The interview data were stored in compliance with the standard ethical-research requirements of linguistic inquiries. The participants' names were anonymised and any sensitive information was removed from the interview transcripts.

3.3.3 Analysis

The following Tables 3.1, 3.2 and 3.3 summarise the quantitative analysis of parts 1 and 2 of our research. They include the number of occurrences of *M/minzu-zhuyi* and *nationalism* in our diachronic corpora:

Table 3.1 *Number of pre-1949 and post-1949 occurrences of* M/minzu-zhuyi *and* nationalism *in the political-speeches corpus*

	Pre-1949 political speeches		Post-1949 political speeches	
	M/minzu-zhuyi	Nationalism	M/minzu-zhuyi	nationalism
Total	26	1	56	4
Negative uses	1 (*minzu-zhuyi*)	1	56 (*minzu-zhuyi*)	4
Positive uses	25 (*Minzu-zhuyi*)	0	0	0

Table 3.2 *Number of occurrences of* M/minzu-zhuyi *and* nationalism *in the media corpus*

Media data	M/minzu-zhuyi	nationalism
Total	460	137
Negative uses	443 (*minzu-zhuyi*)	137
Positive uses	17 (*M/minzu-zhuyi*)	0

Table 3.3 *Number of occurrences of* M/minzu-zhuyi *and* nationalism *in the political speeches and media corpora with numbers of qualifying adjectives*

Both corpora	M/minzu-zhuyi	nationalism
Number of occurrences of *M/minzu-zhuyi and nationalism*	542	142
Number of adjectives collocating with *minzu-zhuyi and nationalism*	506	34
Number of negative adjectives collocating with *minzu-zhuyi and nationalism*	490	24
Number of positive or neutral adjectives collocating with *minzu-zhuyi and nationalism*	16	10

The figures given in Tables 3.1, 3.2 and 3.3 clearly show major cross-cultural contrastive differences between the Chinese and US expressions under investigation – we will revisit this point in more detail later. More importantly here, they also point to the existence of a diachronic rupture in the Chinese data. While Table 3.1 indicates that *M/minzu-zhuyi* was almost always used positively in pre-1949 political speeches, it also shows that, after 1949, Chinese politicians used it only negatively. This is in accordance with the fact that, in pre-1949 Chinese political speeches, *M/minzu-zhuyi* had a dual use: it was used as a proper noun in a positive sense, and (rarely) as a common noun in a negative sense.

After 1949, Chinese politicians only used *minzu-zhuyi* as a common noun (see more below), in a negative sense. Table 3.2 (in conjunction with Table 3.1) shows that this rupture is less valid for post-1949 media texts, in which *M/minzu-zhuyi* can be used in both negative and positive ways, although the negative uses are much more marked than the positive uses. Table 3.2 (in conjunction with Table 3.1) also indicates that it is not always clear in post-1949 media texts whether *M/minzu-zhuyi* is a proper or common noun when used positively. That is, unlike the situation in pre-1949 political speeches, in post-1949 media texts there is a sense of ambiguity surrounding the modern use of this expression. Table 3.3 confirms this ambiguity: while in our corpus of political texts *Minzu-zhuyi* as a proper noun is never modified by an adjective, in the media texts one can observe cases where *M/minzu-zhuyi* has been modified by an adjective and expresses a positive meaning. Table 3.3 also confirms that negative uses of *M/minzu-zhuyi* are substantially more frequent than positive uses. It is worth noting that the ambiguity regarding whether *M/minzu-zhuyi* is a proper or common noun stems from the nature of Chinese writing. Unlike with many other writing systems, when using Chinese characters, one cannot indicate whether a word is a proper or common noun, and so the status of a noun can only be discerned from its context. While we attempted to resolve this ambiguity by carefully analysing the contextual use of *M/minzu-zhuyi* in each example in our corpus, and also by validating our interpretation with the aid of a panel of native speakers, in certain cases the ambiguity could not be completely resolved.

In the following, we first conduct a qualitative interpretation of the above quantitative results and then check the validity of the findings by implementing the third interview-based step in our model.

3.3.3.1 Contrastive Analysis 1: Speeches by Political Figures
In order to interpret the aforementioned quantitative differences between the positive and negative uses of *M/minzu-zhuyi* and *nationalism*, we begin our investigation with an overview of how politicians have used the concepts of *M/minzu-zhuyi* in China and *nationalism* in the US over time.

The term *M/minzu-zhuyi* was coined during the early modern period in China: it was borrowed from Japanese in the late nineteenth century (see Cui 2004; Hao 2004). At this time, the Chinese attempted to modernise the country. As part of this endeavour towards modernisation, Chinese intellectuals borrowed many 'modern' Western expressions, often via Japanese (Fairbank 1982). Japan had earlier undergone modernisation, following the Meiji Restoration in 1868. The Japanese equivalent of *M/minzu-zhuyi* is *minzoku-shugi* 民族主義, which the Chinese directly imported (see Levenson 1953).

M/minzu-zhuyi later became a fundamental 'Principle' under the influence of Sun Yat-sen 孙中山 (1866–1925), the first president of the Republic of China (1911–1949). Sun's political philosophy was based on what he called the Three Principles of Governance (*Sanmin Zhuyi* 三民主义), with the first of these

Principles being *Minzu-zhuyi*. Bearing in mind that, in Sun's work, *Minzu-zhuyi* is a proper noun with a positive meaning, it is not surprising that during the first half of the twentieth century *Minzu-zhuyi* was essentially associated in the Chinese linguaculture with a positive political principle. The fact that during this time *Minzu-zhuyi* was essentially used as a proper noun in Chinese is neatly illustrated by the authoritative *Mathews' Chinese–English Dictionary* (1931), which translates the characters of this expression as 'Principle of Nationalism' rather than just 'nationalism'. In Sun's philosophy, *Minzu-zhuyi* was the political philosophical equivalent of *aiguo-zhuyi* 爱国主义 ('patriotism') – the latter was used by Sun in reference to the feelings of an individual rather than a political principle:

(3.1)   … 做人的最大事情是什么呢?就是要知道怎么样爱国,怎么样可以管国事 … 什么是民族主义呢?就是要中国和外国平等的主义。要中国和英国、法国、美国那些强盛国家都一律平等的主义,就是民族主义。

> … What's the most important thing for a human being? It is to know how to be <u>patriotic</u> (*aiguo*) [as an individual] and how to administer the affairs of our state [in public] … What is <u>Minzu-zhuyi</u>? It is the doctrine of equality between China and foreign countries. <u>Minzu-zhuyi</u> is the doctrine according to which China is an equal of the powerful nations of Britain, France and the United States.
>
> (Sun Yat-sen, speech given at the commemorative meeting of Guangdong First Women's Normal School, 4 April 1924)

In pre-1949 texts, *Minzu-zhuyi* is almost always used in a positive sense (see Table 3.1) as a proper noun, representing a revered Principle. This implies that its positive meaning prevails whenever it appears as a proper noun. The following extract (3.2) illustrates this point. In this case, *minzu-zhuyi* is used as a common noun, in reference to *nationalism* in a foreign sense:

(3.2)   白种人以此为本位,去吞灭别色人种。 … 白种人民族主义很发达。因为白种人的民族主义很发达,所以他们在欧洲住满了,便扩充到西半球的南北美洲,东半球东南方的非洲、澳洲 …

> It is standard for white people to devour other races … White <u>nationalism</u> (*minzu-zhuyi*) is highly developed. Because white people's <u>nationalism</u> (*minzu-zhuyi*) is so much more developed, they have spread beyond Europe, and have colonised the western hemisphere of North and South America, the eastern hemisphere of Africa, Australia …
>
> (Sun Yat-sen, 'On nationalism: The fourth lecture note', 17 February 1924)

Besides the dual meaning of *M/minzu-zhuyi* in Sun's political philosophy, Sun also used another term – *Guozu-zhuyi* 国族主义 – as a synonym of *Minzu-zhuyi* in his works, as the following excerpt illustrates:

(3.3) 我说民族主义就是国族主义,在中国是适当的,在外国便不适当。外国人说民族和国家便有分别。 ... 在中国文中,一个字有两个解释的很多。即如「社会」两个字,就有两个用法:一个是指一般人群而言,一个是指一种有组织之团体而言。本来民族与国家相互的关系很多。不容易分开,但是当中实在有一定界限,我们必须分开什么是国家,什么是民族。我说民族就是国族,何以在中国是适当,在外国便不适当呢?因为中国自秦汉而后,都是一个民族造成一个国家。外国有一个民族造成几个国家,他们国内的民族是用白人为本位,结合棕人、黑人等民族,才成「大不列颠帝国」。所以在英国说民族就是国族,这一句话便不适当。

>When I use my Principle of Minzu-zhuyi I mean Guozu-zhuyi ('equal nations of our country-ism'). This notion [Minzu-zhuyi] is appropriate in China and inappropriate in foreign countries. Foreigners say that there is a difference between a 'nation' and a 'country' ... In Chinese, many more words have two meanings than in foreign languages. For example, the word *shehui* ('society') has two interpretations: it can refer to both the general population and a community. In a similar way, when we talk about Minzu-zhuyi, the relationship between nation and state is intrinsically related in many aspects. It is not easy to separate them, but there is a line between what is a state and what is a nation. I say that 'nation' (*minzu*) includes the nations of our country (*guozu*). Why is it appropriate to use Minzu-zhuyi in China but not in a foreign country? China has been a nation state country since the Qin [221 to 206 BC] and Han [202 BC to 220 AD] Dynasties. This differs from Western countries which consist of various nations, including the white colonising nation and other – brown, black and other races – forming the nation, such as what we can see in the case of 'Great Britain'. This is why, when it comes to Britain, a 'nation' (*minzu*) does not consist of the equal nations (*guozu*) of the country. Therefore 'Minzu is Guozu' is inappropriate in Britain.
>
> (Sun Yat-sen, 'The Three People's Principles: The first lecture note', 27 January 1924)

Sun Yat-sen here provides an insightful metapragmatic analysis of his own conception of *Minzu-zhuyi*. The description in example (3.3) reveals that Sun was fully aware of the potential dangers of using the Chinese equivalent of *nationalism* in a positive way.

As a result of the importance of Sun's political heritage, various political figures continued to use the expression *M/minzu-zhuyi* in the aforementioned dual manner. As our Chinese corpus shows, between Sun's death in 1925 and 1949, leaders of different political parties tried to claim 'ownership' of Sun's legacy, by providing different interpretations of Sun's *Minzu-zhuyi*. Despite the ideological debates surrounding *Minzu-zhuyi* at that time, this expression was used primarily in a positive way, as our data have shown.

In 1949, with the unification of the mainland of China, state socialism became the official form of governance, with Russian Marxism having a fundamental influence on the language used in Chinese politics (e.g. Hodge and Kam 1998: 17). Mao Zedong – and Chinese national leaders after him – used *minzu-zhuyi* as a Marxist common noun, and because of this change the term *minzu-zhuyi* started to be used essentially differently from what we could observe in our pre-1949 corpus. However, as we will later show, this shift in the use of *M/minzu-zhuyi* by Chinese politicians does not mean that *Minzu-zhuyi* as a Principle lost its positive connotation.

It is important to note that, in our post-1949 Chinese corpus of political speeches, *minzu-zhuyi* always collocates with an adjective to indicate a negative meaning. A typical example of this use is *difang minzu-zhuyi* 地方民族主义 ('local nationalism'), featured in example (3.4) below. 'Local' in this context refers to local (domestic) nationalistic opposition to Marxism that needed to be 'overcome':

(3.4) ... 无论是大汉族主义或者<u>地方民族主义</u>,都不利于各族人民的团结 ...

      ... Neither Han chauvinism nor <u>local nationalism</u> (*defang-minzu-zhuyi*) can contribute to the unity of our ethnic groups ...
      (Mao Zedong, 'Correct handling of ethnic minority relations', 27 February 1957)

In summary, we may argue that *M/minzu-zhuyi* changed from an expression used in a dual way to a more ambiguous term, without a clear-cut difference between its 'native' and 'foreign' uses. However, as our follow-up contrastive analysis of media texts will show, the situation is more complex than meets the eye: in other data types featuring Chinese language and politics, such as our post-1949 media corpus, *M/minzu-zhuyi* has retained some of its dual meaning.

In English, the expression *nationalism* was, to the best of our knowledge, first used in 1844, although the concept of 'nationalism' can be traced back to the seventeenth century (Kohn 2005). An early description of *nationalism* in the US appeared in the *New Englander* and the *Yale Review* in July 1845, according to the *Corpus of Historical American English*.[1] In the nineteenth century, *nationalism* in the US was primarily used in relation to European nationalist movements, adopting the negative meaning of 'social unrest' (see Zimmer 2003). *Nationalism* became increasingly negative in the US after the outbreak of the First World War in 1914 (Hayes 1931). Between the end of the First World War and the late 1940s, *nationalism* gradually became a symbol of war and the lack of international co-operation in the US, as the analysis of our corpus of political speeches shows. Furthermore, according to our corpus analysis, from the beginning of the 1950s *nationalism* in the US was associated with social instability in the Soviet bloc during the Cold War, until the collapse of the Soviet Union (see also Fousek 2000). Since then, *nationalism* has been a highly dispreferred term in mainstream US political language use.

---

[1] See www.english-corpora.org/coha.

The following examples represent a pre-1949 and a post-1949 use of *nationalism* taken from our corpus of US political speeches. These examples illustrate that, unlike *M/minzu-zhuyi*, *nationalism* has been used in a consistently negative way by leading US politicians, according to our US corpus.

(3.5) The economic depression has continued and deepened in every part of the world during the past year. In many countries political instability, excessive armaments, debts, governmental expenditures, and taxes have resulted in revolutions, in unbalanced budgets and monetary collapse and financial panics, in dumping of goods upon world markets, and in diminished consumption of commodities . . . In a number of countries there have been acute financial panics or compulsory restraints upon banking. These disturbances have many roots in the dislocations from the World War. Every one of them has reacted upon us . . . Such 'economic nationalism' exacerbates both the international depression and nationalist tensions . . .
       (Herbert Hoover, 3 July 1930, Veterans Administration Act)

(3.6) The disarray of the Communist empire has been heightened by two other formidable forces. One is the historical force of nationalism – and the yearning of all men to be free. The other is the gross inefficiency of their economies. For a closed society is not open to ideas of progress – and a police state finds that it cannot command the grain to grow.
       (John F. Kennedy, 14 January 1963, State of the Union Address)

The use of the English word *nationalism* in examples (3.5) and (3.6) seems to us to represent the main 'Western' pattern of using *nationalism*. Although in the current study we have not dealt with other linguacultures, we may assume that the term *nationalism* is used in an equally negative way in other 'Western' linguacultures such as French and German. Due to the essentially negative meaning of *nationalism*, adjectives cannot 'positively' modify the meaning of this expression. For instance, while 'economic' in *economic nationalism* normally has a neutral meaning, in example (3.5) *economic nationalism* is used in a negative way because the strong negative meaning associated with *nationalism* is projected onto the modifying adjective.

As Table 3.1 shows, after 1949 the Chinese and US uses of *M/minzu-zhuyi* and *nationalism* became much more similar than in the period before 1949, although it is also clear that leading US politicians very rarely used *nationalism* in public speeches, at least as far as our corpus is concerned. If we compare our post-1949 Chinese data with its US counterpart, one can conclude that *minzu-zhuyi* became 'internationalised' in Chinese political speeches.

3.3.3.2 Contrastive Analysis 2: The Media

The examination of our Chinese media corpus shows that, even after 1949, *M/minzu-zhuyi* retained some positive connotations in the Chinese media. However, such positive uses are often more ambiguous than the pre-1949 uses of these expressions, in that it is not always clear whether *M/minzu-zhuyi* is used as a proper or a common noun when it occurs in a positive sense. In some cases, media texts make explicit reference to Sun's Principle, whereas in other cases this reference is either implicit or unclear. This implies that, in modern Chinese media language, *M/minzu-zhuyi* is a somewhat ambiguous term even in the context of domestic politics. The following example illustrates a typical implicit positive use of *M/minzu-zhuyi*:

(3.7) 另一种则是指向现代中国、中华民族层次的<u>民族主义</u>,或者称为"<u>国族主义</u>"。奥运火炬遭遇干扰、激起国人以及海外华人的抗议后,国外一些媒体将这种情绪曲解为政府煽动的民族情绪;... 不加分析地贴上了"<u>民族主义</u>"标签,好像但凡民族主义都是洪水猛兽。

> another sense of <u>*M/minzu-zhuyi*</u> or <u>*Guozu-zhuyi*</u> ('equal nations of our country-ism') should be used in reference to modern China and the Chinese nation. After the disruption of the Olympic torch relay [reference to the politically loaded *éclat* during the 2008 Beijing Olympic torch relay], the people of China and also Chinese people living overseas felt greatly frustrated, and some foreign media outlets smeared their emotions as nationalistic emotions fuelled by the government ... and labelled their feelings as gross '<u>nationalism</u>' (*minzu-zhuyi*), seemingly pulling together various types of *minzu-zhuyi* under a dreadful umbrella.
>
> (See https://mil.huanqiu.com/article/9CaKrnJkrYc, 11 May 2008)

Example (3.7) is interesting not only because here *M/minzu-zhuyi* is used to describe both a Chinese phenomenon and a translational issue, in both cases without an adjective, but also because the author of this text makes an implicit reference to Sun's work, by using the now archaic expression *Guozu-zhuyi* 国族主义 ('nations of our country-ism'), which was coined by Sun as a synonym for *Minzu-zhuyi* (see extract 3.3). The reason why we consider this reference to Sun's principle to be an 'implicit' reference is that, in the present-day Chinese linguaculture, it is not common knowledge that Sun coined the term *Guozu-zhuyi*, and the text does not explicitly mention this fact.

In our Chinese media corpus, the ambiguity triggered by implicit references to Sun's legacy in positive interpretations of *M/minzu-zhuyi* is often skilfully resolved by the author of the text explaining that the positive use of *M/minzu-zhuyi* reflects a domestic tradition. The following example illustrates this point:

(3.8) 民族主义曾是世界潮流,在它的推动下,中国推翻了满清帝制,坚持了八年抗战,创造了今天的经济奇迹。

> *Minzu-zhuyi* used to be a global pattern, which in China triggered the downfall of the Manchu Qing Dynasty, and which gave the Chinese persistence during the eight-year anti-Japanese war and created our current economic miracle.
>
> (See https://opinion.huanqiu.com/article/9CaKrnJJMGK, 10 April 2015)

Sometimes the authors of Chinese media texts engage in intrinsic metapragmatic work to explain why *M/minzu-zhuyi* is a positive expression in the domestic context. This is particularly the case whenever a text does not disambiguate whether *M/minzu-zhuyi* is being used as a proper or common noun. See the following example:

(3.9) 与被侵略的历史同步发展起来的中国人的<u>民族主义</u>,本身就是一个被动型的<u>民族主义</u> … 而在今天 … 依旧是一个不断地向中国的对外<u>民族主义</u>提供着发酵条件的温床。

The Chinese people's *M/minzu-zhuyi* – developed in the historical context of our country being invaded by the colonialist powers – is a <u>non-aggressive type of</u> *M/minzu-zhuyi* … Today … some foreign countries misinterpret *M/minzu-zhuyi* and its foreign counterparts.
(See https://opinion.huanqiu.com/article/9CaKrnJFvLO, 3 September 2014)

The fact that *M/minzu-zhuyi* is used for positive purposes in our Chinese media corpus does not mean that this expression is predominantly used with a positive meaning in the Chinese media (see Table 3.2). It is no coincidence that when it is used in a positive sense, the authors of the media texts practically always provide an explanation for this positive use, as examples (3.8) and (3.9) above have shown.

In comparison, neither any sense of ambiguity nor any positive use of *nationalism* is observed in the US media corpus. The use of *nationalism* in our media corpus is illustrated by extracts (3.10) and (3.11):

(3.10) President Trump delivering a video message to the delegates of the World Jewish Congress Plenary Assembly in New York on Sunday. Credit … Brendan Mcdermid/Reuters

A <u>virulent nationalism</u>, tinged with bigotry, is on the rise across much of the world …
(See https://nyti.ms/4dB5lY9)

(3.11) '… The Department of Justice, as you know, initiated the request for inclusion of the citizenship question,' Ross told the committee. He was referring to a much-debated question that the Trump administration was proposing to add to the 2020 census, asking people whether they were American citizens … But the Justice Department, Ross claimed, 'initiated' the question, because it believed that knowing where citizens lived could somehow help the federal government protect the voting rights of African-Americans. It's almost a perfect distillation of the Trump political philosophy: A mix of <u>white nationalism</u> and falsehoods.
(See https://bit.ly/4dPD7IM)

These examples illustrate that *nationalism* is rarely used ambiguously in 'Western' cultural contexts such as the US. This may be the reason why this

Table 3.3 *Number of occurrences of* M/minzu-zhuyi *and* nationalism *in the political speeches and media corpora with numbers of qualifying adjectives*

Both corpora	M/minzu-zhuyi	nationalism
Number of occurrences of *M/minzu-zhuyi and nationalism*	542	142
Number of adjectives collocating with *minzu-zhuyi and nationalism*	506	34
Number of negative adjectives collocating with *minzu-zhuyi and nationalism*	490	24
Number of positive or neutral adjectives collocating with *minzu-zhuyi and nationalism*	16	10

expression is frequently used in the speech act Complain, as in examples (3.10) and (3.11), in which the producer of a text 'expresses his negative view of a past action' (see Edmondson and House 1981: 144).

At this point, it is worth revisiting Table 3.3, which is inserted again at the top of page 45. In the US corpus, *nationalism* is modified by an adjective in 34 of the 142 cases. Interestingly, while in ten of these cases the modifying adjective itself does not have a negative meaning – witness *white* in *white nationalism* in example (3.11) – the meaning of the *adjective* + *nationalism* sequence remains clearly negative because of the overriding negative meaning of the noun. This differs essentially from the case in Chinese, in which a positive adjective always gives *minzu-zhuyi* a positive meaning, as witnessed in example (3.9) above.

The analysis thus far has shown the benefits of using a multi-layered analysis for the examination of politically relevant expressions such as *nationalism* and *M/minzu-zhuyi*: as the current analysis of media texts has illustrated, once various types of data are considered, the seemingly simple and systematic picture gained from the study of a single type of data becomes much more complex. More specifically, the study of Chinese and US media texts has illustrated that

a *M/minzu-zhuyi* has retained a positive connotation in the Chinese linguaculture due to its specific historical trajectory;
b *nationalism* in the US linguaculture has no comparable positive connotation and is essentially negative in meaning; and
c a major contrastive pragmatic difference continues to exist between the two linguacultures under investigation, as our above analysis of adjectives has also shown.

In the following section, we now turn to the third layer of our analytical model, whereby we attempt to test the findings of our contrastive analyses.

Table 3.4 *Chinese and American interviews on* minzu-zhuyi/nationalism

	Positive	Neutral	Negative
minzu-zhuyi	24	6	0
Age of the Chinese respondents	Under 35: 9	Under 35: 6	n/a
	Over 35: 15	Over 35: 0	
nationalism	0	9	21
Age of the US respondents	n/a	Under 35: 3	Under 35: 12
		Over 35: 6	Over 35: 9

3.3.3.3 Testing the Results of the Contrastive Analyses: Interviews

The following three questions were posed to our interviewees in Chinese and English:

1 Do you think that nationalism (*minzu-zhuyi* for Chinese respondents) is a positive, neutral or negative term?
2 Please describe your understanding of nationalism (*minzu-zhuyi* for Chinese respondents).
3 Would you consider yourself to be a nationalist?

Table 3.4 summarises the results of the responses given by our interviewees to Question 1. As Table 3.4 shows, the Chinese and US respondents differed when assigning positive, neutral or negative values to *minzu-zhuyi* and *nationalism*. While such differences are themselves noteworthy, due to the small size of our corpus – a total of sixty interviews – they should not be overinterpreted. However, the results of the interviews gained further significance when we asked the interviewees to expand on their thoughts regarding the concepts under investigation; that is, when they provided responses to the open-ended questions 2 and 3.

Regarding question 2, the Chinese interviewees stated that they not only considered *minzu-zhuyi* to be a positive notion, but also defined it as being part of the 'Chinese cultural heritage', and associated this 'heritage' with concepts such as 'national unity'. The following extract represents such an association:

(3.12) 嗯(.),就是70周年大庆的时候(.),我感觉这个民族对吧(..),就是到处都插满了国旗(.),民族主义,我觉得挺好的,嗯(.),然后(.)还有一个新冠疫情的时候,一个民族精神,大家很团结(.),我觉得这个也挺好。爱国主义↑情怀,我认为它是积极的,非常好。

uhm (.), It's now the seventieth anniversary of the foundation of our country (.), and I really have a sense of national belonging together (..). There are flags everywhere (.), and nationalism (*minzu-zhuyi*), um, I think it's good, er (.), then (.), in particular in the wake of the COVID-19 outbreak. I think now we are united (*tuanjie*) (.) by our national spirit (*minzu-jingshen*). I think this is an excellent matter. *Minzu-zhuyi* means patriotism (*aiguo-zhuyi*)↑, which I think is positive, it is very good.

(Chinese interviewee, over thirty-five)

Pitfall 1: Following an Ethnocentric View

We were rather surprised by the above interview because it echoes Sun Yat-sen's thinking on *Minzu-zhuyi*: according to the interviewee, the Principle of *Minzu-zhuyi* is closely related to the concept of *aiguo-zhuyi* ('patriotism'). Neither had we revealed any historical information regarding *M/minzu-zhuyi* to our interviewees, nor did we assume that the interviewees were familiar with the specific history of this expression.

In the English interviews, two key notions surrounding *nationalism* were found to be 'superiority' and 'harm'. The following extract (3.13) illustrates this tendency:

(3.13) I believe (.) um, that in the world in which we are living today (..) the concept of <u>nationalism</u> has a <u>very</u> negative! connotation. My understanding (.) of the meaning of <u>nationalism</u>, um, is belief (.) in the act of <u>placing one's own country above those of any other</u> ... This could result in (.) actively <u>harming members of another country</u> (.) or by ignoring the needs of another country ...

(US interviewee, under thirty-five)

As extract (3.13) shows, our US interviewees held very negative views regarding *nationalism*.

With regard to question 3, it emerged that several of the Chinese interviewees considered themselves to be *minzu-zhuyizhe* 民族主义者 ('nationalists'), whereas the US interviewees strongly denied being *nationalists*. The following examples (3.14) and (3.15) from our interview corpus illustrate these two tendencies:

(3.14) 我认为 (.),嗯,什么时候我都可以说自己是一个民族主义者,那个(.)因为一般的民族主义吧,嗯(.),良性?的民族主义,是(.)为了(.)民族的发展和幸福,嗯,能够继承民族的优良传统,(.)并善于向其他民族学习,对<u>本民族</u>有种深沉的爱,但(.)不等于不对本民族的缺点进行批判。

I think (.), er, I can say that I am a nationalist (*minzu-zhuyizhe*) <u>under any circumstance</u>, well (.), because, in general, em (.), nationalism (*minzu-zhuyi*), in particular <u>benign?</u> [sic] nationalism (*liangxing-de-minzu-zhuyi*), serves (.) a nation's development and happiness. Er. It is good way of <u>inheriting</u> excellent national traditions, and (.) learning from another nation's excellent culture. Benign nationalism unfolds a deep love for <u>one's own nation</u>, but (.) it does not mean that one ignores one's nation's shortcomings.

(Chinese interviewee, under thirty-five)

(3.15) I would, um, typically not regard myself as a <u>nationalist</u> again. I would describe myself as a <u>patriot</u>. But under certain circumstances, like, em, if in times of war or as far as rules break and following the rules or line order, then I would consider myself a nationalist (.).

(US interviewee, over thirty-five)

As Table 3.4 shows, the age of the Chinese respondents had implications for the different ways in which they evaluated *minzu-zhuyi*, although clearly our interview corpus is too small to argue that these differences hold for a larger number of Chinese-language users. More specifically, it was only the younger (under thirty-five) respondents who held relatively neutral views about *minzu-zhuyi*, whereas every respondent over the age of thirty-five evaluated this notion positively. A similar generational difference was not observed in the US corpus, which again confirms that a negative meaning is persistently assigned to *nationalism* in the US American linguaculture irrespective of the age of the respondents.

3.4   Reflections

In this chapter, we have proposed a tripartite model, demonstrating how one can avoid Pitfall 1 in the study of language and politics. We have illustrated the use of this model with our case study, providing a contrastive pragmatic analysis of the ideologically loaded expressions *M/minzu-zhuyi* and *nationalism*. The results of the case study have shown that, despite the main diachronic rupture in the Chinese data, the historical trajectory of *M/minzu-zhuyi* continues to influence modern uses and evaluations of this term. The uses and evaluations of *nationalism* in the US corpora are fundamentally different from this: the concept of *nationalism* is essentially negative in nature. A key advantage of using various types of corpora in contrastive pragmatic analysis like ours is the following: if we had only compared Chinese and US political speeches, our conclusion would have been that the understanding of *nationalism* and *M/minzu-zhuyi* in the two linguacultures under investigation became similar after 1949. The results obtained from analysing the media and interview corpora have, however, revealed that the situation is more complex than meets the eye.

In summary, it is clear that the first pitfall type is dangerous because politically relevant notions can have significantly different meanings across linguacultures, which remain hidden unless we look at our data by using a bottom-up methodology. What makes such differences particularly complex is that they are rarely clear-cut: for example, our case study has shown that in modern political speeches *nationalism* and *M/minzu-zhuyi* are *both* negative, in spite of their different connotations.

3.5   Recommended Readings

Paul Chilton. 2004. *Analysing Political Discourse: Theory and Practice.* London and New York: Routledge.

We have already mentioned Paul Chilton's book, which is one of the classics of the field of language and politics, in Chapter 1. In the following section, Chilton (2004: 4) discusses the problematic nature of providing set definitions for the notion of democracy, which is an issue that has emerged in this chapter as well:

How can politics be defined? It is not the business of this book to answer this question definitively. We shall, however, say that politics varies according to one's situation and purposes – a political answer in itself. But if one considers the definitions, implicit and explicit, found both in the traditional study of politics and in discourse studies of politics, there are two broad strands. On the one hand, politics is viewed as a struggle for power, between those who seek to assert and maintain their power and those who seek to resist it. Some states are conspicuously based on struggles for power; whether democracies are essentially so constituted is disputable. On the other hand, politics is viewed as cooperation, as the practices and institutions that a society has for resolving clashes of interest over money, influence, liberty, and the like. Again, whether democracies are intrinsically so constituted is disputed.

Teun van Dijk. 2015. Critical discourse analysis. In Deborah Tannen, Heidi E. Hamilton and Deborah Schiffrin (eds.), *The Handbook of Discourse Analysis, Vol. 2*. London: Wiley, 466–485. https://doi.org/10.1002/9781118584194.ch22.

While our pragmatics-anchored approach is different from CDA, many issues which we pointed out in this chapter are also present in CDA analyses, albeit in a different form. For example, Van Dijk (2015: 476, 477) pointed out that ethnocentrism is a highly problematic phenomenon:

Many studies on ethnic and racial inequality reveal a remarkable similarity among the stereotypes, prejudices, and other forms of verbal derogation across discourse types, media, and national boundaries. For example, in a vast research program carried out at the University of Amsterdam since the early 1980s, we examined how Surinamese, Turks, and Moroccans, and ethnic relations generally, are represented in conversation, everyday stories, news reports, textbooks, parliamentary debates, corporate discourse, and scholarly text and talk ... Besides stereotypical topics of difference, deviation, and threat, story structures, conversational features (such as hesitations and repairs in mentioning Others), semantic moves such as disclaimers ('We have nothing against blacks, but ...', etc.), lexical description of Others, and a host of other discourse features also were studied. The aim of these projects was to show how discourse expresses and reproduces underlying social representations of Others in the social and political context. Ter Wal ... applies this framework in a detailed study of the ways Italian political and media discourse gradually changed, from an antiracist commitment and benign representation of the 'extracommunitari' (non-Europeans) to a more stereotypical and negative portrayal of immigrants in terms of crime, deviance, and threat.

...

The major point of our work is that racism (including antisemitism, xenophobia, and related forms of resentment against 'racially' or ethnically defined Others) is a complex system of social and political inequality that is also reproduced by discourse in general, and by elite discourses in particular ...

4 Pitfall 2
Associating Values with Political Actors and Entities at the Very Outset

4.1 Introduction

In language and politics, the second pitfall covers the practice of the researcher determining at the very outset the nature of how a political actor uses language. There is an assumption here that the linguist is somehow 'objective', and this presumed 'objectivity' allows one to use a morally 'superior' and 'rational' stance to describe the behaviour of an 'irrational' political actor. The sociolinguist Gal (1989: 352) captured this phenomenon as follows:

> It is exactly on the basis of its own supposedly special and superior forms of talking and knowing – which it defines as decontextualized, autonomous, rational, and therefore universal and value-free – that this new class [of Western intellectuals] justifies its claims to power.

Gal refers to the work of the American sociologist Alvin Gouldner, and Gal's arguments here mainly relate to sociolinguistic power. However, we believe that what Gal outlined is also applicable to how certain linguists set out to moralise about political actors and their behaviours.

While this pitfall type very often comes hand in hand with ethnocentrism discussed in Chapter 3, it can also occur in marginally ethnocentric analyses. The following extract from the study of Silva (2019) illustrates such a case:

> Scholars, political commentators and portions of the Brazilian society seem to agree that the success of Jair Bolsonaro's presidency is largely dependent on social chaos and institutional collapse. Brazilian philosopher Marcos Nobre ... has neatly summarized this point: 'To undertake his authoritarian project, Bolsonaro needs to (...) keep the existing democratic institutions in the same state of collapse in which they have been since the mass protests of June 2013 – one of the decisive reasons underlying his election, by the way.' In this article, I resort to some basic principles of linguistic theory in order to explain how Bolsonaro enacts his 'pragmatics of chaos' in language. Inspired by Jacquemet's analysis of Trump's deceitful relation to truth ... my parsing of Bolsonaro's linguistic pragmatics of chaos singles out three levels: Bolsonaro's jocular and incendiary locus of enunciation ...; the texture of chaos and denial in his text and talk ...; and his interested assembling of semiotic and digital resources that produce

a toolkit for recursive and permanent agitation of audiences, both pro and against his politics ...

From the pragmatician's point of view, a major error of descriptions like that outlined above is that they simply do not give a chance to any neutral empirical investigation because the outcome of the investigation is already known at the very beginning. While Jair Bolsonaro, the former president of Brazil, may be an unsympathetic politician whose decisions triggered controversies, by deciding beforehand that he is an authoritarian decision maker who unleashes a 'pragmatics of chaos', Silva already makes a judgement on Bolsonaro's practices of language use before analysing data produced by Bolsonaro himself. Further, Silva's judgement is heavily moralising, as the quasi-academic expression 'pragmatics of chaos' shows.

Pitfall 2 often occurs in top-down comparisons of political actors and entities. For example, in her study of language change in the former Yugoslavia, Šarić (2010: 56) describes various inquiries which presented interaction between politicians in the former Yugoslav state of Slovenia and their colleagues representing the EU (then the European Economic Community, henceforth EEC) as an essentially positive and constructive process, as a result of which 'Slovenia's mission [was] to be the "Europeanization" and "enlightenment" of the Balkans.' A problem with pre-categorising interaction between organisations in the above way is that by doing so an altruistic value is assigned to one of them – in this case, representatives of the EU – and a negative value is assigned to the other organisation, such as the former Yugoslavia in this case. Our case study in this chapter will show that during the break-up of the former Yugoslavia the language behaviour of EU representatives was in certain cases far from altruistic. This outcome, in turn, shows that any pre-assigned altruism is unrealistic in the realm of politics.

4.2 Methodological Approach

When collecting and analysing data featuring how political actors use language, we are faced with a fundamental conflict between the goal of pragmatic analysis and the means of reaching this goal. As Chafe (1994, cited in Chapter 2) argues, on the one hand, we want to recognise, understand, describe and explain systematic, generalisable patterns of language use. On the other hand, every single interaction is a separate linguistic action. This is why it is problematic to project what one thinks one knows on political actors before considering their language use with the aid of case studies. Furthermore, since every single interaction is a separate linguistic action, ultimately it is very difficult to put the language behaviour of a political actor under one single grand umbrella (e.g. Bolsonaro = 'pragmatics of chaos'; see Silva 2019). For instance, in our case studies, featured below, we found that, during the

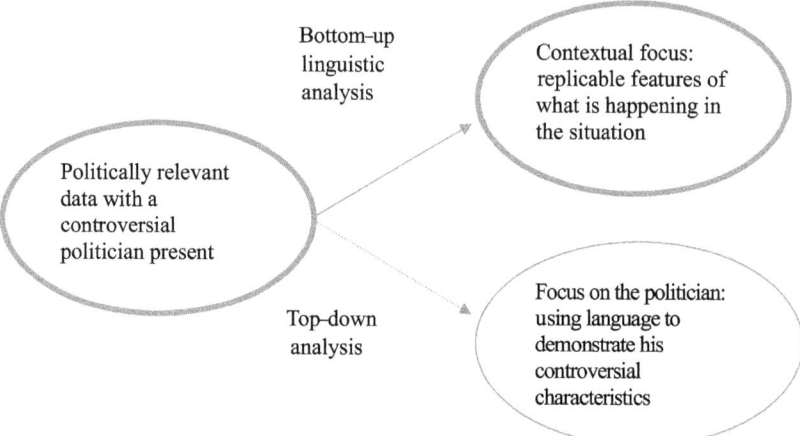

Figure 4.1 Our analytic approach to avoiding Pitfall 2

break-up of Yugoslavia, representatives of the EEC behaved at one point of history in a way which runs counter to the way the behaviour of representatives of the EEC is often perceived. This finding does not, however, lead us to any grand conclusion about the communicative patterns of the EEC; rather it illustrates our main point that it is counterproductive to assign any value to any political actor at the very outset of an analysis.

Figure 4.1 illustrates the methodological take we are proposing here. In Figure 4.1, the bold circles represent our preferred analytic direction, which helps us to avoid falling into Pitfall 2.

We do not intend to argue that aiming to make generalisations about political actors is wrong per se in the study of language and politics. However, we believe that from a pragmatic point of view it is more productive to work out the pragmatic constraints and affordances of a particular political context or situation with the aid of case studies than to make (often predictive) generalisations about how political actors use language.

4.3 Case Study

To illustrate how to put into practice Chafe's methodological recommendation, outlined above, here we present a bipartite case study featuring diplomatic mediation and a follow-up political meeting. In the following, we will refer to elements of this bipartite case study as our 'first' and 'second' case studies. First, we examine the transcript of an unofficial tape recording of a diplomatic exchange between representatives of Slovenia and Croatia and members of an EEC

Pitfall 2: Associating Values 53

delegation in the wake of the Slovenian War of Independence, the first of the ensuing Yugoslav wars in 1991. The representatives of the EEC had agreed with the Yugoslav side before the meeting that the Slovenian and Croatian implementations of the declarations of independence must be postponed and that Yugoslavia must remain intact for the time being, despite the fact that the Slovenians and Croatians had already held plebiscites on independence and had requested a meeting with the EEC exactly because they wanted the EEC to help them to legitimise their independence and persuade the Yugoslav state to stop the ongoing fighting. In this first case study, we investigate patterns of language use through which the mediator with a vested interest in one particular outcome of a diplomatic meeting upheld the tone of 'neutrality' due in the ritual frame of **diplomatic mediation**, which prevents mediators from revealing any partiality. It can be argued that, in such a scenario, there is even a larger pressure on the mediators to uphold the conventions of the frame of ritual mediation than in other – more balanced – diplomatic exchanges, and so their patterns of language use may represent archetypal mediatory conventions of language use. We also consider how the EEC could exert pressure on the Slovenian and Croatian delegates under the **veneer of a 'neutral' style**, using concepts such as 'democracy' as interactional resources (see section 3.2).

Second, we examine the tape recording of a meeting between Slovenian decision makers shortly after the mediation session. During this meeting, the Slovenian politicians reflected on the diplomatic mediatory negotiation with the EEC representatives and discussed what to do next. Studying these two data sets helps us to capture how power manifests itself in the diplomatic mediatory negotiation studied, and how it is judged by the powerless afterwards. We consider whether there is a tension between the ideally 'neutral' language of diplomacy in mediation settings and the presence of a powerful actor who takes up the role of the mediator, with the powerless side facing defeat from the start. Focusing on language behaviour during the mediatory negotiation session and *ex post facto* reflections of the powerless side helps us to achieve a deeper interpretation of the presence of power in a diplomatic situation where it should in theory not be played out.

Through these two case studies, we are able to capture how diplomatic mediatory negotiation operates when there is a salient power difference between the participants. This outcome leads to a language-based and – as such replicable – description of language use in the context of mediation. However, we have no means to generalise about the actors and their patterns of language use beyond the here and now: while representatives of the EEC behaved in a clearly controversial way in our data, we do not think that this behaviour leads to any value judgement about the 'democratic value' of the EEC beyond the actual case.

In terms of the general methodology outlined in Chapter 2, in both our case studies our key unit of analysis is speech act, allowing us to break down our interactional data into replicable components. Further, in the following two case studies we compared various corpora, representing different participation frameworks (see Figure 2.2): in our first case study the Slovenian politicians are members of a delegation, while in our second case study they are in a debriefing session, reflecting on the outcomes of the previous mediatory negotiation. Another contrastive element which emerges here includes the comparison of the behaviour of political actors in different participation roles (Goffman 1981). Our second case study is about a situation in which the participants of a political negotiation where they were powerless report on the outcomes of this negotiation during a debriefing to other politicians. It is interesting to compare their language use during and after the negotiation because such a comparison allows us to capture how the lack of power in diplomacy manifests itself in terms of language use.

4.3.1 Background

Mediatory negotiation as a form of preventive diplomacy has been studied from many angles, such as international relations (e.g. Bercovitch and Rubin 1994; Bercovitch and Gartner 2007), conflict (e.g. Wallensteen and Svensson 2014; Beardsley et al. 2018), history (e.g. Gürkan 2015; Van Gelder and Krstić 2015; Ciftci 2022) and rhetoric and argumentation (e.g. Murau 2012). Some scholars also examined the phenomenon of imbalanced and partial mediation: Wehr and Lederach (1991), Tome (1992), Svensson and Lindgen (2013), Blakemore (2019) and others explored the role of partial mediator in conflict management.[1] Covertly imbalanced diplomatic mediation – where the conflicting sides did not agree that the mediator can be imbalanced – has been studied by Siniver (2022) and Awwad (2023), who considered problems caused by partial mediators in Middle Eastern conflicts. Further, Rosoux (2022) argued that certain seemingly 'democratic' mediation attempts in postcolonial conflicts are doomed to fail due to the mediator's inherently biased position. This latter body of inquiries is particularly relevant for both our case studies because we also consider language use in an event where the mediator was supposed to remain 'neutral'.

Research on back-door diplomatic negotiations is clearly relevant for our study (for an overview see De Lange 2010). In language and politics, negotiation and mediation have been studied in three different areas:

1 various scholars have examined mediation in the context of translation where the interpreter/translator of a diplomatic text is referred to as a 'mediator' (e.g. Ayyad 2012; Pérez-González 2012; Bendazzoli 2023);

---

[1] A particularly interesting study in this area was conducted by Shire (2020), who found that, in many societies, involving partial mediators is part of the ritual of conflict mediation.

Pitfall 2: Associating Values 55

2 others have considered the role of institutionalised media in conflict resolution (see Gilboa 2001; Kampf 2015; Friedman 2017; Friedman et al. 2017);
3 a few scholars have examined the actual face-to-face language use of the mediator in mediation and conflict resolution (e.g. Smith 2012; Barbé et al. 2015).

For us, the third area above is of particular relevance. We hope to contribute to previous research in the field by conducting a pragmatic investigation of what happened to the powerless party during a closed-door diplomatic mediation session, and also by considering *ex post facto* reflections of this powerless side.

Research on mediation in legal contexts (e.g. Maley 1995; Jacobs 2002) and ritual conflict resolution (e.g. Ran and Zhao 2018) also bears relevance for our study. Such research has focused on how the pragmatic conventions through which mediation is realised are constrained by a ritual frame, which cannot be violated due to the institutionalised nature of mediation. Since in our first case such a violation was kept under the veneer of diplomatic 'civility', it is interesting to consider how it was interpreted by the representatives of the powerless side.

Finally, historical research, like the studies conducted by Lyddon (1996) and Glaurdic (2013), provides a detailed outline of the diplomatic strategies of the EEC in the historical events discussed in our case studies.

4.3.2 Data

The data in our first case study consist of the transcript of a tape recording of a mediation event between EEC representatives and the newly established Slovenian and Croatian states. Following the Slovenian and Croatian declaration of independence on 25 June 1991, the Yugoslav People's Army launched an attack on Slovenia. The EEC intervened partly because they had a vested interest in Yugoslavia's remaining intact and politically and economically stable (Repe 2002), and partly out of fear that similar independence movements might occur elsewhere in Europe. On 28 June 1991, after reaching an agreement with Yugoslavian state representatives that they will convince the Slovenian and Croatian representatives to temporarily suspend further steps towards independence, the EEC representatives met with the president of the Presidency of the Republic of Slovenia, Milan Kučan; the Slovenian foreign minister, Dimitrij Rupel; the president of the Republic of Croatia, Franjo Tuđman; and Croatia's representative in the Presidency of Yugoslavia, Stjepan Mesić. Kučan was persuaded to agree to recommend to the Slovenian assembly suspending the independence process for at least three months in the form of the so-called 'Brioni declaration'.

The data in our second case study are a transcript of another tape recording taking place on 8 July 1991, between Kučan and other Slovenian representatives, some of whom were not present in the diplomatic mediation session. The participants in this second meeting faced the following dilemma: implementing the agreement by having the Brioni declaration ratified by the Slovenian parliament meant that Slovenia would militarily put itself at the mercy of Yugoslavia, with no guarantee from the EEC that they would intervene if the Yugoslav state backtracked on what they had promised, blocking Slovenian attempts to reach independence. However, were the Slovenians not to implement the agreement and the declaration, the Yugoslav state would have most likely declared war on Slovenia, and Slovenia would consequently have lost all support from the EEC. In this second meeting, the Slovenian leadership regarded what was said during the first meeting as a 'dictate'. Still, they convinced the Slovenian parliament to ratify the Brioni declaration and suspend the independence process temporarily (for three months) a few days later (Repe 2004: 146–148).

The transcript of the first meeting under investigation consists of approximately 7,000 words, and the second data set consists of approximately 14,500 words. As far as we are aware, the original tape recordings of these events are not available, but owing to Repe's (2004) comprehensive historical work the transcripts of the events are available in Slovenian. While the first data set included speakers of other languages as well, what was said by the EEC representatives is only available in a Slovenian translation (with elements of Serbo-Croat), provided by an interpreter who was present in the meeting.

4.3.3   Methodology

We interpret diplomatic mediatory negotiation as a ritual. As outlined in Chapter 2, following Goffman (1967) and Kádár's (2017; 2024) pragmatic adaptation of Goffman's view, we argue that in ritual situations – which involve both ceremonies and as seemingly more ad hoc interactions – pragmatic conventions follow underlying rights and obligations and a related moral and interactional order. In the context of mediatory negotiation, while such rights and obligations are not set in stone and both the mediator and the conflicting parties have significant leeway to pressurise the others, any form of pressurising needs to be hidden under a veneer of civility (House et al. 2023). Pragmatic constraints are particularly strict for the mediator: provided he has an outsider and non-partial **footing** (i.e. takes such a participant role in an interaction; see Goffman 1979), he is bound by the ritual frame to sound 'neutral', while the other side is not bound by such a pragmatic constraint; that is, the parties in conflict can afford to sound 'subjective'. Setting out from this basic difference, which is in the DNA of the ritual, the contrastive approach is particularly useful in the analysis of our first case study: we aim to capture recurrent patterns in the language use of the EEC representatives and the Slovenian and Croatian representatives and contrast these patterns. In our second case study, we consider how the Slovenian representatives reflected on what happened during the mediatory session once they were not constrained by its ritual frame.

Pitfall 2: Associating Values

We break down our data in both our first and second data sets into speech acts, relying on our finite speech act typology. To help the reader to follow our analysis below, here we present our typology again (see Figure 4.2 below).

Following our bottom-up take, we do not assume that the ritual phenomenon of diplomatic mediation or the *ex post facto* debriefing is realised by one particular speech act. Instead of zeroing in on any speech act, we first examine frequent speech acts in our data from both qualitative and quantitative points of view, and then interpret our outcomes. In quantifying our data, we annotated our corpus manually, and so broader speech act annotation issues relevant to the study of large corpora are not relevant to the current investigation (see here Weisser 2014). To keep our manual annotation rigorous, we used sentences rather than utterances as a unit to be categorised as a speech act.

In both our analyses – in particular in the first case study – we refrain from using the concepts of 'politeness' and 'impoliteness', and instead use the notion of '**covert aggression**' (e.g. House et al. 2023) to refer to cases where significant pressure is exerted on the other in a diplomatic exchange. In diplomatic exchanges, one can rarely observe fully fledged 'politeness' and 'impoliteness' in Brown and Levinson's (1987) sense simply because the participants are

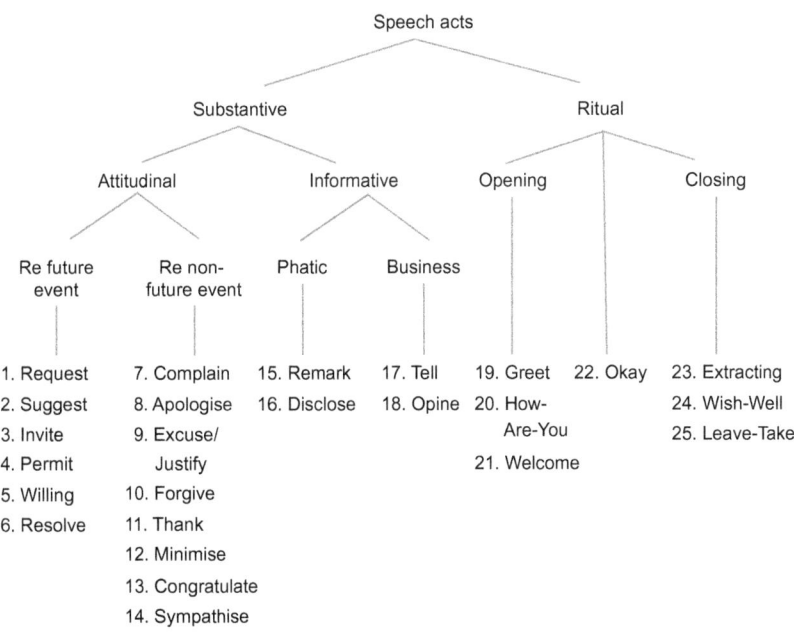

Figure 4.2 Our speech act typology

bound to follow the ritual conventions holding for the situation, so attempts to pressurise the other normally represent a covert form of 'civil' aggression rather than impoliteness. The notion of 'covert aggression' therefore includes instances of language use which have an aggressive overtone but which are not explicitly aggressive and rude, and which do not afford the other's making the speaker accountable.

4.3.4   Case Study 1

Table 4.1 summarises recurrent speech acts in our first data set. As Table 4.1 shows, by far the most frequent speech acts in data set 1 are the Informative speech acts Tell and Opine. While this tendency accords with what we previously observed about the language of diplomatic conflicts in general, it is noteworthy that there are more Opines than Tells in the utterances of the Slovenian and Croatian representatives. Other salient tendencies are the following:
- the EEC representatives realise more Requests than the Slovenian and Croatian representatives;
- Willings are nearly exclusively realised by the Slovenian and Croatian representatives.

In the following, we interpret these tendencies from the point of view of the power imbalance which they reflect in the seemingly 'impartial' procedure of diplomatic mediation in our case.

4.3.4.1   Tells and Opines

As we argued in Edmondson et al. (2023: 169, original emphasis),

> The assumption behind a Tell is that the content of the illocution – the 'fact' communicated – is of interest and relevance to the hearer's concerns and interests, and Tells are therefore made as a response ... to the hearer's explicit or implicit desire to know that fact. If, however, the hearer goes on to *argue* the fact, by doubting or disputing it, then we shall have to say he has treated the preceding illocution as an Opine, and not as a Tell.

If one looks at the proportion of Tells and Opines in our data (see Table 4.1), it becomes clear that the Slovenian and Croatian representatives realised

Table 4.1 *Speech acts in our first data set*

	EEC representatives	Slovenian and Croatian representatives
Tells and Opines	51 and 25 (76 in total)	66 and 106 (172 in total)
Requests	33	21
Willings	1	19

Opines much more frequently than Tells (61.6 per cent of their Informative speech acts are Opines), whereas the EEC representatives frequented Tells (67.1 per cent of their Informative speech acts are Tells). Due to space limitation, in the following we only provide a limited number of extracts to illustrate how the speech acts Tell and Opine are used in our data, in order to cement the superiority of the EEC representatives.

EEC representatives often realise Tells to refer to claimed violations of broader European norms and the international law that the Slovenian and Croatian representatives should have been aware of but failed to observe. Openly criticising the Slovenian and Croatian representatives would normally fly in the face of diplomatic conventions in a mediatory negotiation session (see e.g. various studies in Bercovitch and Rubin 1994). Yet, considering that the EEC delegation included expert diplomats, it can be assumed that their language use only violated the conventions of the event implicitly, and the 'objective' speech act Tell helped them to covertly pressurise the Slovenian and Croatian delegates. Extract (4.1) illustrates such a critical chain of Tells:

(4.1) *Evropska skupnost je izredno zaskrbljena zaradi te situacije zato tudi Evropski svet, ki se danes in jutri sestaja v Luxemburgu razpravlja o tej situaciji. Evropski svet misli, da dogodki, ki so se zgodili v Sloveniji in na Hrvaškem, predstavljajo grožnjo ne le državljanom Jugoslavije predvsem pa slovenskemu in hrvaškemu narodu, kakor tudi ogrožajo stabilnost celotnega kontinenta Evrope čigar del ste tudi vi. Zato danes pozivamo k vašemu čutu odgovornosti.*

The European Community is extremely concerned about this situation, which is why the European Council, which is meeting today and tomorrow in Luxembourg, is discussing the situation. The European Council believes that the events that have taken place in Slovenia and Croatia are a threat not only to the citizens of Yugoslavia, but above all to the Slovenian and Croatian peoples, and a threat to the stability of the whole continent of Europe, of which you are a part of. That is why today we call on your sense of responsibility.

In the above chain of Tells, one of the EEC representatives describes the Slovenian and Croatian policies as 'threats' not only to the citizens of Yugoslavia but also to the whole of Europe. What aggravates aggression here is that this chain of Tells ends with the moralising – and patronising – words 'which you are a part of': clearly the recipients are here given a piece of information which they are supposed to know.

Such Tells are in clear contrast with many Tells realised by the Slovenian and Croatian representatives, which are often self- rather than other-oriented (Blum-Kulka et al. 1989), and which have a much clearer Informative value. This does not mean that Tells realised by the Slovenian and Croatian representatives are always Informative in the fully fledged sense of our typology of speech acts. For instance, as part of exchanging arguments, the leading Slovenian representative Kučan states the following:

(4.2) *Na drugo vprašanje, da sedaj skrajšam, mi smo od našega plebiscita naprej ponujali razgovor o vrsti vprašanj. Nekateri od vas so že imeli priliko govoriti z mano in vedo kakšne so bile naše ponudbe. Šest mesecev od plebiscita do predvčerajšnjim, do razglasitve samostojnosti Slovenije, ni bilo nobene pripravljenosti za razgovor o teh vprašanjih. Praktično se je obšlo, oziroma se ni priznavalo plebiscita, na katerem je 93% udeležencev, teh je bilo pa 86% vseh prebivalcev Slovenije, glasovalo za samostojno in suvereno Slovenijo, ki ne bi bila več v sestavi SFRJ.*

Regarding the second question, in short, we have offered to discuss a range of issues since our plebiscite. Some of you have already had the opportunity to talk to me and know what our offers have been. For six months since the plebiscite until the day before yesterday, until the declaration of Slovenia's independence, there was no willingness to talk about these issues. The plebiscite, where 93% of the attendants voted in favour of an independent and sovereign Slovenia that would no longer be part of the SFRY, which is 86% of the total entire population of Slovenia, was practically bypassed or not recognised.

Here Kučan refers to the fact that although, on 23 December 1990, 93 per cent of the attendants (86 per cent of the entire population of Slovenia) voted for an independent Slovenia, the EEC ignored their requests to negotiate with the Yugoslav state regarding the plebiscite until a military conflict evolved (Osojnik 2022: 464). Yet even this 'non-innocent' Tell is self-oriented, lacking a negative description of the other and reflecting the footing of a powerless participant.

The Slovenian and Croatian representatives realise many Opines. These speech acts reflect on actual events but are realised in a defensive and emotively loaded manner, which makes it difficult to interpret them as merely factual utterances; that is, Tells. Extract (4.3) illustrates such an Opine realisation:

(4.3) *Nismo ogrožali miru in varnosti evropskih držav, nismo ogrožali normalnega pretoka ljudi, blaga, kapitala, idej čez naše meje. Šele ko so se tanki Jugoslovanske armade pojavili na mejah in ko so rakete in lovci šli tudi čez zračni prostor prek Avstrije, je vse to bilo ovirano. Po stališčih dvanajsterice je bilo očitno, da se bojijo, da bi naš odhod sprožil državljansko vojno in etnične konflikte v Jugoslaviji. Etnični konflikti in kršitve pravic so v Jugoslaviji bile že prej.*

We have not threatened the peace and security of European countries; we have not threatened the normal flow of people, goods, capital, ideas across our borders. It was only when the tanks of the Yugoslav army appeared on the borders and when the missiles and fighters also crossed through the airspace via Austria that all this was hindered. It was obvious from the positions of the Twelve that they feared our departure would trigger a civil war and ethnic conflicts in Yugoslavia. Ethnic conflicts and violations of rights had already existed in Yugoslavia.

Pitfall 2: Associating Values   61

Here Slovenian representative Kučan responds to the accusatory Tell that the Slovenians and Croatians destabilised peace in the European continent by declaring independence. He first realises an utterance which we coded as an Opine because it reflects on a perception rather than factual information. Kučan here uses two 'we'-s and states what he believes the Slovenians and Croatians did *not* do, which are typical features of 'subjective' narratives (see e.g. Santora 2013). Following this, he realises two utterances which we coded as Opines because they present the course of perceived events as an interpretation: Kučan uses the formulation 'it was obvious'. In contrast to the Opines of the Slovenian and Croatian representatives, Opine realisations by the EEC representatives are less frequent and represent covert attacks on the Slovenian and Yugoslavian delegates. To keep the present case study analysis focused, we do not cite such Opines here.

4.3.4.2 Requests

Table 4.2 illustrates realisation types of Requests in our first data set. As Table 4.2 shows, the EEC representatives predominantly realise direct Requests with no mitigation (for an overview of the degree of directness of Requests see Blum-Kulka et al. 1989). For example, extract (4.4) features direct Requests uttered by one of the EEC representatives:

(4.4)   *Zato smo vprašali, v naših predhodnih sestankih s predsednikom vlade gospodom Markovićem in predsednikom Srbije gospodom Miloševićem, tri vprašanja. Tudi vam jih bomo zastavili na isti način. Posredovali smo isto sporočilo in uporabili bomo iste besede pri vsebini. Centralno vlado smo prosili, da ukaže takojšnjo prenehanje ognja in da naj še nocoj ukaže vojski, da se vrne v kasarne, da umakne vojsko z vseh okupiranih področij in da se vrne v kasarne. Prosimo vas, da zadržita uresničevanje vaših deklaracij o samostojnosti začasno, ali recimo za obdobje treh mesecev, samo odgodite jih, da boste dosegli demokratičen dialog, za katerega se zavzemate v vašem današnjem sporočilu. In tretjič, prosimo, da spoštujete ustavni red in da se izvrši rotacija v kolektivnem predsedstvu, kakor je zahtevano. To pomeni, da bo gospod Mesić izvoljen in proglašen za predsednika jugoslovanske republike in Jugoslovanov.*

That is why we asked, in our previous meetings with the prime minister, Mr Marković, and the president of Serbia, Mr Milošević, three questions. We will raise them to you in the same manner. We forwarded the same message, and

Table 4.2 *Allocation and realisation types of Requests in our first data set*

	EEC representatives	Slovenian and Croatian representatives
Indirect	5	11
Direct	28	10 (7 realised with formulae)
Total	33	21

62 Language and Politics

> we will use the same wording in their contents. We asked the central government to order an immediate ceasefire and to order the military to retreat to the barracks this very night. <u>We ask you to suspend the implementation of your declarations of independence temporarily, or for example for a period of three months, just postpone them, so you can establish a democratic dialogue for which you are advocating in today's message. And finally, we ask that you respect the constitutional order and that the rotation in the collective presidency is realised as required.</u> This means that Mr Mesić will be elected and proclaimed president of the Yugoslav Republic and Yugoslavs.

As the underlined section shows, after outlining the EEC's previous negotiations with Yugoslavia,[2] an EEC representative, Van den Broek, starts negotiating with the Slovenian and Croatian representatives by uttering two non-mitigated Requests (to-do-x). In this connection, the content of these Requests is also worth mentioning: Van den Broek Requests the Slovenian and Croatian representatives to postpone validating their populations' independence vote in order to 'establish a democratic dialogue' and to 'respect the constitutional order' of a country which essentially ceased to exist due to the plebiscites. In our data, representatives of the EEC recurrently use the expressions 'democracy' and 'order' in a patronising and as such covertly aggressive way, assuming that the Slovenian and Croatian representatives can only uphold these values by providing the requestable. This tactic of pressurising is also reinforced by the supportive move Grounder: Van den Broek tells the Slovenian and Croatian representatives that the same Requests were made to the Yugoslav side, which on the one hand creates an air of 'objective neutrality' (see e.g. Murau 2012), and on the other hand presents a fait accompli for the Slovenian and Croatian representatives.

In contrast to the EEC representatives, the Request realisations of the Slovenian and Croatian representatives are often indirect, as the following extract shows:

(4.5)   *Torej mi smo se na podlagi razglasitve Slovenije, deklaracije oziroma ustavne listine o samostojnosti in suverenosti Slovenije, pripravljeni pogovarjati o postopnem prevzemanju suverenih funkcij z ravni zveznih organov, tako kot smo to predlagali že prej. Moj odgovor na drugo vprašanje je pozitiven, če razumem, da je stališče, da naša ustavna listina velja, da velja to kar je bilo narejeno in da je drugo stvar dogovorov, tako kot smo to sami predlagali.*

So, based on the declaration of Slovenia, the declaration or the constitutional charter on the independence and sovereignty of Slovenia, we are ready to discuss the gradual takeover of sovereign functions from the level of the federal authorities, as we have proposed before. <u>My answer to the second question is positive, if I understand that the position is that our constitutional charter is valid, that what has been done is valid, and that the rest is a matter of arrangements, like we ourselves have proposed.</u>

---

[2] We interpreted this as a supportive move in the form of a Grounder, through which reasons or justifications are provided for a Request (see Edmondson and House 1981).

Pitfall 2: Associating Values

In extract (4.5), Slovenian representative Kučan first realises the speech act Tell ('my answer to the second question is positive'), followed by a Request for the EEC representatives to confirm that what serves as the baseline for negotiations by himself and his Croatian colleague is acceptable. This preference for indirect Requests is logical because tentative/indirect Requests for certain conditions may be preferred in a context where the requestable is granted by the more powerful EEC representatives. This tendency is also reflected by the orientation of the Requests realised by the two sides: Requests realised by the Slovenian and Croatian representatives tend to be speaker-oriented (e.g. 'if *I* understand'), whereas representatives of the EEC prefer addressee-oriented Requests (e.g. 'we demand from *you*') (see also Blum-Kulka et al. 1989).

What makes the contrast between the Request realisations of the two sides even clearer is the following: as the diplomatic meeting unfolds, a negotiation of terms and conditions begins and – as part of this – representatives of the EEC start to reflect on the nature of their own Requests. However, none of these self-reflections is mitigated in any way, as the following extract illustrates:

(4.6)   *V zvezi z drugim vprašanjem moram biti zelo jasen, ko rečemo odgoditi uresničitve, ne zahtevamo od vas, da na kakršenkoli način razveljavite plebiscit vaših ljudi. Suverenost je pri narodu in narod je tisti, ki odloča, mi delamo isto v Evropski skupnosti, da skupno uresničujemo nekatere naše pravice suverenosti. To je delegacija v zvezi skupnosti, federaciji in ni pomembno kako jo imenujete. Torej kar vas zelo precizno prosimo je, da začasno odgodite ...*

        Regarding the second question, <u>I must be very clear, when we say to postpone implementation, we are not asking you to in any way annul the plebiscite of your people</u>. Sovereignty is with the nation and the nation is the one that decides, and we are doing the same in the European Community, so we can exercise some of our sovereign rights together. This is a delegation in a union, in a federation, it does not matter what you call it. So, <u>what we are very precisely asking you to do is to temporarily suspend</u> ...

While here the EEC delegate Van den Broek clarifies the demands he made earlier in the negotiation, he continues to realise the EEC's Requests in a direct and addressee-oriented way ('what we are very precisely asking you ...').

4.3.4.3 Willings

Table 4.3 illustrates the use of Willings in our data.

Table 4.3 *Allocation of Willings in our first data set*

	EEC representatives	Slovenian and Croatian representatives
Willings	1	19

64 Language and Politics

Willing is a speech act through which a speaker communicates that she is in favour of – or at least not against – performing a future act as in the interest of the hearer. The uneven allocation of the speech act Willing in our data is not surprising, considering that it is the Slovenian and Croatian representatives who need to commit themselves to acting according to the outcomes of the mediation event. Yet, considering that in our first data set the Slovenian and Croatian representatives made many different indirect Requests to the mediators to grant that certain conditions be met, the very low frequency of Willings realised by the EEC representatives clearly shows that they had the upper hand throughout the diplomatic mediation event.

Extract (4.7) illustrates a typical Willing realisation in our data:

(4.7) *Prema tome na vaš drugiji prijedlog mi možemo pristati u tom smislu da ostajemo kod svojih odluka o samostalnosti i suverenosti na koji nas obvezuje referendum koji je na najdemokratskiji način izražavanje volje naroda na prava samoodredženje na prava demokratskog odlučivanja o sebi . . .*

> Therefore, we can agree to your second proposal in the sense that we stand by our decisions on independence and sovereignty, which we are obligated to by the referendum, which is in the most democratic way the expression of the people's will on the rights of self-determination and the rights of democratic self-decision . . .

Here the Croatian president Dr Franjo Tuđman states that he is willing to fulfil the EEC's second demand (suspension of declaration), while he keeps reiterating that the referendum is the right of the people to self-determination and self-government, and that this declaration is a direct result of the most democratic form of expression.

4.3.4.4 Summary of Our Analysis of Data Set 1

We found that the uneven power relationship in the diplomatic mediation event studied manifests itself in the following unequal distribution of speech acts:

- Tells are more frequently used by the EEC representatives, who realise them in an other-oriented fashion, while the Slovenian and Croatian representatives more frequently use Opines, with their Tells being mostly self-oriented; the EEC representatives exert pressure on the participants through covert aggression realised with both Tells and Opines.
- The EEC representatives can realise direct Requests, often in a covertly aggressive way; the Slovenian and Croatian participants, on the other hand, frequent indirect realisations of Requests.
- The speech act Willing is frequently used by the powerless participant in the negotiation event – that is, in our case, the Slovenian and Croatian representatives – as it is the powerless side who need to commit themselves to act in a certain way, in order for the mediation event to succeed.

Pitfall 2: Associating Values 65

Since all the EEC representatives were professional politicians, it is safe to argue that their language use represents diplomatic mediation in its quintessential form in a scenario where the mediator has a vested interest in the negotiation's success, and so he may use language in an even more 'objective' way than in other settings. We could also see that the EEC representatives – who actually blocked the implementation of democratic plebiscites – hid their agenda behind a veneer of 'democracy', lecturing the Slovenian and Croatian delegates, who rather sheepishly endured the criticisms. But how did they perceive what happened during the event? In the second case study we investigate this question.

4.3.5 Case Study 2

In the following, we focus on those parts of our second data set which feature a meeting between Slovenian decision makers who reflect on what happened during the diplomatic mediatory meeting. Such *ex post facto* reflections are realised by the speech acts given in Table 4.4 below.

4.3.5.1 Opines

As Table 4.4 shows, the most frequent speech act in our second data set is Opine. Many Opines are negative reflections on the diplomatic style of the EEC representatives, as extract (4.8) illustrates:

(4.8)   *Janez, še enkrat povem: to ni bil rezultat našega pogajanja. To je bil enostranski diktat, ki smo ga mi, kolikor-toliko, moderirali. In nič drugega! In na koncu je bilo rečeno: Ali sprejmite, ali pa pustite. In, če ne sprejmete, mi dvignemo roke in gremo!*

Janez [Defense Minister Janez Janša, one of the participants], I'll say it again: this [the agreement] was not the result of our negotiation. It was a one-sided dictate, which we moderated as far as possible. And nothing else! And in the end it was stated: either take it or leave it. And if you don't accept, we raise our hands and leave!

In this chain of Opines, France Bučar – president of the Slovenian parliament who later declared Slovenian independence – evaluates the veiled aggression of

Table 4.4 *Types of speech act in our second data set*

	Slovenian representatives
Opines	178
Tells	127
Justify	24
Request (for information)	13

the EEC delegates during the mediatory negotiation session. The participants in the meeting in our second data set use such Opines most likely because they were defeated, and also because, through such negative Opines, giving agency exclusively to the EEC, they could minimise their own responsibility for signing the agreement. This latter function of Opines becomes particularly clear in the following excerpt:

(4.9)   *Torej še enkrat jasno in glasno, da to ni rezultat pogajanj, ker pogajanj ni bilo. To je enostranski diktat, ki smo ga s svojim nastopom nekoliko omilili.*

> So once again, loud and clear, this is not the result of negotiations because there were no negotiations. This is a unilateral dictate which we somewhat softened by our performance.

Here Bučar reflects again on the behaviour of the EEC delegates, who did not negotiate with the Slovenian and Croatian delegates but rather handed over a dictate to them. More importantly, he also evaluates their own performance during the diplomatic mediatory meeting as an attempt to 'soften' the impact of the dictate. Such self-evaluations are as frequent in our data as other-evaluating Opines: among the 178 Opine realisations (see Table 4.4), 109 are other-oriented while 69 are self-oriented. Interestingly, as the meeting unfolds some participants move away from negatively evaluating the diplomatic mediation session and begin to reinterpret the way in which the Slovenian delegates handled the negotiations with the EEC representatives. Extract (4.10) illustrates such a case:

(4.10) *Te sestanke bi lahko povzel takole: vi ste politično zmagali, moralno ste zmagali, dajte še probat speljat še te tri mesece, tako da pridemo skozi.*

> I could sum up the meeting as follows: political victory and moral victory, so let's try to get through these next three months so that we get through.

As the above extracts illustrate, a key function of the speech act Opine in our second data set is to negatively evaluate the EEC representatives' behaviour and reinterpret what happened during the diplomatic mediatory negotiation.

4.3.5.2 Tells

Tells in our second data set are used by those participants in the meeting who were present during the diplomatic negotiation with EEC representatives. The following is a typical Tell realisation by Kučan:

(4.11) *Jaz sem povedal, jaz sem na to včeraj pristal z oceno, da je to edino realno, če želimo imeti mednarodno podporo in pogajalsko pot zunaj.*

> I said it: I accepted this [agreement] yesterday because I think that it is the only realistic thing if we want to have international support and a negotiating position abroad.

Here the Tell is followed by the supportive move Grounder, through which Kučan explains the reason behind making the decision reported through the speech act Tell.

As part of the debriefing process, various participants also realise Tells which are in clear contrast with what happened according to our transcript of the first meeting. For example, in response to criticisms of various other participants who were not present in the diplomatic meeting, Bučar realises the following Tell:

(4.12) *Mi smo izrecno rekli ničesar ne sprejemamo, ničesar ne podpišemo o vsem tem bo odločal slovenski parlament.*

> We explicitly said we accept nothing, we sign nothing, the Slovenian parliament will decide about all this.

While indeed the signed agreement with the EEC representatives did not commit the Slovenian parliament to accepting what was agreed, the agreement was in fact signed by the Slovenian and Croatian representatives. We can therefore conclude that, in the present emotively loaded debriefing, seemingly 'objective' Tells are also part of the facework through which the powerless participants in the biased mediation event reconstruct what happened.

4.3.5.3 Justifies

The speech act Justify is also relatively frequent in our second data set featuring the debriefing. Justify is most frequently realised by Kučan, as illustrated by extract (4.13):

(4.13) *Jaz tega nič ne branim, mi ki smo bili zraven, smo presojali vsako stvar, vsako potezo sproti ali z razgovorov ali potem, ko smo dobili informacije kakšni so rezultati teh razgovorov.*

> I am not defending anything; we who were there evaluated every single thing, every single move, either on an ongoing basis, or through discussions, or after we were informed what the results of those discussions were.

Along with the Justifies outlined above, another important Justify realisation type in our second data set involves cases where those who signed the agreement with the EEC representatives distance themselves from the agreement, similar to what we observe with Tell realisations shown in extract (4.13) above. The following extracts illustrate this Justify realisation type:

(4.14) *Jaz pa to nič ne branim, da ne boste mislili, da je to kakšen moj veliki osebi pristanek.*

> I am not defending this [agreement], so that you do not think that this is some kind of personal endorsement.

(4.15) *Ne zagovarjam tega. Hočem stvar samo postaviti v realne okvire.*

I am not advocating that [i.e. proceeding according to the agreement]. I just want to put it in a realistic context.

It is noteworthy that the above utterances were realised by Kučan, who had actually signed the agreement, and Bučar, who had endorsed it.

4.3.5.4   Requests (for Information)

Although most Requests in our second data set occur as the participants in the meeting begin to discuss how to proceed, in the present *ex post facto* discussion Requests are also realised either as Requests (for information) addressed to those who conduct the debriefing, or Requests (for information) through which the participants speculate about the mindset of the EEC representatives. The following extract illustrates the latter case:

(4.16) *Mislite da si oni predstavljajo Slovenijo neodvisno čez tri mesece?*

Do you think they [the EEC representatives] imagine an independent Slovenia in three months' time?

This Request (for information) concerns an issue that the other has no way of answering, and as such it is clearly speculative in nature.

4.3.5.5   Summary of Our Analysis of Data Set Two

We found that *ex post facto* reflections of the powerless side manifest themselves in the realisation of the following speech act types:

- Opines through which the participants either negatively evaluate the diplomatic behaviour of the EEC representatives or reinterpret what happened during the negotiation.
- Tells through which the participants – especially those who lead the debriefing – report what happened. In spite of the seemingly 'factual' way in which such Tells are realised, they often refer to an alternative reality, helping those who led the powerless delegation to reinterpret and thus reconstruct what happened and minimise loss of face.
- Justifies through which those who led the powerless delegation present their course of action to others, and others through which they distance themselves from what happened.
- Requests (for information) through which other participants ask for information from those who participated in the meeting, and others through which the participants speculate about the mindset of the powerful EEC delegates.

4.3.6 Reflections

In this section, we have considered how to avoid Pitfall 2 with the aid of a bipartite analysis, featuring two closely related case studies. We investigated whether there is a tension between the ideally 'neutral' language of diplomatic negotiation during mediation and the presence of a powerful actor who takes up the role of the mediator, with the powerless side facing defeat from the start. We studied this tension by using a **speech act-anchored approach**, allowing us to precisely capture differences between the behaviour of the powerful and the powerless sides in our first data set, and to interpret *ex post facto* reflections by the powerless side in our second data set. Figure 4.3 summarises our findings from a contrastive pragmatic point of view.

As Figure 4.3 shows, while only a small variety of speech acts are frequented in both our data sets, looking at the realisation patterns of these speech acts has still allowed us to tease out the power dynamics underlying the first meeting and reflections about this during the second meeting.

Our findings suggest that although diplomatic language use on the part of a mediator – like the EEC representatives in our case – is ideally 'neutral', such

First dataset		Second dataset
Powerful side	Powerless side	Powerless side
(arrows indicate decreasing frequency)		
Tells (other-oriented)	Tells (self-oriented)	Opines Negatively evaluate the behaviour of the powerful party or reinterpret the behaviour of the powerless side
Opines (covert attacks on the powerless)	Opines (defensive and emotively loaded)	Tells Negatively evaluate the behaviour of the powerful party or reinterpret and thus reconstruct the behaviour of the powerless side
Requests (predominantly direct)	Requests (often indirect)	Justify Realised by those who led the powerless delegation either to present their course of action positively or to distance themselves from what happened
Willings (very few and non-committing uses)	Willings (the powerless party commits itself to act according to the outcomes of the mediation event)	Request (for information) Realised by participants who ask for information from those who participated in the meeting, and others through which the participants speculate about the mindset of the powerful side

Figure 4.3 Outcomes of our analysis

'neutrality' is often covertly violated. While various scholars, such as Rosoux (2022), have noted that diplomatic negotiation is often biased, here we have been able to capture such a bias from a speech act point of view. Furthermore, we have found that representatives of the powerless side are often clearly aware of such violations. The powerless side may also reinterpret their own behaviour after the diplomatic event, in order to save face. For example, we were able to witness various cases when negatively reflecting on the aggressive behaviour of the powerful side also prompted representatives of the powerless side to reinterpret very basic facts, such as whether the agreement was signed or not.

Through these case studies, we are able to capture how diplomatic mediatory negotiation operates when there is a salient power difference between the participants, which is often the case in such settings. This outcome led to a replicable description of this context, but not so much of the actors: while in our case studies the representatives of the EEC behaved in a controversial – not to say arrogant – way, we do not think that this behaviour should lead to any grandiose value judgement about the 'democratic values' of the EEC beyond the actual case.

4.4 Recommended Readings

Julian Aichholzer and Johanna Willmann. 2020. Desired personality traits in politicians: Similar to me but more of a leader. *Journal of Research in Personality* 88: 103990. https://doi.org/10.1016/j.jrp.2020.103990.

Not only is it futile to associate a political actor with a value from a linguistic point of view, but also psychology experts often argue that it is more productive to examine the values that electors expect from a politician than the values of the politician himself. The contrastive study of Aichholzer and Willman represents such a psychological investigation, as the following extract illustrates:

> From citizens' perspective, what kind of a personality should the ideal politician have? We suggest two answers. First, to carry out leadership duties, politicians are expected to have exceptional traits that distinguish them from the general population. As a consequence, we expect that voters, on average, design the *ideal politician* to hold more of those traits that are commonly associated with leadership qualities. Second, we argue that voters will differ in preferred candidate traits, because they seek personality congruence with their candidates. This is partly due to the well-known similarity-attraction principle or attachment to likeness. In the realm of politics, however, personality congruence may also ensure ideological representation of citizens by their legislators. In particular, we expect that citizens seek representation (congruence) in basic value-related personality traits that, at the same time, mirror the content of core ideological attitudes.
>
> We examine our research questions and test our hypotheses in two samples surveyed in Germany and Austria. The two countries represent very similar socio-political contexts of multi-party systems with a relatively stable and long-lasting democratic regime. (Aichholzer and Willmann 2020: 1–2, original emphasis)

Jennifer Sclafani. 2017. *Talking Donald Trump: A Sociolinguistic Study of Style, Metadiscourse, and Political Identity.* London: Routledge.

While we do not advise approaching the language use of individual politicians through pre-held assumptions, this argument does not mean that one cannot tease out invaluable information regarding political actors and their language use patterns with the aid of rigorous language-based analysis. A good example is the work of Sclafani, who examined the language use of Donald Trump without starting from the personality traits of Trump. In the following section, Sclafani (2017: 1, original emphasis, references elided) discusses why the style of what Trump says – rather than exactly what he said – triggered controversies:

Donald Trump became famous, and infamous, not so much for his political stances, which were rarely expressed in any detail during his primary campaign. It was rather *how* he expressed his stances linguistically that fascinated pundits and the public alike. The language of Donald Trump – at the time of writing, President Trump – has been the subject of much debate, both in terms of the rhetorical style in which he has delivered criticism of various individuals and groups, and what some have referred to as the candidate's general oratorical lack of coherence and substance.

It is not the case that Mr. Trump was the first American presidential candidate in history to have received criticism for his oratorical skills or lack thereof. In recent presidential history, President George W. Bush became known for his 'folksy' style and awkward diction. In fact, as Lim ... has documented, presidential rhetoric has been considered to be on a downhill path since the birth of the nation. However, the presidential candidacy of Donald Trump has brought studies on the declining discourse of American presidential figures into the mainstream media limelight over the past two years, and has even spurred new studies and commentary in academic and journalistic circles. Scholars of language and gender have weighed in on the sexism and misogyny ... prevalent in his speech; others have homed in on Trump's racist discourse ...

5 Pitfall 3

Using One's Research to Demonstrate a Pre-held Conviction

5.1 Introduction

When it comes to Pitfall 3, ideological beliefs tend to be present in language and politics in two different ways. First, scholars often put the behaviour of political actors under one particular preset ideological umbrella, representing beliefs held about these ideologies and their role by the researchers. As an example, let us refer here to the study of Winfield et al. (2000: 329, 332) who examined how press systems and their language operate in China and Japan:

> The strong focus on the collective in both China and Japan stems largely from Confucianism and, to a lesser extent, from Buddhism. Confucianism, founded by Confucius (551–479 B.C.) during the Han Dynasty, became a system of social ethics more than a religion. Confucianism persisted as a great and pervasive ethical tradition. In western societies, politics and economics have been influenced by industrial, business and trade groups, but in China, such matters, as well as the general conceptions of family and cultural life, still have Confucian roots. Those values today blend with the needs of the village economy ...
>
> Such [social] ranking [of Confucianism] extends to politics and society as a whole. In Analects 1.2, Confucius wrote: 'Master Yu said, "Those who in private life behave well toward their parents and elder brothers, in public life seldom show a disposition to resist the authority of their superiors."' A role for an individual or the press as a type of 'watch-dog' in an American sense would be difficult to obtain in such a philosophy.

While we agree with Winfield et al. (2000) that an ideology like Confucianism may strongly influence the language of politics, the argument above is heavily overgeneralising, representing a conviction about the social role of one particular ideology. That is, Winfield et al. essentially claim that press systems in China and Japan are somehow 'prisoners' of the ideology of Confucianism. This, in turn, flies in the face of a body of inquiries dedicated to power negotiation between spokespersons and journalists and other related issues in East Asian press events (see e.g. Gu 2018; Mao and Zhao 2020). A particular problem in our view is that grand ideological assumptions often emerge when language and politics are discussed with reference to non-Western – in particular East Asian – linguacultures. Because of this, academic accounts like that of Winfield et al. (2000) are **postcolonial** in nature and ignore more complex research on the influence of ideology on language use (e.g. Cameron 2006; Fairclough 2010; Verschueren 2012). The exoticising postcolonial nature of such descriptions becomes clear once one begins to hypothetically twist them, such as by making a hypothetical claim that all European press conferences are Judaeo-Christian in nature. Should we have made such a claim, it would have been dismissed on the grounds that press conferences are secular in Europe, and so it is clear that in many academic accounts exotic ideologies somehow 'belong' to certain countries and not others.

Second, beliefs also emerge in the study of language and politics whenever scholars set out to prove convictions held by many at the outset. In this book, we have already referred to cases where significant energy is devoted to proving that political actors like Trump and Bolsonaro use language in ways that are non-ethical, disturbing and so on. Since in academia there is a relative consensus about the problematic nature of the language use of these political actors, any attempt to unveil this problem is, in a sense, futile. However, not all academic convictions which are to be proven by the researcher are so straightforward. For example, a noteworthy conviction – which we also consider in the present case study – includes the belief that **colonialism** is evil. What is wrong with an academic inquiry motivated by an attempt to reveal the evils of colonialism? The linguist Mufwene (2002: 163) answers this question clearly:

> I submit that the subject matter of language endangerment will be better understood if discussed in the broader context of language vitality, with more attention paid to factors that have favoured particular languages at the expense of others, factors which lie in the changing socio-economic conditions to which speakers respond adaptively for their survival. Linguists have typically bemoaned the loss of ancestral languages and cultures especially among populations colonised by Europeans, arguing that relevant languages and cultures must be revitalised or preserved by all means. Missing from the same literature are assessments of the costs and benefits that the affected populations have derived from language shift in their particular socio-economic ecologies.

Indeed, it is not problematic to accept that colonialism and neo-colonialism are evil – we ourselves are of this opinion. However, once we build our actual analysis to prove such an argument, we may lose our objectivity and are thus prevented from unearthing hitherto neglected phenomena, such as the issue of cost and benefit insightfully pointed out by Mufwene.

5.2 Methodological Approach

In order to avoid proving pre-held convictions, a self-reflexive procedure which we recommend here is to look at the subject of conviction in actual politically relevant interactional events from both quantitative and qualitative angles. Figure 5.1 represents our approach.

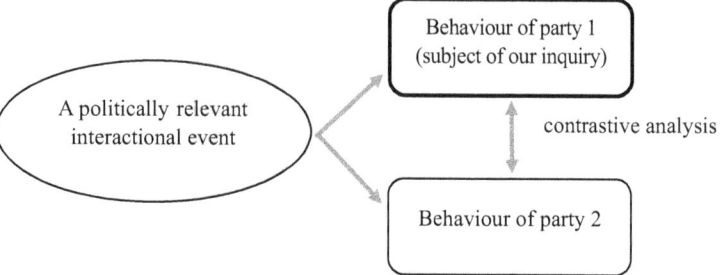

Figure 5.1 Our analytic approach to resolving Pitfall 3

Politically relevant events are those in which one of the participants enacts or represents behaviour which falls under the umbrella of the (usually negative) conviction that the researcher may hold at the beginning of his study. For example, typical politically relevant events in our interpretation would involve interactions between Bolsonaro and another politician, a coloniser, representatives of the colonised party and so on. In this approach, our question is naturally not so much whether the politically relevant interactional event is 'positive' or 'negative', but rather how the subject of our inquiry who enacts a form of behaviour which reinforces a conviction actually behaves. By contrastively examining such an interaction, we may reach outcomes beyond what we know at the outset of our analysis. For example, in the following case study we attempt to tease out recurrent pragmatic behavioural forms of the ruthless coloniser, by looking at the speech act realisation patterns of a typical coloniser. In Figure 3.5, the upper box is indicated in bold because in the procedure outlined above the central figure of the analysis is an actor like a coloniser whose behaviour we hope to systematically and critically analyse, by contrasting his behaviour with the other participant – in our case, the colonised.

5.3   Case Study

In the current case study, we examine the operation of veiled aggression in diplomatic language use from the point of view of speech acts. In particular, we explore how what we define as the speech act Tell is deployed to realise aggression in a nineteenth-century exchange of diplomatic notes between representatives of China and the United States, at a time when the US wanted to join other Western nations in colonising China. As already noted, Tell is an informative illocution which can simultaneously convey information and become **intertwined** with other speech acts to realise threat.

5.3.1 Key Concepts

We use the collective term *diplomatic note* to refer to a note deployed in national conflicts of interest. In modern diplomacy, this subgenre of **diplomatic notes** is often known as *démarche* (*zhaohui* 照會 in historical Chinese). In diplomatic notes, aggression is veiled through the operation of a conventionalised ritual frame (Kádár and House 2019): as already pointed out, covert aggression in diplomacy always occurs under a veneer of civil diplomatic language. In our present case study, the intensity of veiled aggression correlates with the power of the coloniser over the colonised.

In diplomacy, especially exchanges of written discourse studied here, interaction often takes place in the form of genres with strict **conventionalised ritual features** (see Kádár 2017; 2024), including

- the intensive use of expressions of deference, such as ceremonial forms of address;
- the operation of complex participation and ratification in Goffman's (1967; 1974) sense: while a diplomat may exchange seemingly 'personal' remarks with the recipient, ultimately he corresponds as a representative of a country rather than as an individual;
- the operation of a ritual frame, which manifests itself in participants' rights and obligations (see also our previous case studies).

In diplomatic notes, aggression tends to be realised in the form of **veiled threats**; that is, aggressive behaviour hidden behind conventional diplomatic civility with the goal of coercing representatives of the other state to do what the aggressor wants. As Culpeper et al. (2002: 1572) argue, veiling threats is usually 'insincere', provided that the goal of the language user is to realise a real threat. Considering that the veneer of diplomatic 'civility' precludes being explicitly impolite while at the same time affording aggression, in the current study we use the term 'covert aggression', similar to our previous case study. The aggressive veneer in written diplomatic language studied in our present case study resembles what Watts (1999) defined as the 'iron fist in a velvet glove'. The 'velvet glove' implies that the aggressor uses insincere 'politeness' to frame his aggression as 'civil', but also allows him to morally legitimise the aggression (see Kádár et al. 2019).

The ritual characteristics of diplomatic notes mentioned above manifest themselves in the operation of a ritual frame, imposing a certain sense of ritual 'constraint' (Goffman 1967) on aggressive language use: what a diplomat can and cannot do is tightly regulated, and it is practically impossible to cross a certain invisible conventionalised threshold in a ritual diplomatic genre.

76   Language and Politics

5.3.2   Positioning the Case Study

The genre of diplomatic notes has received limited attention in pragmatics, and it has been mostly examined by historians and political scientists (e.g. Fendrick 2012; Beres 2015). A major contribution to this area involves research on 'coercive diplomacy', such as George (1991), Jakobsen (2011) and Schettino (2011). Our study relates to this latter body of research: we examine a case in which a colonising state coerces a state to be colonised into 'coping' with the claimed needs of the so-called 'international community'. Such claimed needs involve the coloniser's demand to be allowed to represent himself in the capital of the colonised and establish free trade, only benefitting the coloniser. From a contemporary point of view, enforcing such demands may be more than sheer 'diplomacy', in that such coercive behaviour violates what we today understand as normal international diplomacy. However, at the time of colonialism many Western countries officially claimed that they were entitled to colonise 'underdeveloped' nations, and when making threats their representatives often argued that they were simply enforcing their countries' perceived diplomatic 'rights' (see Fitzmaurice 2003).

Chinese linguists have devoted particular attention to diplomatic notes, due to the humiliating role such notes played in the nineteenth-century colonisation of the country. For example, various scholars have used such notes to explore diplomatic issues surrounding translation problems in late imperial China (see e.g. Qu 2017). Another interesting line of inquiry in this area is represented by the study of Ding and Mao (2000), who investigated the diachronic development of diplomatic documents in China and explored the diplomatic issues which the archaic style inherited from ancient China triggered during nineteenth-century Chinese diplomatic encounters with Western nations. Other scholars, such as Guo (2003), explored how diplomatic notes evolved in late imperial China under the influence of exchanges with Westerners. Guan (2017), on the other hand, explored Chinese influence on British diplomatic notes written to the Chinese government. Our present case study fills a knowledge gap by approaching nineteenth-century diplomatic notes between China and a Western power, the US, and by focusing on the ways in which an American diplomat realised aggression through veiled threats. While we mostly focus on covert aggression in our US corpus because we are interested in the behaviour of the coloniser (see Figure 3.4), we also briefly examine Chinese diplomatic responses to the US diplomatic notes to enrich our analysis from a cross-cultural pragmatic point of view.

The context of colonialism provides insights into the relationship between aggressive threats and aggression (see Kádár et al. 2019). In our case study, the coloniser who has the military might to cause significant harm and loss of face to the other practically always embeds threats in his realisation of diplomatic 'politeness' rather than impoliteness proper. In this respect, the data under investigation are very different from what (im)politeness and impoliteness-anchored research studied in the realm of language and politics. That is, while a small body of studies touched on aggressive language use in diplomacy (e.g. Swain 2015) and other political settings (see e.g. Bull 2013), such analyses mostly focused on impoliteness rather than on the role of politeness as a veneer of civility – our phenomenon of covert aggression. Also, while ritual has received considerable attention in pragmatic research on language and politics (see e.g. Chilton 1990; Kampf 2019), little work has been done on ritual as an interactional frame facilitating and condoning aggressive political exchanges under the polite veneer discussed above.

Furthermore, while a number of scholars have studied the role of aggression in institutional language use (see e.g. Harris 2001; Grainger 2002; Archer 2008), little attention has been devoted to the institution of diplomacy. Also, in terms of the mode of realising aggression, pragmaticians frequently examine spoken and computer-mediated modes of interaction (see e.g. Vladimirou et al. 2021), while the type of written interaction which we analyse in our case study has been backgrounded.

5.3.3 Methodology

In the present case study, we investigate the following research question: 'How is aggression realised in the ritual genre of diplomatic notes?' The rationale behind asking this question is that one may assume that diplomatic communication is blandly professional, avoiding aggression and conflict, considering that diplomats are responsible for upholding international relationships.

As elsewhere, we follow the logic of Karl Popper's empirical research methodology, which we already discussed in detail in Chapter 2. An advantage of such an empirical procedure is that it often leads us to falsify our own assumptions. For example, when conducting the present case study we had an initial assumption, namely that aggression in diplomatic notes is essentially realised through upgraded Requests (see Blum-Kulka et al. 1989). This was a logical assumption because, in a context where a more powerful party wants the powerless side to do something, the speech act Request is a 'natural' choice. This is all the more because Request can be realised on a wide scale of (in)directness. Notwithstanding our assumption, we decided to explore our corpus without any pre-categorisation, by basing our work on our typology of speech acts. Our examination has shown that the speech act Tell is by far the most frequent speech act in our corpus; that is, our initial assumption turned out to be completely wrong.

As already noted, in our speech act typology Tell is an Informative illocution, which is defined as follows:

The Tell we might call the most 'neutral' informative illocution ... The assumption behind a Tell is that the content of the illocution – the 'fact' communicated – is of interest and relevance to the hearer's concerns and interests, and Tells are therefore made as a response ... to the hearer's explicit or implicit desire to know the fact. (Edmondson and House 1981: 177–178)

Our category Tell is close to what Searle (1979) in his classic study defines as 'Representatives (Assertives)'; that is, a speech act category consisting of speech acts committing the speaker to the truth of his proposition. The reason why we use the category of Tell rather than 'Representatives (Assertives)' is that we pursue interest in the interactional features of Tell following our typology of speech acts and related analytic system; that is, we do not assume that Tell is always informative. More specifically, we focus on cases when Tell is not about committing the speaker to the truth, but rather serves other pragmatic functions.

Our analysis will reveal that in the US corpus (see below) the coloniser's aggression is overwhelmingly realised through the Informative speech act of Tell, which not only changes its default Informative function as a means of covert aggression, but also is often intertwined with other speech acts, such as Request and Complain. By the 'intertwinedness' of speech acts we mean that the speech acts under investigation in our diplomatic data cannot always be rigorously disentangled. This has a significant implication for the understanding of covert aggression in the ritual genre of diplomatic notes: whenever diplomats have the power to act as aggressors and realise threats, they often 'package' aggression in the insincerely 'harmless' informative speech act Tell.

5.3.4   The Historical Background of Our Corpus

In 1842, the First Opium War ended with the Treaty of Nanking between Britain and the Qing Dynasty (1644–1911), through which Britain forced China to open its ports. This was not a harmless 'opening of trade': the British ruthlessly swamped China with opium. Following this treaty, many Western powers, including the US, decided to follow the example of Britain. The US government appointed Caleb Cushing (1800–1879) as envoy extraordinary and minister plenipotentiary and dispatched him to the south of China to negotiate a treaty similar to the one signed between the British and the Chinese. In February 1844, Cushing arrived at Macao, then a Portuguese colony. He immediately contacted Ching Yucai (Pinyin: Cheng Yucai 程矞採, 1783–1858) – China's acting governor general of Guangdong and Guangxi Provinces – with a series of diplomatic notes. Cushing demanded that Ching allow him to proceed to Peking (Beijing) to negotiate a 'treaty of peace' (i.e. an open-trade arrangement) with the imperial government. Cushing's demands rang alarm bells in the Chinese government, and Ching responded to Cushing's notes by attempting to prevent, or at least delay, Cushing's proceeding to the capital. Cushing, on the other hand, was very

Table 5.1 *Our corpus*

Diplomatic notes	Number of English words/Chinese characters
Cushing's diplomatic notes	6,700
Ching's diplomatic notes	7,315

well aware that China, having recently suffered a humiliating defeat by the British, had essentially no power to prevent him signing a treaty for his government. Because of this, Cushing's diplomatic notes became increasingly assertive. Not surprisingly, the exchange ended with the Chinese government giving in to Cushing's demands.

5.3.5 Data

Our corpus consists of the twenty-five diplomatic notes exchanged between Cushing and Ching, between 27 February and 24 May 1844. Within this corpus, we devote special attention to the twelve notes written by Cushing, with occasional references (for contrastive purposes) to Ching's diplomatic notes. Originally Cushing's diplomatic notes were translated into Classical Chinese, and a sinologist in Cushing's team translated the Chinese diplomatic notes into English. In this case study we only mention translational problems in passing, as they do not relate to the main issue we wish to investigate – how the coloniser behaves. The translations of the examples featured in this case study are the original translations. The size of our corpus is given in Table 5.1.

Diplomatic notes in our corpus are publicly available.[1] Note that while our corpus is relatively small, we agree with Sharoff et al. (2013) that a certain degree of 'imperfection' of corpora does not invalidate pragmatic research, in particular if we look at historical data.

5.3.6 Analysis

5.3.6.1 Cushing's Diplomatic Notes through the Lens of Speech Acts

As already noted, our analysis of Cushing's diplomatic notes has shown that an overwhelmingly frequent speech act type in these notes is Tell. As our analysis of the corpus has shown, Cushing realises many Tells to deliver covertly aggressive threats in a seemingly informative way, often as a fait accompli;

---

[1] See Public Documents Printed by Order of the Senate of the United States, Second Session of the Twenty-Eighth Congress, Begun and Held at the City of Washington, December 2, 1844, Vol. 2. Gales and Seaton, Washington, DC; History of Sino-American Relations. Institute of Modern History, Academia Sinica, Taipei, 1968.

that is, he simply announces a menacing piece of information to Ching without bothering to justify it. Considering the importance of Tell in our corpus, in the following we examine realisation patterns of aggression in Cushing's diplomatic notes by centring our analysis on Tell.

The Speech Act Tell as an Instrument of Aggression

The analysis of the Cushing corpus shows that many of Cushing's Tells are not purely informative, but also simultaneously fulfil non-informative functions. Such uses are typically covertly aggressive, and they are not to be confounded with argumentation. The following extract (5.1) illustrates this use of Tell:

(5.1) SIR: I have the honor to inform your excellency that the United States frigate Brandywine, bearing the broad pennant of Commodore Parker, proceeds this day to Whampoa [a port in Guangzhou], on a visit, for a few days, of courtesy and civility to the capital of the Province.

In order to contextualise the Tell in extract (5.1), it is relevant to note that straight after the first note in which Cushing greeted Ching and initiated an exchange of diplomatic notes, he immediately started to demand to be permitted to proceed to the capital in person, to sign a treaty with the emperor. Ching tried to gain time and requested that Cushing stay in extraterritorial Macau, which was a Portuguese colony at the time. However, following Ching's response, Cushing informed him in extract (5.1) above that his military officer, Commodore Parker, is actually already en route to Whampoa to prepare the ground for Cushing's journey to the north. That is, in extract (5.1) Cushing realises a diplomatic Tell presenting the other with a fait accompli, which is a form of threatening aggression as it signals that the previous prohibition of the other's coming is ignored. It is exactly due to this aggressive character that the Tell does not merely fulfil its default Informative function in this context. Importantly, extract (5.1) does not represent an intertwine between Tell and another speech act, such as Request, but rather it provides information tainted with covertly aggressive threatening and related threat to face. To use a colloquial example, diplomatic Tell here resembles a mafia person uttering 'We are coming' in a sing-song voice.

Extract (5.1) represents a relatively 'restrained' Tell in the Cushing corpus. The following extract (5.2) represents a less ambiguously aggressive Tell, in which threat is cleverly packaged as informing the other about a hypothetical situation in a manner-of-fact voice:

(5.2) The rules of politeness and ceremony observed by Sir Henry Pottinger were doubtless just and proper in the particular circumstances of the case. But, to render them fully applicable to the United States, it would be necessary for my Government, in the first instance, to subject the people of China to all the calamities of war, and especially to take possession of some island on the coast of China, as a place of residence for its Minister.

Here Cushing demands that his warship to be allowed to anchor close to Peking and dismisses Ching's argument that not even the British colonisers have ever been allowed to do this.[2] In extract (5.2), Cushing does not explicitly threaten his interlocutor: rather, his veiled threat outlines in detail a hypothetical situation, basically telling the other what he, as an aggressor, might be capable of doing.

If we observe the Cushing corpus from a sequential point of view, it emerges that Tells in Cushing's notes become increasingly aggressive, albeit within the realm of covert aggression; that is, there is a sense of **escalation** in the manner in which Tells are realised across the individual notes. While in the first three of the twelve notes in our corpus Tells are relatively 'moderate' in tone, in that they simply announce what Cushing plans to do, in later notes various Tells gradually become underhandedly more menacing, and also the information they convey increasingly becomes an arrogant lecturing of the other about 'Western diplomatic manners', hence reflecting the face-threatening power talk of the coloniser. Interestingly, at the same time Cushing does not openly violate the norms of diplomacy by being overtly aggressive. The following example illustrates the way in which increasingly menacing Tells manifest themselves in our data:

(5.3) It is customary, among all the nations of the West, for the ships of war of one country to visit the ports of another in time of peace, and, in doing so, for the commodore to exchange salutes with the local authorities, and to pay his compliments in person to the principal public functionary. To omit these testimonies of good will is considered as evidence of a hostile or at least of an unfriendly feeling.

What makes Tell particularly threatening here is that Cushing basically announces that his warship *will be* anchored in a Chinese port close to Peking, hence precluding any objection. The lecturing on the part of the coloniser in this Tell operates as an escalatory mechanism; witness the negative terms 'hostile' and 'unfriendly'.

Other Speech Acts Intertwined with Tell: Complains

Tells in Cushing's notes are often intertwined with other speech acts, with the most frequent ones being Complains and Requests. As already noted, by 'intertwining' we mean not only that Tell sequentially precedes other speech acts, but also that there is a pragmatic 'co-operation' between Tell and other speech acts in the realisation of covert aggression. Let us start the analysis of these speech acts and their relationship with Tell by first focusing on the speech act Complain (see also Vásquez 2011). Our definition of Complain is as follows. The speech act Complain occurs when the speaker expresses his negative view of a past action by the addressee (i.e. for which he holds the

---

[2] Both Cushing and Ching refer in their notes to Pottinger, the British diplomat in charge of signing the treaty after the Opium War.

addressee responsible), in view of the negative effects or consequences of that action for himself. Clearly, the scope of this speech act may include Complains made of third parties.

Complains are frequently employed in diplomatic notes because they point to the rationale triggering the note. Such a basic use of a Complain, combined with a Tell, is illustrated by the following extract (5.4), where the Complain is underlined:

(5.4) When I addressed your excellency on the 13th, thanking you for copies of the treaty of Nanking and of that of Portugal, I was not aware of the fact, which I have since discovered with much regret, that <u>your excellency did not deem it convenient to communicate to me the whole of the treaty of Nanking</u>.

Extract (5.4) shows a neat transition from the speech act Tell to the subsequent Complain. In our corpus the use of Complains intertwined with Tells is often more complex than we can observe in extract (5.4). That is, Cushing often uses Tell–Complain intertwines to make Ching accountable for the threat realised by the Tell. The following extract (5.5) illustrates this phenomenon (Complain is underlined):

(5.5) The people of America have been accustomed to consider China the most refined and the most enlightened of the nations of the East; and they will demand, how it is possible, if China be thus refined, she should allow herself to be wanting in courtesy to their Envoy; and, if China be thus enlightened, <u>how it is possible that, having just emerged from a war with England, and being in the daily expectation of the arrival of the Envoy of the French, she should suffer herself to slight and repel the good will of the United States</u>. And the people of America will be disposed indignantly to draw back the proffered hand of friendship, when they learn <u>how imperfectly the favor is appreciated by the Chinese Government</u>.

Here the Complain is intimately intertwined with a menacing and lecturing Tell: this Tell does not simply ground the Complain, but rather describes a dreadful consequence which may be the respondent's responsibility. Here we can witness a fully fledged intertwine between the speech acts Tell and Complain, in that there is no one single transition between the two speech acts, but rather the intertwined speech acts recur in the threatening message.

Other Speech Acts Intertwined with Tell: Requests

Another speech act which frequently recurs in Cushing's diplomatic notes is Request. We define Request as follows (Edmondson and House, 1981; Edmondson et al. 2023: 42):

In performing a Request, the speaker wants his hearer to do P, which is in the speaker's own interest; that is, not in the hearer's interest. When we analyse Requests, we need to distinguish between the types of goods requested – between Requests for *non-verbal* goods and services, and Requests for *verbal* goods and services. Some requests are realised as *Request to-do-x*, while others are realised as *Request not-to-do-x*.

Pitfall 3: Demonstrating a Pre-held Conviction

Cushing's diplomatic notes reveal the following pragmatic pattern: he rarely uses Requests (to-do-x) and rather frequently uses Requests (not-to-do-x). This pattern is logical if one considers the aforementioned argument that Cushing often realises demands through his Tells announcing a fait accompli. Thus Requests in his diplomatic notes often concern prohibitive behaviour, with Ching being Requested, in a rather menacing way, not to do certain things. Such Requests (not-to-do-x) are always intertwined with face-threatening lecturing Tells, as the following extract (5.6) illustrates (Request is underlined):

(5.6) Least of all, should such apprehension be entertained in reference to any ships of war belonging to the United States, which now feels, and <u>(unless ill treatment of our public agents should produce a change of sentiments)</u> will continue to feel, the most hearty and sincere good will towards China.

In his Tell, Cushing once again announces the fait accompli that his warship *will be* anchored close to the capital of China. At the same time, Cushing inserts – literally, in brackets – a Request (not-to-do-x), warning the Chinese not to try to 'ill treat' the crew of the American ship.

In many cases in Cushing's notes, the Tell is intertwined not only with Request (not-to-do-x), but also with the speech act Complain. More specifically, the Request (not-to-do-x) in such Tells often fulfils a dual Requestive and Complain-like function. This fits into a broader pragmatic pattern which Blum-Kulka et al. (1989) have already pointed out in the Cross-cultural Speech Act Realisation Project (CCSARP). The following extract (5.7) illustrates this point (Request is underlined):

(5.7) Foreign ambassadors represent the sovereignty of their nation. Any disrespect shown to them, is disrespect to their nation, Government, or sovereign. They possess the right, in the discharge of their public duty, to come and go, without let or hinderance. <u>Causelessly to molest them</u>, is a national injury of the gravest character.

Unlike in his other Tells (see above), Cushing here not only refers to a hypothetical clash between the US and China. Rather, his Tell is a response to a move by the Chinese, and so the strongly worded phrase 'Causelessly to molest them' is a face-threatening Request for Ching not to dare to make similar attempts at 'molestation' in the future, with the negatively connoted verb 'molest' also entailing a Complain.

In our corpus, Tells including information about Ching's Requests (not-to-do-x) can also become Complains. In such cases, Cushing usually gives Ching a face-threatening 'lecture' about the 'inappropriacy' of the latter's Request (not-to-do-x), as in the following case (we underline that part of the Tell where Cushing informs Ching about Chiang's own Request, framing it as 'importunate'):

(5.8) Permit me to observe, that your excellency misapprehends the nature of my communications, if you look upon them as conveying an importunate request on any subject whatever; not having understood that your excellency has any power to negotiate with foreign Ministers; and having contented myself with courteously replying to what seemed to me the <u>importunate request of your excellency to have me abstain from going to Peking.</u>

Indeed, my sole object, originally, in addressing your excellency was, to signify my high personal respect, and that of my Government, for the August Sovereign, by seizing the earliest moment, after my arrival in China, to make inquiry for his health.

Cushing's Requests (to-do-x) in his notes mainly concern Requests (for information), which are Requests for 'verbal goods'. The following extract (5.9) represents such a Request intertwined with a Tell (Request is underlined):

(5.9) The United States are at peace alike with China, Great Britain, and Portugal; and I trust that this happy state of things may long continue as to all these Powers, and especially as between the United States and China.

But the Government of the United States would be liable to commit errors injurious to a good understanding, and capable of disturbing mutual good will, <u>unless it were fully and exactly informed as to the terms of the treaties existing between Great Britain and Portugal on the one hand, and China on the other, by which their political as well as their commercial relations are regulated.</u>

In extract (5.9), the Request legitimises the threatening Tell; that is, the potential that the US 'would be liable to commit errors' and end the 'peaceful' relationship with China.

Other Speech Acts Intertwined with Tell: Suggests

Another speech act which occurs intertwined with Tells in our corpus is Suggest, a speech act category which in other research has also been referred to as the speech act of 'advice' (see e.g. Hinkel 1997). We define Suggest as follows. In the speech act Suggest, the speaker states that she is in favour of the addressee's performing a future action, which is in the addressee's own interest. Suggest is therefore essentially different from the speaker-oriented speech act category Request.

In Cushing's notes, Tells can be intertwined with Suggests which are apparently in the interest of the recipient but are certainly not 'innocent': such Suggests are often deployed as aggressive threats. The following extract (5.10) illustrates such a use of a Suggest embedded in a Tell (the Suggest is underlined):

(5.10) Accordingly, in the West, foreign ministers, on arriving at the borders of the Government to which they are sent, are accustomed to enter the country immediately, and to proceed, without delay or obstacle, to the Court, where, after paying their respects to the sovereign, they address themselves at once to the appropriate minister of State, for the transaction of the business of the mission. Such are the usages followed by the West, in the general interests of humanity. For, when great nations deal together as such, they must deal through

Pitfall 3: Demonstrating a Pre-held Conviction   85

> the medium either of ambassadors, the instruments of friendship, or of fleets and armies, the instruments of hostility. <u>There is no other alternative. And thus it is, that the agency of ambassadors is found to be of the greatest utility, not only as the means of terminating the calamities of war, but also as the means of securing the continuance of the blessings of peace.</u>

Such uses of Suggest are not only aggressively threatening because they are intertwined with face-threateningly lecturing Tells, but also because the recipient's 'interest' here is ambiguous at best: Ching is provided with a choice between being assaulted (unsuggested outcome) and avoiding the assault (suggested outcome).

Other Speech Acts Intertwined with Tell: Excuse/Justify and Sympathise

Tells in Cushing's diplomatic notes can also be intertwined with the speech acts Excuse/Justify (see also Searle 1975) and Sympathise (see also Nakajima 2002). While in 'ordinary' interpersonal interaction these non-Future-related speech acts are typically positively connoted and relationally constructive, in Cushing's correspondence they are part of realising aggression because they tend to be embedded in threating and 'lecturing' Tells.

We define Excuse/Justify and Sympathise as follows (Edmondson et al. 2023: 152–153):

> If we seek to interactionally distinguish between an Excuse and a Justify, we might say that in the first case a speaker admits that what she did was undesirable but suggests that there are or were mitigating circumstances which lessen the blame attached to herself. With a Justify, however, the speaker seeks to persuade someone that what she did was 'justified', such that *no* blame attaches to herself for having done it. When we analyse naturally occurring interaction, it is often difficult to rigorously distinguish between these two speech acts. A Sympathise is an appropriate response whenever the speaker hears that something unfortunate has happened to the addressee.

While in daily interaction Excuse/Justify tends to be relationally constructive because it relates to the producer of a given Excuse/Justify, in Cushing's notes this speech act always occurs in reference to other colonising powers, such as the British. Thus, in Cushing's notes, this speech act aggravates lecturing Tells, usually 'educating' Ching about why his worries regarding the aggressive US moves, and his Complains about the actions of the British and other colonisers, are unjustified. The following extract (5.11) illustrates this use of Excuse/Justify (Excuse/Justify is underlined in the extract):

(5.11)   I have examined the article referred to; and find that by it England is required to keep a Government vessel at anchor in each of the five ports of Kwangchow, Fuchow, Amoy, Ningpo, and Shanghai; but I find nothing in the article to limit the size and the armament of that vessel, and <u>nothing which prohibits England from keeping two or ten Government vessels in each of the five ports, if it suits her pleasure. I presume she consults her</u>

> own convenience in keeping at present only one Government vessel, and that of small size, anchored at Kwangchow, which she may well do having a fleet of large vessels so near at hand, at Hong Kong.

Cushing's argument here is that the British are justified keeping warships in Chinese ports. This argument also validates the US demand to anchor military ships in Chinese ports.

While Sympathise is relatively rare in our corpus, whenever it occurs it expresses anything but sympathy for Ching. Rather, Cushing's realisations of Sympathise are typical expressions of the face-threatening condescension which is typical of an interaction between the powerful coloniser and the essentially powerless colonised. The following extract (5.12) shows this use:

(5.12) I have only to add, that when the Brandywine went to Whampoa, it was the intention of Commodore Parker to return so soon as the state of the tide should admit of her crossing the bar in safety; and to this original intention he will still adhere. <u>I have no disposition to increase the embarrassments to which your excellency is already subjected</u>, by the grave omission of the Imperial Government in neglecting to make proper provision for the American legation, immediately on receiving notice of its intended arrival.

5.3.7 Summary of Analysis

Our analysis has shown that Tells are fundamental in our US data for realising aggression under a veneer of civility. We have also examined other speech acts which, being intertwined with Tells, are also used to realise covert aggression. In the following, we summarise the results of our analysis from a quantitative point of view. Note that in this analysis we only count the approximate length of covertly aggressive speech acts in our corpus, bearing in mind all the difficulties which speech act annotation entails, and also that intertwinedness only allows us to quantify our data for illustrative purposes.[3] Based on our annotation of the data, here we simply refer to the number of words representing speech acts in our annotation, rather than arguing that Cushing used a particular 'quantity' of speech acts. In annotating our data, we manually distinguished sections which are relevant for the realisation of aggression from others which we regarded as 'neutral'; we dismissed the latter from our quantitative analysis. Table 5.2 provides a summary of our quantitative findings.

In the following, we will conduct a comparison of the outcomes of our analysis of Cushing's notes with the pragmatic features of Ching's responsive

---

[3] We have not studied the 'frequency' of speech acts in the conventional sense of the word. Unlike either in naturally occurring face-to-face interaction or elicited spoken data, diplomatic notes represent longer stretches of written discourse and, as our analysis has illustrated, one particular Tell unfolds by using many words; that is, it often takes a significant portion of the text. This is

Table 5.2 *Quantitative features of aggression realisation in Cushing's diplomatic notes*

Type of aggression-relevant speech acts	Distribution of aggression-relevant speech acts (in words)	Proportion (overall size of the Cushing corpus: 6,700 words)
Tell	3,165	47.23%
Complains (intertwined with Tell)	587	8.76%
Requests (intertwined with Tell)	470	7.01%
Suggests (intertwined with Tell)	186	2.77%
Excuse/Justify and Sympathise (intertwined with Tell)	121	1.80%
Total	4,529	67.57%

diplomatic notes. We keep this comparison brief because in the procedure provided for resolving Pitfall 3, we propose to analytically prioritise the behaviour of the actor whose behaviour we aim to investigate.

5.3.7.1 Ching's Diplomatic Notes through the Lens of Speech Acts

Before engaging in an analysis of speech acts in Ching's diplomatic notes, it is worth noting that the aggression in Cushing's Tells appears to be at the same time exaggerated and mitigated by the Chinese translators of Cushing's notes. That is, the Chinese translators not only translated but also liberally interpreted Cushing's notes, reflecting Chinese assessments of these notes (see House 2024 on the evaluation of translations):

1 *Exaggeration:* The translators added a 'militant' exaggerating interpretation to both the personnel and ships of Cushing. For example, while Cushing often refers to his own ship simply as 'Brandywine' in his own diplomatic notes, in the Chinese version of these notes the Chinese translators always refer to 'Brandywine' as 'warship Brandywine' (*Bolandiwan bingchuan* 沒蘭的灣兵船).

2 *Mitigation:* The translators attempted to mitigate the face-threat of Cushing's notes to the emperor by adding honorific nouns and verbs. For example, Cushing's menacing Tell that he will 'deliver a letter ... addressed to his Imperial Majesty' was translated into Chinese as *chengxian Dahuang yulan* 呈獻大皇帝御覽 (lit. 'presenting humbly for the majestic reading of the Heavenly Emperor').

All Tells in Ching's notes are 'innocent'; that is, devoid of aggression. The following example illustrates this point:

why we counted the number of words instead of considering how 'many' Tells there might be in a particular text.

(5.13) 現在大皇帝福壽安康,遐邇同慶,理合复知貴公使,以答慕義之忱。

> At the present time, the great Emperor is in the enjoyment of happy old age and quiet health, and is at peace with all, both far and near; of which it is proper, in reply, to inform the honorable Plenipotentiary, in order to answer his sincere desire of what is just and proper.

Here the Tell simply operates in its default informative function.

An additional pragmatic function of such 'innocent' Tells is the following: in various cases, Ching realises Tells essentially to appease the aggressor. For example, in the following extract (5.14) Ching realises a Tell to inform Cushing that he is trying his best to cope with Cushing's wish.

(5.14) 又本兼護部堂於二月十四日具奏貴公使仍請進京,並願由內河行走一案,本月十九日,接奉軍機大臣字寄大皇帝諭旨,頒給調任兩廣總督耆欽差大臣關防,與貴公使酌商定議。

> Again: I, the acting Governor General, upon the 2nd moon, and the 4th day, (April 1, 1844) memorialized the Emperor, that the honorable Plenipotentiary still requests to go to Peking, and is willing to go by the inner rivers. This, too, is on record. Upon the 19th of the present month (May 6) I received a communication from the Privy Council, stating that the August Emperor's will has been promulgated, to deliver over the seal of Imperial High Commissioner to Tsiyeng, Governor General of the two Kwang, in order that with the honorable Plenipotentiary he may negotiate and settle deliberations.

When it comes to other speech acts, our analysis has not only shown that they are rather defensive in nature, but also, and more importantly for the present analysis, that they are rarely intertwined with a Tell. Rather, Tell simply occurs in a sequential preparatory relationship with other speech acts, providing necessary informational background for an ensuing speech act. Thus the pragmatic dynamics of Ching's diplomatic notes are very different from those of Cushing's notes: Ching responds with speech acts such as Request and Complain to Cushing's menacing Tells, instead of reciprocating with similar Tells. Let us here refer to two Chinese examples including first a Request (not-to-do-x) and then a Complain:

(5.15) 若不待奏請,徑以兵船駛往天津,殊與體制未協。

> Again: if [the Plenipotentiary] presumes to go the capital, still he must stop; for if he do not wait to memorialize the Emperor, and request permission, but proceed hastily, by a narrow passage, with a man-of-war to Tien Tsin, this will be to put an end to civility, and to rule without harmony.

The Request (not-to-do-x) in extract (5.15) is a direct 'hedge performative' (Blum-Kulka et al. 1989). However, this level of directness does not translate into aggression; rather, it represents an attempt to fend off Cushing's aggressive fait accompli. The following Complain, in extract (5.16) fulfils a similar function:

(5.16) 軍機大臣字寄。道光二十四年三月初五日,奉上諭:據程奏米利堅仍復籲請進京,並願由內河行走等語。

> We, great Ministers of State, Members of the Privy Council, communicate that, on Taou Kwang, 24th year, 3rd moon, and 5th day, (22nd April) we received the Imperial mandate, that whereas Ching has memorialized the Throne, that the American Envoy still again <u>importunately</u> requests to enter Peking, and is willing, by the inner rivers, to make the journey,

While the speech act Complain in extract (5.16) is upgraded, it again represents an attempt to fend off aggression. The word 'importunately' in the English text was added by the American translator, supposedly to escalate the conflict between the two parties.

Our Chinese corpus reveals a major cross-cultural pragmatic difference between the two corpora of diplomatic notes under investigation. While Cushing produces mainly Tells, often intertwined with other speech acts, he refrains from realising these other speech acts in a direct manner. As an aggressor with power, it might simply not have been necessary for him to do this. The Chinese respond to Cushing's Tells by realising speech acts in a rather direct manner. While there is very little upgrading (see Blum-Kulka et al. 1989) in Cushing's notes, Ching's responses are generally upgraded: he uses many expressions such as *xu* 須 ('must') and *bude* 不得 ('should not').

From a quantitative point of view, if one counts attempts at fending off the American aggression as aggressive behaviour and dismisses non-aggressive language use, the quantitative properties of aggression realisation in our Chinese corpus are given in Table 5.3. As Table 5.3 also indicates, the aggression-related speech acts in Ching's notes are Complains and Requests.

5.4 Reflections

In the current case study, we have examined the use of the Informative speech act Tell in diplomatic notes, by focusing on its role in the realisation of aggression in Cushing's notes. We investigated the research question 'How is

Table 5.3 *Quantitative features of aggression realisation in Ching's diplomatic notes*

Type of speech acts fending off aggression	Distribution of speech act occurrences fending off aggression (in characters)	Proportion (overall size of the Ching corpus: 7,315 words)
Complains	2,251	30.77%
Requests	1,927	26.34%
Total	4,178	57.11%

aggression realised in the ritual genre of diplomatic notes?' Our analysis has shown that, in the US corpus, realisations of aggression are centred on the particular speech act type Tell, which in the context of covert aggression is often used beyond its default Informative function. More specifically, when a Tell is used to announce a forthcoming menacing action, it gains an aggressive character. There is a cluster of speech acts which are deployed intertwined with Tell to realise covert aggression in our data. The prevalence of Tell in the genre of diplomatic notes is due to the fact that diplomats are supposed to uphold a veneer of civility, especially when they realise covertly aggressive threats. Our analysis of the Chinese corpus has shown that Tells in Ching's notes are only realised with their original 'innocent' Informative function. It is not a coincidence that the pragmatic qualities of Cushing's and Ching's notes are not in parallel, given the power difference between these two politicians.

In summary, this case study has shown that it is possible to pin down the *behaviour* of the coloniser from a pragmatic point of view. Any negative predisposition towards colonialism has not (and could not have) influenced our perceptions of this behaviour because we had no way to know at the outset of our research exactly what to expect in our data. Therein resides, in our view, the effectiveness of a strictly language-anchored bottom-up approach to language and politics.

In Chapter 3, 4 and 5 we have discussed how the methodology proposed in Chapter 2 can be used to avoid the three major pitfall types we outlined for the study of language and politics. Having presented our methodology and its application in Part One of this book, in the following Part Two we move on to cover what we regard as the key topics in the pragmatic study of language and politics.

5.5   Recommended Readings

Popper, Karl. 1954. *The Logic of Scientific Discovery*. London and New York: Routledge.

Karl Popper's seminal work has influenced our framework enormously, and most ideas outlined in Chapters 3, 4 and 5 have their roots in Popperian thought. We therefore highly recommend Popper's above book for readers with interest in empirical research. In the following section, Popper discusses the problem of pre-held convictions influencing the research procedure – an issue at the heart of Pitfall 3 discussed in this chapter:

We may now return to a point made in the previous section: to my thesis that a subjective experience, or a feeling of conviction, can never justify a scientific statement, and that within science it can play no part except that of an object of an empirical (a psychological) inquiry. No matter how intense a feeling of conviction it may be, it can never justify a statement. Thus I may be utterly convinced of the truth of a statement; certain of

Pitfall 3: Demonstrating a Pre-held Conviction

the evidence of my perceptions; overwhelmed by the intensity of my experience: every doubt may seem to me absurd. But does this afford the slightest reason for science to accept my statement?

... Even the fact, for me to so firmly established, that I am experiencing this feeling of conviction, cannot appear within the field of objective science except in the form of a *psychological hypothesis* which, of course, calls for intersubjective testing: from the conjecture that I have this feeling of conviction the psychologist may deduce, with the help of psychological and other theories, certain predictions about my behaviour; and these may be confirmed or refuted in the course of experimental tests. But from the epistemological point of view, it is quite irrelevant whether my feeling of conviction was strong or weak; whether it came from a strong or even irresistible impression of indubitable certainty (or 'self-evidence'), or merely from a doubtful surmise. None of this has any bearing on the question of how scientific statements can be justified.

Considerations like these do not, of course, provide an answer to the problem of the empirical basis. But at least they help us to see its main difficulty. In demanding objectivity for basic statements as well as for other scientific statements, we deprive ourselves of any logical means by which we might have hoped to reduce the truth of scientific statements to our experiences. Moreover, we debar ourselves from granting any favoured status to statements which describe experiences, such as those statements which describe our perceptions (and which are sometimes called 'protocol sentences'). They can occur in science only as psychological statements; and this means, as hypotheses of a kind whose standards of inter-subjective testing (considering the present state of psychology) are certainly not very high.

Whatever may be our eventual answer to the question of the empirical basis, one thing must be clear: if we adhere to our demand that scientific statements must be objective, then those statements which belong to the empirical basis of science must also be objective, i.e. inter-subjectively testable. Yet inter-subjective testability always implies that, from the statements which are to be tested, other testable statements can be deduced. Thus if the basic statements in their turn are to be inter-subjectively testable, there can be no ultimate statements in science: there can be no statements in science which cannot be tested, and therefore none which cannot in principle be refuted, by falsifying some of the conclusions which can be deduced from them. (Popper 1954: 24–25, original emphasis)

Part Two

Key Topics

6   Research Involving Sensitive Topics

6.1   Introduction

A key area in the study of language and politics is concerned with the study of sensitive topics. Since politics influences our lives, the researcher may easily encounter data types and phenomena which are sensitive to certain social members or social groups, and as such are delicate to study. In fact, there are various types of **sensitivity in language and politics** which the analyst may have to consider.

6.1.1   Sensitivity Type 1: Studying Politically Relevant Data in Countries Which Do Not Support Such Work

The analyst may have to work with data in contexts where such research is considered unwanted. For example, the Russian scholar Yusupova (2019: 1–2) argues as follows in her study of sensitive topics in Russia:

> The study of minority groups can be particularly sensitive since illiberal regimes often seek to homogenize their populations and portray minority groups as a threat to justify the state's increasing control over the population. Exploring even mundane, everyday manifestations of ethnicity in such situations can become highly sensitive and raise methodological problems such as limitation of available academic literature and funding, greater responsibility for research and participants' safety, and forced partisanship.

6.1.2   Sensitivity Type 2: Studying Secretive Data Produced by Politicians

There are data types which are sensitive because they are produced by politicians for internal use only; that is, they are designed to be kept away from the public eye. In the study of such sensitive data, the main question for the researcher is how to access it. For example, Coetzee (2020: 65), in his study on arms deals, notes the following:

> [There is] a small but established body of literature on elite interviewing regarding 'sensitive' topics . . . providing a reflexive and methodological account of the processes,

practices and challenges associated with researching one highly politicised policy domain, namely the conventional arms trade. I draw on examples from a study that was designed to explore ideals and interests (and their interrelationship) in foreign policy. An in-depth case study of this issue examined Sweden's 1999 JAS-39 Gripen fighter aircraft deal with South Africa.

6.1.3 Sensitivity Type 3: Studying Painful Topics

The third type of sensitivity – which in our view is the most important sensitivity type in the field of language and politics – includes the study of painful topics. Cornejo et al. (2019) summarise this type of sensitivity as follows:

> Research on sensitive topics comprises studies that examine potentially delicate issues, since they focus on experiences that are painful or emotional for participants. Studying these topics also causes researchers to be affected by the sensitive contents and meanings of the participants' experiences. Research on sensitive topics can also be regarded as that which, given the nature of what is examined, involves research processes in which each stage must be carefully designed and implemented, so that the methods employed in sampling, data production and analysis, and results generation, take into account the sensitive nature of the research object.

The reason why this type of sensitivity is particularly relevant for the field of language and politics is that political decisions may lead to outcomes which cause suffering and are painful for many to talk about later on, including, for example, wars and mass murders. Thus the way in which politicians reflect on such events is important to study from a pragmatic point of view.

In the remainder of this chapter, we will deal with this third type of sensitivity in language and politics, by focusing on the phenomenon of **public ritual apology**. We believe that such apologies are illuminating in the study of the third sensitivity type outlined above due to two reasons:

1. Such apologies are triggered if and when an event which is painful for many leads to some form of outcome whereby either a responsible politician or a representative of the perpetrator is held to account.
2. Methodologically speaking, the speech act Apologise represents a phenomenon which has been broadly studied in pragmatics (see more below), and so the study of public ritual apologies allows us to consider how apologies representing public political language use relate to everyday apologies.

To provide a representative example to illustrate how such Apologise realisations are formulated, it is worth here referring to the trial of Kaing Guek Eav, alias 'Comrade Duch'. Duch was one of the most notorious perpetrators of mass murders committed by the Khmer regime. He was tried openly by the Supreme Court Chamber of the Extraordinary Chambers in the Courts of

Cambodia in 2009. Duch realised a public ritual apology towards the victims. His public apology can be described as excessive by nature: along with recurrently emphasising his own responsibility and admitting his guilt through apologising, the paralinguistic and non-linguistic features of his chain of Apologise realisations display intensified emotions: Duch maintained long pauses between his apologies, and he also sobbed many times during his public ritual apology. Although the public apology took place in Khmer, we cite here a brief excerpt of its English translation with paralinguistic and non-linguistic annotations:

(6.1)
1 Mr President, my remorse and suffering continue unabated.
2 Every time I recall the past I am racked by the same anguish.
   (thirty-six seconds, altogether six longer pauses, one taking seven seconds)

Duch looks grave and gulps various times; he squeezes his lips over some of the breaks:

(Retrieved from www.youtube.com/watch?v=zN9R-DaXJ-A)

Duch's Apologise realisations show the typical communal feature of apology as a public ritual 'performance' (Goffman 1971): Duch apologises also on his subordinates' behalf and towards all the victims of the Khmer terror, and as such his two Apologise realisations in the excerpt above aim not so much to resolve any actual conflict as rather to reposition the performer as a repentant. It is clear from the paralinguistic signs of long pauses and his faltering voice that – emotively speaking – he is highly involved in the ritual 'performance'. Some of his pauses are extremely long, which indicate that the event is dramatic; in addition, Duch's facial signs also express dramatic tension. In summary, the observer of this ritual may have no doubt about the sincerity and excessive nature of Duch's ritual public apology, and yet this public apology has received mostly negative reactions in the media, due to the fact that various commenters argued that no apology would be sufficient to be accepted and it came only *after* Duch was brought to court. Thus this ritual apology may not be regarded as 'manipulative', or 'strategic' in the sense of Brown and Levinson (1987). That is, many might have expected Duch, as an 'animator' of the voice of the Khmer Rouge, to make a profound public apology, and as such this excessive apology was regarded as appropriate. The nature of this public apology as a ritual to admit guilt rather than to obtain pardon is illustrated by the following excerpt from an online article, which was written as a reflection on this event:

(6.2)   He's called Kaing Guek Eav, but he's better known as Comrade Duch. As head of Tuol Sleng prison from 1975 to 1979, he was the Khmer Rouge's executioner-in-chief. The prisoners in his care were beaten, mutilated and subjected to electric shocks, and then bludgeoned to death and buried in mass graves. 'I am,' he calmly told a packed courtroom this week, 'solely and individually responsible for the loss of at least 12,380 lives.' ...
There has, apparently, been no great rush.

(Retrieved from https://bit.ly/3APfi5V)

In this chapter, we look into the phenomenon of public ritual apologies in greater detail and from a contrastive angle, by examining a case study of Japanese and German apologies following war crimes committed during the Second World War by members of these two countries. In terms of our framework, studying these data represents a procedure whereby we examine a discourse-level phenomenon with the aid of speech acts and expressions, and by contrasting data drawn from Japanese and German corpora. Unlike in various other speech act analyses presented in this book, here we focus on a single speech act – namely Apologise sequences emerging as public apologies – and examine and compare the realisation patterns of Apologise speech acts in our corpora. Furthermore, we capture patterns of pragmatic behaviour in a ritual setting. In the study of this topic, the bottom-up view we are following in all the studies presented in this book is particularly important because, when it comes to Japanese and German Second World War apologies, there are many long-standing ethnocentric beliefs and prejudices, which are worth challenging (see e.g. Luke 1997; Brooks 1999; Smith 2013).

6.2   Our Case Study

The term 'war crime apology' (or simply **'war apology'**) refers to a public ritual speech centring on the speech act category of Apologise, delivered by a ratified person (Goffman 1967) – usually a representative of the state or a state minister – following crimes which have been perpetrated during a wartime situation. Generally, these single-source apology speeches are realised after negotiations have taken place between the government issuing the apology and representatives of the victims of war crimes (see Renner 2015). In one respect, war apologies conform to Goffman's (1956: 113) definition of apology, which he describes as being an act during which the apologiser splits himself into two parts: the guilty side and the side that 'stands back and sympathizes with the blame giving'. Admitting guilt (responsibility) and the expression of regret are both quintessential parts of a war apology. However, war apologies represent a form of political rather than interpersonal apology, which can bring about reconciliation, but does not necessarily do so. While every speech act Apologise is, in a sense, paradoxical, in that no matter how sincere it might appear it cannot undo the acts that have been committed, a war apology emerges following a major moral transgression which cannot be healed (Benoit 1995). As Tavuchis (1991: 102) notes, such apologies are invariably made in public:

Publicity ... at once defines and distinguishes this form of apology, namely, to amplify what was said earlier, the primacy of the record in regard to the production and registration of the speech. And it is ultimately this necessity, a speech whose sole *raison d'être* is the record, that takes us to the heart of collective apology.

In terms of pragmatic realisation, ritual war apology discourse displays a number of features which are typical of public rituals: (a) they operate with conventionalised and recurrent features, (b) they are emotively invested and (c) they can only be performed by a ratified person at specific times and spaces. In addition, as with many political rituals, war apologies are 'staged'; that is, they operate with a complex cluster of dramaturgical elements. It goes without saying that the quintessential component of such ritual speeches is the category 'Apologise'.

In pragmatics, Apologise has often been approached from an interpersonal perspective, following the CCSARP (see Chapter 5). The interpersonal view of Apologise has often assumed that, when an Apologise is realised, a definite relationship exists between expressions associated with Apologise and defined as **Illocutionary Force Indicating Devices (IFIDs)** and the pragmatic success of the Apologise. For instance, Bergman and Kasper (1991: 160) argue the following:

The theoretically interesting point emerging from the highly variable use of IFIDs is its intricate relationship with Severity of offence. By responding to low Severity offenses with an explicit apologetic formula, the offender symbolically emphasizes her eagerness to repair whatever minor norm infringement has occurred. Not using IFIDs to remedy high Severity offenses may have either of two functions: an offender may avoid admitting responsibility for the offense committed, which would be concomitant with an explicit apology. Conversely, where the offender is prepared to assume responsibility, an all-purpose apologetic formula, which is also used for ritualistic apology, might not be felt to adequately convey a substantive apology for a major offence. An expression of apology which is propositionally related to the specific offence might be more apt to convey the sincerity of the speaker's regret.

As our study of war apologies will show, while IFIDs are important for understanding the development and linguacultural specificity of these apologies, the argument that the severity of an Apologise negatively correlates with the presence of an IFID is an assumption which needs to be reinvestigated from a contrastive angle, in particular by exploring non-interpersonal data – such as public single-source discourses – drawn from typologically distant linguacultures. Although the historical reasons that prompt nations to apologise may have many similar features, the study of war apologies reveals that there is significant linguacultural variation in their linguistic realisations. Further, the case study shows that political apologies like war apologies are different from interpersonal daily apologies.

In the present case study, we investigate the following three research questions:

1 Interpersonal apologies consist of a set of Apologise strategies. Which Apologise strategies are present or absent in war apologies?

2 Has the presence or absence of certain Apologise strategies changed over time?

3 Are there Apologise strategies in war apology data which have not been identified in previous research on interpersonal apology?

6.2.1 Background

War crime apologies have long been studied by journalists, anthropologists, historians, political scientists and psycholinguists (see e.g. Brooks 1999; Yamazaki 2006; Marrus 2007; Gibney et al. 2008; Nobles 2008; Celermajer 2009; Lind 2009; Hein 2010; Páez 2010; Horelt 2019). Areas with particular relevance to be mentioned here include social psychology and cultural pragmatics – in these areas scholars have often fallen into the pitfalls outlined in Part One of this book because they have held overgeneralising views on countries performing such apologies. For example, Zoodsma et al. (2021) conducted a large-scale social-psychological contrastive study of political apologies by comparing the Apologise realisation patterns of fifty different countries. While this study is relevant for our work, Zoodsma et al. followed a largely overgeneralising view, by associating certain countries with Apologise realisation patterns, hence ignoring the diachronic development and variation of Apologise realisation in individual political linguacultures. In the social-psychological study of public ritual apologies, another problem has been that scholars often predetermined what is an 'appropriate' political apology. For example, the social psychologist Páez (2010: 106) argues as follows:

A 'good' apology asks implicitly for forgiveness but does not demand nor impose it openly, and puts the decision of forgiving freely in the hands of the other person or the out-group. An effective apology puts the offender in a position of vulnerability, and redresses partially the usually asymmetrical relationship in terms of power, status and resources between the perpetrator and victim groups.

Similar to social psychologists, various cultural pragmaticians like Saito (2015: 15) also made similar overgeneralising claims about political apologies, as the following extract shows:

When past conflicts, such as the Asia-Pacific War, involved multiple countries, apology cannot simply be dyadic because identities of some parties can be doubled. The majority of Japanese citizens, for example, see Japan as the victim as well as the perpetrator because of the atomic bombings of Hiroshima and Nagasaki and the fire-bombings of other cities, among other atrocities that the Allied Powers committed against Japanese civilians.

We believe that it is rather futile to attribute certain beliefs to 'the majority' of a population without quantitative evidence. Even more importantly, such assumed beliefs have very little to do with public ritual apologies realised by politicians.

Importantly for the methodology proposed in this book, various scholars compared Japanese with German Second World War apologies by using culturally biased views and relying on pre-held convictions; that is, in the study of this area the pitfalls outlined in Part One of this book have been lurking. Hein (2010: 155–156) summarised this phenomenon as follows:

> The stereotype antagonism between Eastern shame cultures versus Western guilt culture needs to be reevaluated in a comparative context if one wants to understand why Japan went a different path facing its aggressor war legacy compared to Germany. The assumption has been made that Japanese cannot apologize because, as members of a shame society, they have no sense of guilt. The Germans on the other side felt guilty but were not ashamed of what they had done. Ruth Benedict has argued that the West operated as a guilt culture concerned with strict morality and personal responsibility whereas Japan reflected a Confucian shame culture, in which the individual was concerned with external public shame exposure rather than with internal guilt feelings. Benedict's outdated concept has continued to influence Western as well as Japanese scholars even though the culturally simplistic dichotomy cannot be maintained from both a psychological and philosophical modern viewpoint.

A key advantage of our pragmatically anchored contrastive approach is that it allows us to avoid such pitfalls.

In pragmatics, political apologies and the related issue of reconciliation have received some degree of attention, with relevant research in this area being conducted by Harris et al. (2006), Kampf (2008; 2009) and Kampf and Löwenheim (2012). Although this research has been invaluable for understanding the relationship between apology and public discourse, it has not focused on war apologies or adopted a cross-cultural contrastive pragmatic approach. In addition, these studies have been based on communication and media studies and, consequently, have pursued more of an interest in the macro sociocultural features of political apologies than in micro-level componential analysis. Furthermore, while Kampf (2012) has studied how political apologies have developed over time in a particular linguaculture, his historical analysis has been confined to the development of attitudes towards apologising. Therefore he reveals relatively little about the evolution of the features which are used to realise a political apology in particular linguacultures. To date, the historical changes in political apologies, particularly war apologies, have remained somewhat under-investigated, despite historical pragmaticians like Jucker and Taavitsainen (2008) highlighting that the realisation of Apologise is subject to extensive diachronic change. Such a change is particularly relevant to the political arena and is worth investigating from a cross-cultural contrastive pragmatic point of view, because even seemingly 'small' issues, such as the exact wording used in an Apologise, can have major consequences in the sensitive context of a war apology.

It is pertinent here also to briefly consider how the CCSARP (Blum-Kulka et al. 1989) defined Apologise strategies:

1. IFID,
2. taking on responsibility,
3. explanation or account,
4. offer of repair,
5. promise of forbearance.

IFID is the most explicit realisation of an Apologise and consists of routinised formulaic expressions of regret. The other four components (2–5) are interactionally constructed. All five Apologise strategies can be modified by 'Upgraders' and 'Downgraders'. Typical examples of an Upgrader are words such as 'very', 'really' and so on, while Downgraders include expressions such as hedges. As our analysis will illustrate, a war apology invariably operates with varying degrees of Upgrading, although the way in which Upgrading operates differs significantly across linguacultures. We include Upgrading in the tables summarising the components of the apologies studied in this chapter. As previously noted, the CCSARP framework has been developed for the examination of interpersonal apologies. However, pragmatic research on political apologies, such as Murphy (2015) and Kádár et al. (2018), has shown that the components of this type of Apologise differ from the components of Apologise in interpersonal multiple-source interaction.

6.2.2 Methodology and Data

Our methodology focuses on the aforementioned components of the speech act Apologise. We explore both the frequency and the use of these components from a contrastive point of view. To examine how the components under investigation have developed, we divide our corpora into a number of decades. Using decades to measure the diachronic development of war crime apologies helps us to map the changes that have occurred in German and Japanese Second World War apologies, over approximately seven decades.

Our corpus of Japanese and German Second World War apologies was obtained from official online sources, such as the website of the Gaimusho 外務省 (Ministry of Foreign Affairs) in Japan,[1] and German governmental websites which granted access to speeches given by representatives of the German state.[2] Japanese apologies were generally in a multilingual (Japanese, English, Chinese and Korean) format, whereas German apologies were only accompanied by English translations. From these websites, we

---

[1] See www.mofa.go.jp.   [2] See www.bundespraesident.de and www.bundesregierung.de.

Research Involving Sensitive Topics

collected forty valid Japanese apologies; by 'valid' we mean that we excluded governmental reports on apologies in which a representative of the state was not directly quoted. The German corpus comprised twenty-six valid apologies.

We conducted a twofold investigation of these corpora. First, we examined the pragmatic features of all the apologies in the corpora to provide answers to the first two research questions. This helped us to capture those pragmatic features that best represented war apologies in the linguacultures being studied, and also the diachronic development of these features. Second, to answer research question 3, we investigated what we considered to be the fifteen best-known and typical war apologies in each linguaculture. The two sets of apologies were not distributed equally over the different decades because the release of war apologies has been more frequent during certain time periods than in others. We attempted to mirror this variation in frequency by selecting the number of representative apologies in each decade in correlation with the frequency of war apologies in general in the particular decade.

6.2.3 Analysis

6.2.3.1 Japanese War Apologies

Table 6.1 summarises the main pragmatic properties of the Japanese war apologies in our corpus.

In the following discussion, we will analyse the occurrence of each Apologise strategy and other components in the various Japanese public apologies.

IFIDs

From Table 6.1, it is immediately evident that Japanese apologies generally operate with IFIDs. The following extract illustrates how IFIDs are deployed in a typical Japanese war crime apology:

(6.3) 2001年4月3日 – 福田康夫内閣官房長官。
因みに、我が国政府の歴史に関する基本認識については、戦後50周年の平成7年8月15日に発出された内閣総理大臣談話にあるとおり、我が国は、遠くない過去の一時期、植民地支配と侵略によって、多くの国々、とりわけアジア諸国の人々に対して多大の損害と苦痛を与えた事実を謙虚に受け止め、そのことについて<u>痛切な反省と心からのお詫びの気持ち</u>を表明するというものである。こうした認識は、その後の歴代内閣においても引き継がれてきており、現内閣においても、この点に何ら変わりはない。

3 April 2001: Chief Cabinet Secretary Yasuo Fukuda said: 'Japan humbly accepts that for a period in the not too distant past, it caused tremendous damage and suffering to the people of many countries, particularly to those of Asian nations, through its colonial rule and aggression, and <u>expresses its deep remorse</u> and <u>heartfelt apology</u> for this. Such recognition has been succeeded

Table 6.1 Apology components in the Japanese corpus

	1957 Prime Minister Kishi Nobusuke to Burma	1965 Minister of Foreign Affairs Shiina Etsusaburo to Australia	1972 Prime Minister Kakuei Tanaka to the People's Republic of China (communiqué)	1982 Chief Cabinet Secretary Kiichi Miyazawa to the Republic of Korea (communiqué)	1984 Prime Minister Yasuhiro Nakasone to China	1989 Prime Minister Takeshita Noboru to the nations of Asia (Japanese Diet)	1990 Prime Minister Toshiki Kaifu to Korea	1992 Chief Cabinet Secretary Koichi Kato to Korea (comfort women)	1998 Prime Minister Keizo Obuchi to China (communiqué)	2001 Chief Cabinet Secretary Yasuo Fukuda to the nations of Asia	2001 Prime Minister Junichiro Koizumi to Korea (comfort women)	2003 Prime Minister Junichiro Koizumi to Asian Nations	2005 Prime Minister Junichiro Koizumi to Asian Nations	2010 Prime Minister Naoto Kan to Korea (comfort women)	2015 Foreign Minister Fumio Kishida to South Korea
IFID	×	✓	✓	×	×	✓	✓	✓	✓	✓	✓	✓	✓	✓	✓
Accepting responsibility	✓	✓	✓	✓	✓	✓	✓	✓	✓	✓	✓	✓	✓	✓	✓
Explanation or account	×	×	×	×	×	×	×	×	×	×	×	×	×	×	×
Offer of repair	×	×	✓	×	×	×	×	×	✓	×	×	×	×	×	×
Promise of forbearance	×	×	×	×	×	✓	×	✓	✓	×	✓	×	×	✓	✓
META	×	×	×	×	×	×	×	×	×	✓	✓	✓	✓	✓	✓
UPGRADER	✓	✓	✓	✓	✓	✓	✓	✓	✓	✓	✓	✓	✓	✓	✓

by subsequent Cabinets and there is no change regarding this point in the present Cabinet.'

This apology includes the following recurrent and formulaic IFIDs:

tsuusetsuna hanshoo 痛切な反省: lit. 'keen heart-searching', and

owabi no kimochi お詫びの気持ち: lit. 'feeling of apology'

It is worth noting that certain Japanese war apologies have proved controversial because of translational disagreements about their choice of IFID (see e.g. He 2007). These debates have occurred mainly in those linguacultures which were affected by the war atrocities perpetrated by Japan and which adopt the Chinese writing system, typically China and Korea. In these writing systems, the choice of a particular character in a sensitive context, such as that of a war apology, is of fundamental importance. Putting debates triggered by translation in this sensitive setting to one side, the Japanese war apology corpus demonstrates the claim that an IFID is not used to realise Apologise for a serious offence (see Bergman and Kasper 1991) is based on an assumption which turns out to be false as far as our data are concerned. In linguacultures which are influenced by traditional Chinese moral philosophy, serious offence usually triggers a particularly deferential style (see Kádár 2012), and the frequency of the IFIDs in our Japanese corpus complies with this linguacultural pattern.

Accepting Responsibility

The Apologise strategy 'accepting responsibility' is a 'super-Apologise strategy' of Japanese war apologies, in that it is present in every apology in our corpus. The following extract illustrates the operation of this Apologise strategy:

(6.4)　1990年5月25日 – 海部俊樹首相。
「私は、大統領閣下をお迎えしたこの機会に、過去の一時期,朝鮮半島の方々が我が国の行為により耐え難い苦しみと悲しみを体験されたことについて謙虚に反省し、率直にお詫びの気持を申し述べたいと存じます。」

25 May 1990: Prime Minister Toshiki Kaifu, in a meeting with President Roh Tae Woo, said: 'I would like to take the opportunity here to humbly reflect upon how the people of the Korean peninsula went through unbearable pain and sorrow as a result of our country's actions during a certain period in the past and to express that we are sorry.'

The issue of Japanese 'war responsibility' (*sensoo no sekinin* 戦争の責任) has been the subject of much ideological debate (for an overview see e.g. Field 1995). However, on the basis of pragmatic evidence we can confirm that the Apologise strategy of 'accepting responsibility' is always present in Japanese war apologies. Thus this Apologise strategy appears to be a precondition for the realisation of the ritual speech act Apologise in Japanese public rituals, provided that such a ritual is performed in the highly sensitive war crimes context. In the case of Japanese war apologies, it should be noted that it is generally 'Japan' as entity, and not 'the Japanese people', that is discursively positioned as a party accepting responsibility for war crimes (in contrast, see the analysis of the German corpus below).

Explanation or Account and Offer of Repair

The component 'explanation or account' is the only Apologise strategy which is completely absent from the Japanese war apology corpus. This absence is related to the severity of the moral transgressions: essentially, providing an explanation for the crimes that have been committed would violate the moral order of the ritual of public apology (Kádár 2017), as this action could be interpreted as an excuse. Equally, it would be improper to give a lengthy account of the murderous details of the war crimes that have been perpetrated. Bearing in mind that, in many cases, the rite of war apology is realised following extensive negotiations (involving war reparations), it is very likely that countries receiving a war apology would object to the use of this Apologise strategy.

When it comes to the Apologise strategy of 'offer of repair', although it is also used infrequently, it still occurs twice in the Japanese corpus. The following extract illustrates its use:

(6.5) 1972年9月29日 – 田中角栄内閣総理大臣。
また、日本側は、中華人民共和国政府が提起した『復交三原則』を十分理解する立場に立って国交正常化の実現をはかるという見解を再確認する。

29 September 1972, Prime Minister Kakuei Tanaka stated the following in the joint China–Japan communiqué:
Further, the Japanese side reaffirms its position that it intends to realise the normalisation of relations between the two countries from the standpoint of fully understanding 'the three principles for the restoration of relations' put forward by the Government of the People's Republic of China.

In our corpus, this Apologise strategy only occurs in communiqués which have been jointly issued by Japan and the country to whom the apology is being offered – China in the above example. This Apologise strategy does not occur in other forms of Apologise because extensive negotiations of repair are most likely to have taken place before the rite of official apology is performed. This claim is validated by the fact that, in those cases where this component occurs, the offer of repair is made in a rather vague manner; that is, it does not include details of the reparations that have been agreed during the negotiations. This also correlates with the ritual power of these public apologies: it would decrease the pragmatic efficiency of a war apology if 'practical details' were to be included.

Promise of Forbearance

The Apologise strategy 'promise of forbearance' occurs frequently in the Japanese corpus (it appears in seven of the fifteen apologies). The following extract illustrates the use of this Apologise strategy:

(6.6) 小泉純一郎首相。「我が国は、かつて植民地支配と侵略によって、多くの国々、
とりわけアジア諸国の人々に対して多大の損害と苦痛を与えました。こうした歴史の事実を謙虚に受けとめ、痛切なる反省と心からのお詫びの気持ちを常に心に刻みつつ、我が国は第二次世界大戦後一貫して、経済大国になっても軍事大国にはならず、いかなる問題も、武力に依らず平和的に解決するとの立場を堅持しています。 … 」

22 April 2005: Prime Minister Junichiro Koizumi said: 'Japan squarely faces these facts of history in a spirit of humility. And with feelings of deep remorse and heartfelt apology always engraved in mind, Japan has resolutely maintained, consistently since the end of the Second World War, <u>never turning into a military power but an economic power, its principle of resolving all matters by peaceful means, without recourse to use of force.</u>'

As Table 6.1 indicates, this Apologise strategy only begins to feature in Japanese war apologies during the late 1980s. We will revisit the notion of diachronic development in our contrastive analysis of the corpora, but at this stage it can be argued – without referring to contrastive evidence – that certain Apologise strategies become more acceptable with the passing of time. This is in accordance with what social psychologists, such as McCullough et al. (2003), argue about apologies that follow more general moral trespasses.

META

In the Japanese corpus, one can observe an Apologise strategy which does not feature in the definition of the interpersonal speech act of Apologise provided by the CCSARP (1989), namely metacomments on the continuity of war apologies. The following extract illustrates the operation of this situated Apologise strategy:

(6.7) 田中眞紀子外務大臣。「日本は、先の大戦において多くの国の人々に対して多大な損害と苦痛を与えたことを決して忘れてはおりません。多くの人々が貴重な命を失ったり、傷を負われました。また、元戦争捕虜を含む多くの人々の間に癒しがたい傷跡を残しています。こうした歴史の事実を謙虚に受け止め、<u>1995年の村山内閣総理大臣談話の痛切な反省の意及び心からのお詫びの気持ちをここに再確認いたします。</u>」

8 September 2001: Minister for Foreign Affairs Makiko Tanaka said in a speech: 'We have never forgotten that Japan caused tremendous damage and suffering to the people of many countries during the last war. Many lost their precious

lives and many were wounded. The war has left an incurable scar on many people, including former prisoners of war. <u>Facing these facts of history in a spirit of humility, I reaffirm today our feelings of deep remorse and heartfelt apology expressed in Prime Minister Murayama's statement of 1995.</u>'

As our Japanese corpus reveals, this situated Apologise strategy became important in Japanese war apologies at the beginning of the twenty-first century; since then, almost every Japanese war apology features the 'META' Apologise strategy. There could be a number of socio-historical reasons for this development, including the increasing controversy which surrounds Japanese war apologies that characterise the relationship between Japan and its East Asian neighbours. From a narrower pragmatic point of view, we argue that this Apologise strategy can only be deployed following a number of preceding apologies, and thus it has the potential to increase the strength of ritual war apologies.

Upgrader

As Table 6.1 illustrates, all Japanese war apologies operate with a specific upgrader, namely **honorifics**. As Ide (1989) argues, it is almost impossible in the Japanese linguaculture not to use honorifics in certain ritual contexts, and in this respect the use of honorifics can be seen as a compulsory Upgrader in a highly ceremonial event, such as a public war apology. However, in the Japanese data, it was observed that the actors performing the apology deploy honorifics rather solemnly, in a somewhat different manner to how they are used in ordinary ceremonial contexts. This has the effect of boosting the force of the Apologise, as the following example (6.8) demonstrates:

(6.8) 中曽根康弘首相。「<u>貴国</u>および<u>貴国民</u>に多大な困難をもたらした ... 深い遺憾の念を<u>覚える</u>」

> 7 September 1984, Prime Minister Yasuhiro Nakasone: There was a period in this century when Japan brought to bear great sufferings upon <u>your precious country</u> and its <u>precious people</u> ... I would like to state here that the government and people of Japan feel a deep regret for this error.

By default, Japanese honorific nouns, such as *kikoku* ('your precious country') in the above example, are used in conjunction with honorific verbal inflection. However, this is not the case in our Japanese corpus – war apologies are deployed with 'plain' verbal inflection; that is, honorifics are used in these explicit performatives in a different way to how they are used in interpersonal interactions.

6.2.3.2 German War Apologies

Table 6.2 summarises the main pragmatic properties of the German war apologies in our corpus.

IFIDs

As illustrated by Table 6.2, the Apologise strategy of IFID is relatively rare in the German corpus: two-thirds of the German apologies (ten of the fifteen apologies) do not feature an IFID. This Apologise strategy appears to be a recent 'development', only appearing for the first time in German war apologies in 1994. The following example illustrates its use:

(6.9) 1 September 2019, Bundespräsident Frank Walter Steinmeier:
Die Vergangenheit vergeht nicht. Und unsere Vergangenheit vergeht nicht. Das wissen wir. Als deutscher Bundespraesident will ich Ihnen versichern: Wir werden nicht vergessen. Wir wollen und werden uns erinnern. Wir nehmen die Verantwortung an. Ich verneige mich vor den Opfern des Überfalls auf Wielun. Ich verneige mich vor den polnischen Opfern der deutschen Gewaltherrschaft. <u>Und ich bitte um Vergebung.</u>

The past is not gone, and our responsibility will not end. This we know. As President of the German state, I want to assure you we will never forget. We want and will remember. We accept responsibility. I bow in front of the victims of the attack on Wieluń. I bow in front of the Polish victims of the German terror regime. <u>And I beg for forgiveness.</u> [Switches code]

Interestingly, in our corpus the representatives of the German state deploy only one particular IFID token – *bitte um Vergebung* ('beg for forgiveness') – no other standard apology IFIDs are used. As Vollmer and Olshtain (1989: 207–208) argue, this IFID is a typical 'German' expression which is pragmatically heavy, and so its use accords with the particularly heavy weight of the war crimes triggering the apology.

It is also remarkable that this IFID only emerged some fifty years after the end of the Second World War. This 'delay' could be due to the enormity of German war crimes. It is worthwhile here to refer to Bergman and Kasper's (1991) claim that IFIDs are not the preferred choice when Apologise follows a severe offence.

Accepting Responsibility

As the Japanese corpus has already shown, accepting responsibility is a 'super-Apologise strategy' in war crime apologies. The following example illustrates the use of this Apologise strategy in the German corpus:

(6.10) Roman Herzog, 8 May 1995
Den Holocaust an den Unschuldigen vieler Völker haben Deutsche begangen
Germans perpetrated the Holocaust on many innocent people

A notable feature of this Apologise strategy in the German corpus is that the apologiser delivers the statement on behalf of the entire German people and not Germany itself, and in this respect German war apologies differ from their Japanese counterparts. This is connected to another Apologise strategy of German apologies, the 'expression of guilt and shame', which we will discuss in more detail later in this chapter.

Table 6.2 Apology components in the German data

	1952 Bundespräsident Theodor Heuss	1964 Chancellor Ludwig Erhard	1964 Chancellor Ludwig Erhard	1970 Chancellor Willy Brandt	1970 Chancellor Willy Brandt	1985 Bundespräsident Richard von Weizsäcker	1988 Bundespräsident Phillip Jenninger	1994 Bundespräsident Roman Herzog	2000 Bundespräsident Johannes Rau	2000 Bundespräsident Johannes Rau	2008 Chancellor Angela Merkel	2014 Bundespräsident Joachim Gauck	2014 Bundespräsident Joachim Gauck	2019 Bundespräsident Frank Walter Steinmeier	2019 Bundespräsident Frank Walter Steinmeier
IFID	×	×	×	×	×	×	×	✓	×	×	×	✓	×	✓	✓
Accepting responsibility	✓	✓	✓	✓	✓	✓	✓	✓	✓	✓	✓	✓	✓	✓	✓
Explanation or account	×	×	×	×	×	×	×	×	×	×	×	×	×	×	×
Offer of repair	×	×	×	×	×	×	×	×	×	×	×	×	×	×	×
Promise of forbearance	×	×	×	×	×	×	×	×	×	×	×	×	×	×	×
Guilt/shame (self-oriented component)	✓	✓	✓	×	✓	✓	✓	✓	✓	✓	✓	✓	✓	✓	✓
Upgrader	✓	✓	✓	×	✓	✓	✓	✓	✓	✓	✓	✓	✓	✓	✓

The Missing Components

German war apologies are 'minimalist' in that three of the main conventional Apologise strategies – 'explanation or account', 'offer of repair' and 'promise of forbearance' – are completely missing. The lack of the Apologise strategy 'explanation or account' is not surprising when the nature of war apologies is considered: the presence of an explanation or account would violate the moral order of the rite of war apology because it could be interpreted as an attempt to rationalise what has taken place (see Kádár 2017).

The Apologise strategy 'offer of repair' is a completely different matter. Germany has a long history of negotiating war reparations with various other countries, such as Israel and Poland. As in the case of Japanese war apologies, these negotiations took place outside the rite of war apology.

The Apologise strategy of 'promise of forbearance' is also missing from the German corpus, supposedly because it is regarded as a 'forward-looking' component. As illustrated in the next section, the rhetoric of German war apologies is essentially inward-looking and self-oriented.

'Expression of Guilt and Shame' and the Use of Upgraders

All German war apologies are centred on what we define as the 'expression of guilt and shame', which appears to be a linguaculturally specific fundamental Apologise strategy. Together with 'accepting responsibility', this Apologise strategy appears to be another 'super-Apologise strategy' as far as German war apologies are concerned; that is, it appears in all the war apologies in our corpus. This Apologise strategy already appears as a central feature of the first war apology in our corpus, delivered by the first German president after the Second World War, Theodor Heuss in 1952:

(6.11) 30 September 1952, Theodor Heuss

> *Und dies ist unsere Scham, daß sich solches im Raum der Volksgeschichte vollzog, aus der Lessing, Kant, Goethe und Schiller in das Weltbewusstsein traten. <u>Diese Scham nimmt uns niemand ab.</u>*
> And this is our shame, that such things have happened in the history of a people, from whom Lessing, Kant, Goethe and Schiller came into the world consciousness. <u>Nobody can take this shame from us.</u>

The importance of the self-reflective expression of guilt and shame fits into a broader linguacultural pattern, defined by the first author of this book as a cross-cultural discourse dimension of German (see House 1996; 2006). That is, German interactional behaviour appears to be more self- than other-oriented, in particular if we contrast it with other linguacultures such as English. In the context of war apologies, this self-oriented character implies that the explicit Apologise is backgrounded and it is the perpetrator's feelings of guilt and shame that are foregrounded.

This self-orientation is also manifested in the way in which Upgrading operates in the German corpus. German heads of state lexically Upgrade war apologies by using negative comparatives and superlatives about the war crimes that have been committed. Upgrading expressions increase the pragmatic power of the super-Apologise strategy 'expression of guilt and shame'.

The prevalence of the Apologise strategy 'expression of guilt and shame' in the German corpus already implies that it is worthwhile to engage in a contrastive analysis of Japanese and German war apologies. For example, although, conventionally, the Japanese linguaculture is described in an essentialist manner as a 'shame and guilt culture' (see Benedict 1946; Sugiyama Lebra 1983), our analysis of the Japanese corpus has already illustrated that shame and guilt do not appear as an Apologise strategy in our Japanese corpus and it is the German corpus where the 'expression of guilt and shame' is a clear-cut Apologise strategy. This shows that attributing conventional and stereotypical notions, such as shame and guilt, to linguacultures apparently does not hold for a serious, cross-cultural pragmatic analysis.

6.2.4 Contrastive Analysis

In contrasting our Japanese and German corpora of war apologies, it is relevant to consider whether there is a direct relationship between the Apologise strategies and the seriousness of the war crime that triggers the Apologise. As per our first research question, we have pursued an interest in the question 'Which Apologise strategies are present or absent in war apologies?' Thus far, our analysis has illustrated that, while certain Apologise strategies, which we have described as a 'super-Apologise strategy', are necessary constituents of a war apology, certain other Apologise strategies – such as 'explanation or account' – are missing from such apologies.

It is also interesting to consider whether the seriousness of the moral transgression triggering the Apologise implies that using more Apologise strategies is preferred. To investigate this question, in the following let us contrastively examine what we believe are the two most renowned apologies in our Japanese and German corpora. These apologies are denoted in bold in Tables 6.1 and 6.2.

Tanaka Kakuei's 1972 war apology (in a Chinese–Japanese communiqué) is widely regarded as the most effective Japanese war apology, as it benchmarked the normalisation of the international relationship between China and Japan.

(6.12) 「日本側は、過去において日本国が戦争を通じて中国国民に重大な損害を与えたことについての責任を痛感し、深く反省する。また、日本側は、中華人民共和国政府が提起した『復交三原則』を十分理解する立場に立って国交正常化の実現をはかるという見解を再確認する。」

'The Japanese side is keenly conscious of the responsibility for the serious damage that Japan caused in the past to the Chinese people through war, and deeply reproaches itself. Further, the Japanese side reaffirms its position that it intends to realise the normalisation of relations between the two countries from the standpoint of fully understanding "the three principles for the restoration of relations" put forward by the Government of the People's Republic of China.'

The above Japanese war apology operates with four Apologise strategies: (1) 'IFID' (*fukaku hanshoosuru* 深く反省する, 'deeply reproaches itself'), (2) 'offer of repair' ('the Japanese side reaffirms its position that it intends to realise the normalisation of relations between the two countries'), (3) 'accepting responsibility' ('The Japanese side is keenly conscious of the responsibility for the serious damage that Japan caused in the past to the Chinese people through war') and (4) 'Upgrader' (honorific style). This war apology is thus realised by a rich cluster of different Apologise strategies.

In contrast to its Japanese counterpart, German chancellor Willy Brandt's war apology in 1970 (which became viral) was perhaps the most minimalistic war apology ever made. He dropped silently to his knees (*Kniefall* in German) in a gesture of humility and penance:

(6.13)

Figure 6.1 *Der Kniefall*
Source: Bettmann/Contributor/Getty Images

In the realisation of a political ritual, non-verbal communication is every bit as important as its verbal counterpart (see Kádár 2017), and this is particularly valid for repentance rituals (Braithwaite 2000). Kneeling in the 'West' represents a Judaeo-Christian ritual (e.g. Carvalhaes 2011) which is typically associated with repentance, and therefore it is clear that Brandt's apology was deeply culturally embedded. While kneeling is also witnessed in East Asia (called *dogeza* 土下座 in Japanese), and various Japanese politicians have performed a respectful bow when delivering their war apologies, we were unable to observe an apology similar to Brandt's in the Japanese corpus. This indicates that the number of Apologise strategies, or even their presence, does not correlate with the moral transgression triggering the war apology. Tables 6.1 and 6.2 also indicate that in 'ordinary' cases (unlike Brandt's apology) where the apologiser uses Apologise strategies, there is a certain degree of variation between the number of Apologise strategies across various apologies in the corpora studied, in particular in the Japanese corpus. That is, while there are super-Apologise strategies that are invariably present in any war apology, other Apologise strategies are subject to variation, at least to a certain degree.

In sum, the following similarities emerge between our Japanese and German corpora.

- In both linguacultures, war apologies have been realised by using the super-Apologise strategy 'accepting responsibility'. This reveals that, as far as our data are concerned, this Apologise strategy is a prime constituent of a war apology.
- Together with the use of this super-Apologise strategy, a permanent feature of a war apology in both corpora is 'Upgrading', although our research has illustrated that Upgrading operates quite differently in the two linguacultures studied. While Japanese politicians engage in the solemn use of honorifics, their German counterparts use Upgraders to increase the pragmatic force of the 'expression of guilt and shame'.
- Both linguacultures have their own 'localised' components for realising a war apology. In the Japanese corpus, we observed the use of what we have defined as the 'META' Apologise strategy. This refers to those instances when a politician discusses or emphasises the diachronic continuity of the apologising and expresses a commitment to upholding the rite of war apology in the future. In the case of the German corpus, it is the explicit 'expression of guilt and shame' which is a distinctive 'super-Apologise strategy'. This points to a central characteristic of the German corpus, namely that German war apologies are more explicitly self-oriented than their Japanese counterparts (witness the importance of the German term *Vergangenheitsbewältigung*, 'coping with the past', which is often used

when referring to the expected post-war behaviour of Germans in relation to Second World War war crimes).

Let us now look at the main differences between the Japanese and German corpora.

- An important contrastive pragmatic difference between the Japanese and German corpora is the spread of Apologise strategies. Japanese war apologies are 'richer' in such Apologise strategies. German war apologies are based on the 'expression of guilt and shame', an Apologise strategy which is not explicitly present in the Japanese corpus (guilt and shame may be interpreted as being implied by the deployment of apology IFIDs).
- Japanese war apologies employ many IFIDs (twelve of the fifteen cases), which is in stark contrast to what is observed in the German corpus.
- In terms of Apologise strategies, Japanese apologies have changed more dynamically over time than their German counterparts. This could be due to various historical reasons, such as the controversy surrounding the war apologies that Japan has made to its neighbours, and it might also have prompted the 'intensification' of Japanese war apologies. German apologies have remained more constant, apart from the fact that early apologies did not include the Apologise strategy 'asking for forgiveness', which is a typical German IFID. Because in cross-cultural pragmatics we pursue an interest in the diachronic development of the pragmatic components of phenomena such as war apologies, we should not normally engage in any form of socio-historical, sociocultural or psychological rationalisation endeavour. Thus we should not try to offer a definitive explanation for these historical changes, other than the fact that Japanese war apologies have been more controversial than their German counterparts.

Figure 6.2 illustrates our main findings regarding the differences between the Japanese and German war apologies in our corpora.

As Figure 6.2 shows, Japanese war apologies are realised more explicitly because they consist of a complex cluster of IFIDs and other Apologise strategies. German war apologies focus on explicitly admitting guilt and expressing shame, which is a super-Apologise strategy in these apologies. While, of course, guilt and shame are inseparable from apology, in German political discourse national guilt and shame have become keywords when discussing past German events (see Assmann and Schwarz 2012). It is evident that German war apologies are embedded in this broader social discourse.

In terms of the moral dimension of these war apologies, both corpora are imbued with linguaculturally specific elements, such as the importance of IFIDs in the Japanese corpus, which has roots in the Confucian tradition of expressing repentance by adopting deference (see Kádár 2012). The German

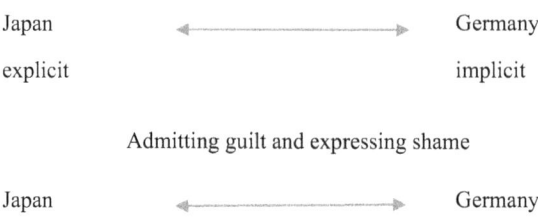

Figure 6.2 Contrastive differences between the pragmatic dynamics of Japanese and German war apologies

data have Judaeo-Christian elements, such as the importance of guilt and asking for forgiveness. What is important to emphasise here is that the generalisations we present in Figure 6.2 are very different from the generalisations we have criticised at the beginning of the case study because they are outcomes of a detailed bottom-up pragmatic investigation; that is, we did not hold them at the outset of our analysis.

6.2.5 Summary

During our examination of the two corpora, we have investigated the following three questions:

1. Interpersonal apologies consist of a set of Apologise strategies. Which Apologise strategies are present or absent in war apologies?
2. Has the presence or absence of certain Apologise strategies changed over time?
3. Are there Apologise strategies in war apology data which have not been identified in previous research on interpersonal apology?

In response to research question 1, our investigation has shown that war apologies are realised through certain 'super-Apologise strategies'. In addition, certain Apologise strategies are underrepresented in certain corpora – such as 'IFIDs' in the German corpus – while other Apologise strategies, such as 'explanation or account', are entirely missing from war apologies in our corpora. Regarding research question 2, our analysis has also shown that clear diachronic developmental patterns can be discerned in our corpora, but the degrees of this development are very different across the two corpora studied. As to research question 3, the presence of 'super-Apologise strategies' revealed that war apologies are realised by alternative Apologise strategies which are infrequently discussed in the context of interpersonal Apologise.

This case study has shown that our pragmatic take on language and politics enables us to stay away from emotively loaded and essentialist arguments. For instance, in both popular and academic discourse one can often encounter questions such as 'Have the Japanese really apologised?', 'Why have German apologies received so much praise?', and so on. For the cross-cultural pragmatician, such questions are, at best, only of secondary interest, as cross-cultural pragmatics draws attention to the linguistic realisation of wartime apologies and similar discursive data.

In this chapter, we examined the key issue of sensitivities. We argued that there are various types of sensitivity in the field of language and politics, and we focused on what we believe is the most important manifestation of sensitivities – events which are painful for many to remember and talk about. We examined Second World War apologies realised by representatives of the Japanese and German states, which can be said to be archetypes of sensitive data. Examining Second World War apologies allowed us to consider how language in sensitive events is used from a contrastive angle. This contrastive approach allowed us to avoid certain pitfalls which we outlined in Chapters 3, 4 and 5 of this book. For example, we have shown that the behaviour of Japanese politicians should not be put under an orientalist cultural umbrella; that is, our findings have shown that overgeneralising views, such as that the Japanese is a 'guilt and shame culture' (Benedict 1946; Sugiyama Lebra 1983), are clearly wrong when it comes to our data.

6.3 Recommended Readings

Marcela Cornejo, Gabriela Rubilar and Pamela Zapata-Sepúlveda. 2019. Researching sensitive topics in sensitive zones: Exploring silences, 'The Normal,' and tolerance in Chile. *International Journal of Qualitative Methods* 18. https://doi.org/10.1177/1609406919849355.

We already referred to Cornejo et al.'s (2019) research above, as it provides an excellent overview of the issue of doing research on sensitive topics. In the following section, Cornejo et al. provide an overview of previous studies in this area (references elided):

We can trace concerns about sensitive topics in research back to the work of Lee and Renzetti ... From the beginning, researchers have regarded 'the sensitive' as a characteristic of the research topic or a feature of the research process ... This field of inquiry, also referred to as sensitive issues or sensitive subjects ... can be organized around two main topics: their impact on the actors who take part in the research process and the way in which researchers reflect on how research on sensitive topics manifests itself methodologically.

In qualitative inquiry, the actors involved are both the researchers and their teams, as well as the participants. The consequences of their involvement have been defined based largely on their risks. There are concerns about possible emotional damage or difficulties arising during the research process ... 'research harm' ... that is, the physical and emotional suffering experienced by researchers, and the implementation of care strategies by researchers ...

Dickson-Swift, James, Kippen, and Liamputtong ... note that suffering or distress may occur when researching personal experiences such as emotions and suffering ... when studying deviation, marginalization, and/or social control, as in the case of vulnerable young people ... when examining politically complex issues involving people or institutions with power interests regarding research ... and when dealing with sacred elements, which become desecrated as a result of research, according to participants ... Overall, working with sensitive topics has important effects for certain ethical and methodological dilemmas of research, which require practices that exceed traditional ethical expectations ...

Research on how studies on sensitive topics are methodologically influenced by their research objects suggests a positive impact on reflective processes: Sensitive topics enrich data analysis and generate new questions and reflections linked to the topic studied. It has been hypothesized that reflectiveness operates as a care strategy that makes it possible to explore the impact of knowledge construction ... while paying close attention to how the sensitive influences the research approach adopted.

Research on sensitive topics is not simply circumscribed to a limited number of topics. Rather, it encompasses particular reflectiveness-related processes and dynamics in research, regarding subjectivity and emotionality as elements involved in the production of knowledge. This leads to the problematization of traditional research methods and results in creative new devices tailored to each particular field of research.

Zohar Kampf. 2009. Public (non-)apologies: The discourse of minimizing responsibility. *Journal of Pragmatics* 41(11): 2257–2270.

Kampf's study is relevant to readers with interest in public apologies studied in this chapter. Unlike our study, this paper examines cases in which the public apologiser attempts to decrease rather than increase his or her responsibility. In the following section, Kampf provides an overview of the phenomenon of public apology:

It seems that the dictum 'Never apologize, Never explain' has lost its illustrative power in the last two decades. Hundreds of apologies made by states, organizations, and public figures have turned the dictum into an archaism and brought academic scholars to claim that we are living in the Age of Apology ... Admittedly, when made genuinely, motivated by moral concerns, public apologies can be considered moral acts ... However, studies that have focused on several problems stemming from the public context of apology realization have undermined to various degrees the sincerity and authenticity of many of these gestures. Those studies point to problems such as issuing delegated apologies (i.e. apologizing for acts that the speaker was not involved in directly ...), limiting the regret to symbolic restitution (without material compensation ...), manipulating the form of the rhetorical genre ... and evaluating apologies by public actors and social groups in a cynical and distrusting manner ... In spite of the fact that more often than not the moral core of public apologies is doubtful ... frequent realizations of the speech act in the global arena since the 1990s have turned apologies into a common device for image restoration as well as a legitimate tool for managing social relationships with others in the public sphere. The practice has been conventionalized through its recurrent realizations in the international and national discourse, and the norm of apologizing for misdeeds in the distant and recent past has been established through this process. The constraining aspect of this norm is apparent in the reflexive designation of verbal responses by public figures, which conforms to the contemporary moral discursive standard (i.e. expressing the 'right' feelings of sorrow following transgressions of human justice). This compliance in the discourse level with the constructed norm of apologizing contributes in its turn to the expansion of the age of apology ... (cited from Kampf 2009: 2257–2258)

7 Communicative Strategies in News Reports

7.1 Introduction

In language and politics, a key issue has been how to analyse news reports. A main difficulty with analysing news reports is that they are forms of single-source discourse, reporting on events which took place in the past, and so from the pragmatician's point of view often seemingly no communicative action is taking place in them apart from conveying of information, especially if they do not directly quote interaction between political actors. The word 'seemingly' needs to be emphasised here because experts in language and politics have developed different solutions through which it is possible to capture linguistic action in news reports. For example, Schäffner proposed to look at **stance** in politically relevant single-source media data such as news reports, arguing that it is fruitful to consider the choice of phenomena such as political metaphors which contribute to 'the positioning and construction of the political actors' (Schäffner 2012: 115). Furthermore, Bednarek and Caple (2012) pointed out that by looking at the style of headlines of news items it is possible to capture the pragmatic characteristics of various types of news discourse; Molek-Kozakowska (2013) proposed a corpus-based pragmalinguistic approach, allowing the scholar to pin down sensationalism in news discourse; Chovanec (2014) offered a framework through which tense and time can be studied in news discourse from a pragmatic point of view; and Weizman and Dori-Hacohen (2017) discussed how to capture the pragmatic dynamics of news editorials by looking at online commenting.[1] As this brief summary already shows, in news discourse, unlike in multiple-source discourse, the scholar cannot simply look at interaction in the conventional sense of the word, such as by considering the realisation of speech acts in turn-by-turn exchanges. Further, in the study of news report data, the analyst needs to resolve the problem that the communicative product often cannot be uncritically accepted as interactional data produced by a political actor. For example, while news articles often report the actual words of politicians and other

---

[1] For an overview of research on stance in single-source media see Jacobs et al. (2008: 1).

actors, they also narrate events, and both reported and narrated speech news items often take different stances, meaning that certain information is **foregrounded** and other information is backgrounded (see also Leech 2008). Thus communicative action in news discourse is often that of a more abstract actor than an individual person.

Provided that one studies single-source news discourse for its own sake, without pursuing an interest in language and politics, the features of news discourse outlined above do not pose any problem. For example, historical pragmaticians like Jucker (2005) treated historical news articles as simple data sources, without conducting any in-depth investigation of the political relevance of their data. Yet, given our framework, studying news reports implies that we attempt to capture a communicative action in news reports in order to relate news corpora to the study of language and politics. Furthermore, in the spirit of our bottom-up view of language use, we aim to avoid attributing any communicative strategy to a political actor without proper evidence. Here our approach is closely related to that of KhosraviNik (2010), who argued as follows: in order to capture communicative strategies in newspaper data, it is recommended that one relies on both quantitative and qualitative evidence, as well as on some form of comparative view. For instance, KhosraviNik (2010: 6) examined the representation of refugees, asylum seekers and immigrants in British newspapers by comparing data drawn from different newspapers such as *The Guardian* and the *Daily Mail*, in order to compare the communicative strategies used by media with different ideological leanings.

Along with taking a contrastive view, it is also important to carefully consider exactly how we define **communicative strategy** when it comes to news discourse. When using the technical term 'strategy' in pragmatics, many associate it with politeness due to the influence of Brown and Levinson's (1987) classic in the field. However, politeness as an individual and interpersonal phenomenon has little relevance for the language of newspaper reports where the author of a news article communicates with a large number of readers in an indirect way, often by seemingly acting only as the **animator** (Goffman 1981) of something to be 'objectively' reported, in particular if a news article is not an opinion piece. Even citizen journalists with online fans (see e.g. Hills 2015) primarily take the role of the animator; that is, their language use is rarely interpersonal in the fully fledged sense of the word. Thus the aim of a communicative strategy in a news report is usually something more general than building any interpersonal relationship between the author and his readers: it is to create a sense of alignment and rapport between the writer and the political entities she represents and the readers of the news. As Breeze (2016: 1, added emphasis) pointed out about the genre of newspaper editorials,

Newspaper editorials are known to use an extensive array of discursive resources which operate continuously through the text. They are shaped by the need for the writer to negotiate *alignment* and *rapport* with a particular readership, which in turn requires the writer to take a position with respect to other parties or voices ... This is achieved by moderating the participation of different voices through the use of reported speech, and by opening and closing different lines of argument using a range of resources, which include modal verbs, reporting verbs, attribution, attitude markers, graduation, conjunctions and so on, and a variety of rhetorical strategies.

Since in pragmatics 'rapport' has a specific interpersonal meaning (see Spencer-Oatey 2000), in what follows we focus on the phenomenon of **alignment** mentioned above.

Alignment originates in Goffman's discussion of the participation framework. Goffman (1981: 128) argued that 'footing' is 'the alignment we take up to ourselves and the others present as expressed in the way we manage the production or reception of an utterance'. According to Goffman, the participants in an interaction may shift footings as they change their alignment with each other and with others who may not be present in the interaction, and they indicate such changes with contextual and linguistic cues. As Fetzer (2008) argues, alignment and non-alignment with a particular political actor or political action is fundamental in multiple-source political interaction. Fetzer (2008: 37) illustrates the operation of non-alignment with the following extract:

INTERVIEWER: *Under a new leader, presumably?*
INTERVIEWEE: *Well, I think the leadership question is frankly a secondary question ...*

Here the second interactant uses the gambit or discourse marker 'well' to indicate hesitation, and then expresses non-alignment with a question (see also Edmondson and House 1981). Unlike in such multiple-source interactions, in single-source discourse like newspapers the alignment of the audience with an actor prioritised by the author of the discourse is something to be 'negotiated' by the author, as Breeze (2016) pointed out; that is, alignment refers to the attitude of accepting the line of discourse presented in the newspaper (Kádár 2024). An author of a newspaper article can both prompt others to align themselves with himself or a third party and, as part of this, may also align himself with a political actor or entity.

Alignment may be negotiated through many phenomena, such as humour (Laineste 2011), foregrounding (Dagtas 2020), deference and so on. For example, in our case study below we feature a situation where the authors of news reports in the Chinese linguaculture use deference to confirm their alignment with political actors, and also to negotiate the readers' alignment with the same actors. Relying on the concept of alignment in the study of the language of news reports implies that the analyst needs to try to look beyond the apparent function of the words uttered. This is a train of thought that various experts in language and politics have advocated through the notion of implicitness (see, in particular, Harris et al.'s 2006 seminal study). Implicitness is particularly relevant if one aims to study single-source news discourse, such as Chinese public governmental announcements in newspapers featured in the case study below (see also Jiang 2006; Dou and Zhang 2007).

In terms of our model outlined in Chapter 2, in this chapter we present a case study in which we follow a discourse-analytic point of view and also consider and quantify pragmatically relevant expressions – honorifics – in the data. Such honorifics also indicate awareness of the ritual frame of the discourse; that is, they are **ritual frame indicating expressions** (RFIEs; see House and Kádár 2021b). We also engage in a specific contrastive approach whereby we compare the way in which news outlets with different authority attempt to negotiate the readers' alignment with political actors.

7.2   Case Study

In this case study, we examine Chinese **public announcements (*gong'gao*)** made in the wake of major crises. Such announcements tend to be made as news released at various governmental-level newspapers, including national, provincial and local (city) ones. The level at which a particular announcement is made bears relevance for its style, considering that in Chinese politics different governmental levels and associated newspapers have strictly defined and clearly different power and related rights and obligations (Ma 2005), unlike in many 'Western' countries.[2] Chinese public announcements typically represent a public ritual where the author's goal is to reassure the public that political decision makers can resolve a situation in an orderly and hierarchical fashion (see Yang 1997; Kádár and Zhang 2019), hence aiming to trigger the public's alignment with the decision makers. The authors of such texts also often make promises of action to the public. The right of 'reporting' the details of an action plan is unevenly allocated across the news releases produced by the various administrative levels.

The data of the present case study consist of official Chinese releases of *gong'gao* during the vaccine scandal that erupted in China in the summer of 2018. This incident began when the national media cautiously released information about a 'potential' problem with 'a limited number of vaccines'. It quickly became evident that the situation was significantly more serious than this euphemistic wording had suggested: a vast number of patients had been improperly vaccinated against life-threatening illnesses such as rabies. This was not the first vaccine scandal in recent Chinese history: there had been a chain of similar events, including an incident in 2007–2008 (Shanxi Province), one in 2009 (Jiangsu and Hebei Provinces) and one in 2016 (Shandong Province). The gravity of such cases

---

[2] For instance, one has no way of witnessing autonomous communicative actions on the city level, not to mention conflict between various administrative levels.

was exacerbated by the fact that many felt that the companies involved had not been sufficiently sanctioned. For instance, Changchun Changsheng, the company responsible for the 2018 incident, only received a penalty of several million yuan, an extremely modest sum compared to the size of the company and its annual profit. From the outset of the 2018 incident, authorities and decision makers at various levels of the state administration were prompt to react: immediately after the release of the first report on the incident, they repeatedly promised a thorough investigation of the case and the strict punishment of those responsible for the production of substandard medicine. The reactions of these leaders and other Chinese political figures were portrayed to the public primarily through *gong'gao* announcements featured in official newspaper releases.

Our study was conducted on the basis of a corpus consisting of thirty national-level public announcements, five provincial-level announcements and five local-level announcements that were made in the media following the outbreak of the incident. Using news reports representing different levels of authority allowed us to engage in a contrastive analysis of our data, following our framework. The overall size of the corpus is 32,891 Chinese characters. The thirty public announcements mentioned above were released during a period of fifteen days between 16 and 30 July 2018, following the earliest report of the incident on 12 July. This limited timeline stems from the nature of *gong'gao*, which is a ritual genre that conventionally operates in contexts where formal legal action has *yet to take place* and appears mainly in the official media, which has been permitted to act as the voice of the authorities. As the incident developed, actors at various administrative levels – from the highest-level decision makers such as Xi Jinping (general secretary) and Li Keqiang (premier) to the leaders of the cities affected – announced their reactions to the incident. Their announcements were disseminated by the main official media outlets: Chinese official national-level news agencies, such as Xinhua, released details of the *gong'gao* made by Xi Jinping, Li Keqiang and the national governing body, while, for example, provincial news, such as the official news site of Jilin Province, released reports that included both information on the *gong'gao* and the local government reaction to the incident. By 30 July 2018, the case was passed on to criminal investigators, and so formally ceased to be a part of the *gong'gao* agenda.

In the current study, we compare language use in national and provincial *gong'gao* newspaper releases to illustrate how alignment with members of the public is triggered in such data. Along with quantitative evidence, we examine excerpts drawn from Chinese newspapers.

7.2.1   Analysis

The study of the present *gong'gao* corpus has shown that Chinese public announcements always follow a bipartite structure:

1 The first section of *gong'gao* reports tends to provide a deferential discussion of the actions that Chinese authorities have taken at the time of the report. Without exception, this narrative is centred on the political leaders of China by emphasising their individual agency. In the corpus studied, the authors discuss the immediate measures that Xi Jinping and Li Keqiang had taken by the time the event was reported in the official media. This focus on the agency of those who hold leadership positions has its roots in the hierarchical structure of Chinese politics. Importantly, such descriptions of the leaders' actions are heavily loaded with deferential forms – most typically, formal expressions that gain a conventional honorific function. Further, as the analysis below will show, the use of such forms closely relates to the level of the news release; that is, the lower a news outlet is in the governmental hierarchy (national > provincial > local), the more ubiquitous and intricate the use of deferential forms it provides.

2 The second section of *gong'gao* announcements focuses on the collective action that decision makers and investigators intend to take in the future. As the analysis will illustrate, this second section of the reports is not simply an 'objective' announcement of action plans, but rather features a further implicit attempt – along with the first part – to trigger the public's alignment with the leadership, without addressing members of the public directly. The manner of reporting correlates with the position of the given news outlet in the administrative hierarchy.

7.2.1.1 *The Language of Public Announcements Featured in National-Level Chinese News*

Let us commence the analysis by introducing the original Chinese and gloss of a *gong'gao* news text which was released at the national level. The text includes both the first and second parts of this news item for illustrative purposes, but the analysis will only focus on the first section.[3]

(7.1) 新华社北京7月25日电 为贯彻落实习近平总书记、李克强总理关于长春长生生物科技有限责任公司违法违规生产狂犬病疫苗案件的重要指示批示精神, 7月23日国务院调查组赶赴吉林, 开展长春长生违法违规生产狂犬病疫苗案件调查工作。 7月24日, 国务院调查组组长、市场监管总局党组书记、副局长毕井泉主持召开调查组第一次全体会议, 传达学习习近平总书记、李克强总理等中央领导同志 重要指示批示精神, 要求调查组深入学习领会习近平总书记重要指示精神, 坚决贯彻落实李克强总理重要批示要求 ...

---

[3] Various expressions in the first part of text with relevance for the analysis are featured in boxes in the Chinese original and are underlined in the English gloss.

会议要求，要重点围绕七个方面开展工作。一是彻查涉案企业违法违规行为，全面查清违法违规事实和涉案疫苗流向，做好调查取证工作；二是依法严惩违法犯罪行为，严肃查处涉案企业，对直接责任人等涉案人员要依法严惩；三是对公职人员履职尽责进行调查，发现失职渎职行为的要严肃问责；四是科学开展风险评估，研究提出分类处理救济措施；五是要妥善处理涉案企业后续工作；六是要回应社会关切，及时公布案件调查进展情况，普及疫苗安全科学知识；七是要研究改革完善疫苗管理体制的工作举措，建立健全保障疫苗质量安全的长效机制。根据工作需要，调查组下设案件调查组、监管责任组、综合组和专家组等工作组。

Xinhua News reports on 25 July: the State Council Investigation Unit [immediately] implements the instructions of General Secretary Xi Jinping and Premier Li Keqiang about the illegal activities of Changchun Changsheng Biotech Ltd. Based on the higher instructions of the general secretary and the premier, on 23 July the Investigation Unit proceeded to Jilin Province to investigate the matter of substandard rabies vaccines produced by the named company.

On 24 July, Bi Jingquan – the principal investigator of the State Council Investigation Unit and Party secretary and deputy director of the State Administration for Market Regulation Bureau – held the first comprehensive meeting to study the instructions of General Secretary Xi Jinping, Premier Li Keqiang and other important cadres. Based on their higher instructions, the principal investigator demanded that the Investigation Unit was to intensively learn from General Secretary Xi Jinping and to determinedly implement the instructions and requirements in the key comments of Premier Li Keqiang ... As an outcome of the conference, the delegates confirmed that they will deliver work on the following seven areas: first, they will thoroughly investigate the illegal actions of the corporation involved and will comprehensively investigate criminal activities in the corporation and the market flow of vaccines produced by the named company. Second, an action will be initiated to severely punish any behaviour that turns out to be illegal, in compliance with law. They will seriously examine the corporation involved in the incident and impose severe sanctions on persons directly responsible for the incident. Third, they will investigate the public officials' fulfilment of their duties. Acts of dereliction should be seriously investigated. Fourth, they will conduct a risk assessment, propose classified measures for disposal and remedies based on research. Five, they will address the social crisis caused by the incident. Six, they will respond to public concerns with the timely disclosure of information on the investigation and disseminate scientific knowledge about vaccine safety. Seven, they will carry out research on operational measures to improve and reform the current vaccine management system and establish and develop long-term mechanisms for the maintenance of vaccine quality (and) safety. The Investigation Unit constitutes subordinate working units including a case investigation unit, a regulatory responsibility unit, an integrated unit and an expert unit.

(Retrieved from www.gov.cn/xinwen/201807/25/content_5309213.html)

The announcement in extract (7.1) features an active form of deferential ritual rhetoric which may be somewhat alien to foreign (non-Chinese) readers.

Table 7.1 *Expressions in the case study which gain deferential meaning in the ritual context*

1	贯彻落实 落实 坚决贯彻落实	guanche-luoshi luoshi jianjue-guanche-luoshi	'to implement higher orders'
2	重要指示批示精神 重要批示要求 重要指示精神	zhongyao-zhishi pishi-jingshen zhongyao-pishi-yaoqiu zhongyao-zhishi-jingshen	lit. 'very important comments and instructions' (in reference to the actions of a higher-ranking person)
3	传达贯彻 传达学习	chuanda-guanche chuanda-xuexi	lit. 'to transfer the words of a higher-ranking person to others for study' and implement (their important instructions and comments)
4	深入学习领会	shenru-xuexi-linghui	lit. 'to deeply learn and comprehend' (from a higher-ranking person)
5	领导同志	lingdao-tongzhi	lit. 'leading comrade'
6	要求 讲话要求	yaoqiu jianghua-yaoqiu	lit. 'demand', a verbal form which indexes power and expresses respect
7	高度重视	gaodu-zhongshi	'to attach a great importance to'
8	全力配合	quanli-peihe	'to co-operate fully'

Xinhua News, being the voice of the national-level authorities, here ritually endorses the individual actions of the leaders by emphasising their agency in resolving the crisis. Due to its national status, the news release remains silent about the actions of individuals below the leadership level: the only other person mentioned alongside Xi Jinping and Li Keqiang is the principal investigator. However, his action is also framed as being of a subordinate status: the text only states that he 'demanded that the Investigation Unit' implement the higher-order actions of the leaders.

One can distinguish two types of social protocol in announcements like extract (7.1) above. First, such reports tend to be heavily loaded with set forms that express a deferential meaning in the ritual context in which they occur. Table 7.1 provides an overview of such expressions which occur in the examples featured in this case study. While these expressions may be used in written – and some in spoken – interaction, they are different from what can be regarded as the 'standard' lexical inventory of Chinese etiquette. Further, the repetitive way in which the authors of Chinese public announcements like extract (7.1) use such expressions shows that these expressions are part of a social ritual: for instance, in the two relatively short texts that are featured in the current analysis, there is a total of fourteen such expressions. The use of these expressions shows that they are not 'polite' in the proper sense of the word: the direct recipient of these expressions is not a leader or an individual; that is, these deferential expressions occur in ritual narratives which tell the readers about the ways in which a community of decision makers (e.g. 'State Council Investigation Unit' in extract (7.1)) position their prospective actions with regard to the individual instructions of the leaders. In the context of a crisis in a hierarchical political linguaculture like the Chinese, this sense of indirect deference triggers acceptance of the leaders' authority in the management of the crisis. In turn, this acceptance communicated in a ritual frame in the media gains the capacity to implicitly trigger the public's alignment with the leaders and their actions.[4]

Second, social protocols are also present in national-level *gong'gao* announcements beyond the use of expressions; that is, in the way in which actions are temporally positioned. When discussing the reactions of the national leaders, *gong'gao* reports indicate the promptness of their responses. Notably, the authors do not use such words as 'quick' in this context to refer to the actions of Xi Jinping or Li Keqiang; that is, it remains the reader's task to make this inference. However, when one considers that the text states that the agenda which has been established for the meeting of the State Council Investigation Unit follows the already available reflections of the national leaders, it is evident that these leaders are being positioned as acting promptly. Once again, since *gong'gao* does not represent a form of interpersonal communication in the strict sense, it is very likely that these manifestations of 'politeness' are being aimed at the public; that is, they form part of alignment triggering.

7.2.1.2 *Social Protocols in Public Announcements Featured in Provincial-Level Chinese News*

Public *gong'gao* announcements made at lower administrative levels operate with more complex forms of deference than their national-level counterparts, as illustrated by the following extract:

(7.2) 长春长生生物科技有限责任公司违法违规生产疫苗案件发生以来，省委副书记、省长景俊海高度重视，先后16次作出具体批示指示，并于7月22日、23日主持召开专题会议，全面调度处置工作。7月23日晚上，景俊海连夜主持召开案件处置工作指导组第一次会议，传达贯彻习近平总书记重要批示指示精神，落实李克强总理批示指示精神，按照巴音朝鲁书记在省委常委会议上的讲话要求，研究具体举措。他强调，要全力配合国家调查组 ...

---

[4] While it has been argued (Pan and Kádár 2011) that modern Chinese communication no longer uses the system of traditional honorifics, several of the deferential expressions here are archaic and follow the format of 'four-character' set phrases (*sizi-shuyu* 四字熟语). This formal style may also increase the alignment-triggering function of such texts, as in the wake of a national social crisis it implies that the authorities are handling the situation professionally and with a sense of gravity.

Since the incident of illegal vaccine production of Changchun Changsheng Biotech Ltd, the vice secretary of the Provincial Committee of the Chinese Communist Party and the governor of the province Jing Junhai <u>attached great importance to the incident;</u> [so far, he has released <u>as many as 16 specific instructions and comments relating to</u> the incident. In addition, he also held two subsequent special meetings on <u>22 and 23 July</u> respectively, to thoroughly take care (of the incident). On the <u>very night</u> of 23 July, Mr Jing hosted the first meeting of the Guidance Group for the dissemination of the Changsheng vaccine incident, in order to <u>study and implement the important instructions and comments</u> made respectively by General Secretary Xi Jinping and Premier Li Keqiang. Furthermore, he emphasised that actions need to be made in accordance with the <u>demand</u> made by Provincial Party Secretary <u>Bayinchaolu</u> in his speech to the Standing Committee of the Provincial Party Committee. He stressed that we <u>must co-operate fully</u> with the State (Council) Investigation Unit to thoroughly investigate the facts ...

(Retrieved from www.jl.gov.cn/zw/yw/jlyw/201807/t20180724_4945608.html)

One can observe at least three different types of social protocol in this brief text:

1 The text expresses deference towards Jing Junhai, the governor of Jilin Province. While in national-level news reports, such as extract (7.1), only national leaders are featured with individual agency, in this case Jing occurs both as an 'author' and as an 'animator' in Goffman's (1981) terms. On the one hand, he is positioned as a *loyal* animator: the news article emphasises that he 'attaches great importance' to, and works the 'whole night' on, the implementation of the policies of the higher authorities. On the other hand, he is also positioned as an 'author' at the local level: the news report emphasises his agency in resolving the crisis, for example by stating that he has released as many as sixteen public comments and has held subsequent meetings immediately after the onset of the incident.

2 The text mediates deference towards the higher authorities, by directly quoting Jing Junhai's words, such as 'must co-operate fully' (*quanli-peihe* 全力配合). Such narrations represent a form of deference that is recurrent in provincial- and local-level reports.

3 Finally, the text also mediates camaraderie between actors at the local level: it features camaraderie between Governor Jing and the Provincial Party Secretary Bayinchaolu, who are peers at the provincial administrative level. The expression of such camaraderie reinforces the message that political decision makers are actively collaborating to resolve the crisis.

The relative abundance of deferential expression and the attribution of agency to local political actors in newspaper *gong'gao* announcements released at lower administrative levels shows that the frequency and pragmatic characteristics of such forms of language use negatively correlate with administrative power. This does not imply that organisations with less power are supposed to communicate in a more 'deferential' way than their more powerful counterparts in crises. The situation is rather that such announcements at various levels are released as part of a major social ritual where authors of texts dispatched on the lower level tend to be more actively engaged in expressing deference in order to showcase their solidarity with, and loyalty to, higher-level organisations, hence attempting to trigger the public's similar alignment with those who make decisions.

In summary, the results of the above case study have shown that it is possible for the linguist to pin down communicative actions in newspaper data, without speculating about such actions. There are various methodologies to do this, as we have argued in the introduction, and in the case study we presented one of these methodologies, by considering how alignment is negotiated between readers, the newswriter and the politicians and political entities represented by the newswriter. We focused on a linguacultural setting in which alignment is negotiated by using forms of deference, including honorifics, playing on agency and so on. Clearly, in other linguacultural settings the triggering of alignment may involve the use of other pragmatic phenomena, such as humour and sarcasm. The present study of alignment has also drawn attention to the fact that many phenomena, like politeness, which are important in interpersonal interaction should be looked at with critical eyes when it comes to the study of language and politics. While such phenomena often emerge in politically relevant data, very often they lose their default function because they have a different goal in political settings than in interpersonal scenarios.

7.3   Recommended Readings

Erving Goffman. 1979. Footing. *Semiotica* 25(1–2): 1–29.

While Goffman's interpretation of alignment is more complex than we have used it in this chapter, the following example features alignment in the exact way in which it has been interpreted in this chapter; that is, as a way of accepting an authoritative line of discourse.

Consider a journalistically reported strip of interaction, a news bureau release of 1973 on presidential doings. The scene is the Oval Office, the participants an assemblage of government officers and newspaper reporters gathered in their professional capacities for a political ritual, the witnessing of the signing of a bill:

WASHINGTON – (UPI) – President Nixon, a gentleman of the old school, teased a newspaper woman yesterday about wearing slacks to the White House and made it clear that he prefers dresses on women.

After a bill-signing ceremony in the Oval Office, the President stood up from his desk and in a teasing voice said to UPPs Helen Thomas: 'Helen, are you still wearing slacks? Do you prefer them actually? Every time 1 see girls in slacks it reminds me of China.'

Miss Thomas, somewhat abashed, told the President that Chinese women were moving toward Western dress.

'This is not said in an uncomplimentary way, but slacks can do something for some people and some it can't.' He hastened to add, 'but I think you do very well. Turn around.'

As Nixon, Attorney General Elliott L. Richardson, FBI Director Clarence Kelley and other high-ranking law enforcement officials smil[ed], Miss Thomas did a pirouette for the President. She was wearing white pants, a navy blue jersey shirt, long white beads and navy blue patent leather shoes with red trim.

Nixon asked Miss Thomas how her husband, Douglas Cornell, liked her wearing pants outfits.

'He doesn't mind,' she replied.

'Do they cost less than gowns?'

'No,' said Miss Thomas.

'Then change,' commanded the President with a wide grin as other reporters and cameramen roared with laughter. (*The Evening Bulletin* [Philadelphia], 1973)

This incident points to the power of the President to force an individual who is female from her occupational capacity into a sexual, domestic one during an occasion in which she (and the many women who could accord her the role of symbolic representative) might well be very concerned that she be given her full professional due, and that due only. And, of course, the incident points to a moment in gender politics when a President might unthinkingly exert such power. Behind this fact is something much more significant: the contemporary social definition that women must always be ready to receive comments on their 'appearance', the chief constraints being that the remarks should be favorable, delivered by someone with whom they are acquainted, and not interpretable as sarcasm. Implied, structurally, is that a woman must ever be ready to change ground, or, rather, have the ground changed for her, by virtue of being subject to becoming momentarily an object of approving attention, not – or not merely – a participant in it. (Goffman 1979: 1–2)

Ruth Breeze. 2016. Negotiating alignment in newspaper editorials: The role of concur–counter patterns. *Pragmatics* 26(1): 1–19. https://doi.org/10.1075/prag.26.1.01bre.

Breeze's study provides an excellent overview of how alignment is negotiated by authors of news articles, and we recommend it for readers with interest in this phenomenon, especially because it studies alignment in a very different political linguaculture than the one we studied in this chapter. In the following section, Breeze provides a summary of her observations regarding pragmatic patterns in her data:

In the most frequent combination of certainty adverbial with contrastive found in this corpus, the locution used to signal concurrence ('obviously', 'of course') is placed in theme position. In other cases, it is placed later in the sentence, but still has the function of modifying the whole proposition to some degree. The use of such sentence adverbials in these examples appears to prime the reader to expect one of two things. Either the certainty marker reinforces the writer's main point, and the contrastive that follows usually introduces a statement of fact that runs counter to the writer's opinion. Or the certainty adverbial is used to authorise certain views which the writer is going to consider, then reject. In the former case, the pattern that emerges might be termed 'concur–disalign', because the main function is to build common ground with the reader in order to reject a contrary position. In the latter case, the pattern may be termed 'concede–align'. (Breeze 2016: 5)

8 Ideological Convictions and Language Use

8.1 Introduction

In this chapter, we consider how **ideological convictions** influence sociopolitically relevant language use. Ideological convictions include a wide variety of morally loaded beliefs, either clearly political ones relating to political actors and parties, or others which are more related to sociopolitical causes than to actors and parties. Political and sociopolitical ideologies influence the behaviour of an individual by becoming her convictions (Tagar et al. 2014). For the scholar of language and politics, the concept of ideological conviction is important because it explains how politics manifests itself in the language use of non-professional political actors, such as activists and other 'lay' members discussing and arguing about political and sociopolitical matters. The concept of ideological conviction is a psychological one, and in this chapter we consider how it can be pinned down from the linguist's point of view, and how ideologically loaded language use may differ from 'ordinary' language use.

The phenomenon of ideological conviction is closely related to the broader phenomenon of ideology, which we have already mentioned at various points in this book. Verschueren (2012: 7, original emphasis) defines ideology as follows:

> Ideology is no longer an academic discipline, but rather an object of investigation. It is related to *ideas*, *beliefs*, and *opinions*, but this relationship is not a straightforward one. Ideas, beliefs, and opinions, as such, do not make ideology. Simplifying a bit, they are merely 'contents of thinking', whereas ideology is associated with *underlying patterns of meaning, frames of interpretation, world views,* or *forms of everyday thinking and explanation*. Thus the ways in which beliefs, ideas, or opinions are discursively used, i.e. their *forms of expression* as well as the *rhetorical purposes* they serve, are just as important for ideology as the contents of thinking for which these three terms serve as labels.

The study of ideologies in the field encompasses various different areas, such as the following:
- The effect of ideologies on the practices of organisations and political parties. For instance, Wodak et al. (2012) examined how Members of the European

Parliament and officials at the European Commission practice and perform multilingualism in their everyday work, and how such pragmatic practices are influenced by ideologies. In a similar fashion, Diermeier et al. (2012) studied how ideologies influence behaviour in the US Congress.
- The influence of ideology on multiple-source political discourse such as the media. For example, Furko (2017) examined the way in which ideologies influence political interviews across linguacultures, Vessey (2016) considered the effect of language ideologies on social media discourse, and Brady et al. (2019) explored how ideologies influence the language use of political decision makers in media discourse.
- The influence of ideologies on single-source news discourse. For example, Van Dijk (2008: 115, original emphasis) pointed out that 'news structure analysis shows us *where* and *how* ideologies preferably manifest themselves in news reports'.

What interconnects such inquiries is that researchers considered how ideologies influence the language use of *professional* politicians. Yet another and more pragmatically relevant area – which we will investigate in this chapter – is how ideologies influence the sociopolitically relevant language use of individuals outside the narrowly defined political arena. We believe that the way in which sociopolitical issues emerge in the interactional behaviour of social members outside professional politics is a fundamental topic to talk about. Why is this so?

As the psychologist Jonathan Haidt argued in his now classic (2012) book, ideological convictions tend to trigger deep-seated divisions between ordinary people discussing politics. The way in which ideological convictions influence the language use of ordinary social members is heavily intertwined with morality and moral order (see Kádár 2017; 2024): essentially, social members often hold religion-like convictions as to what is politically and sociopolitically right and wrong, and these moral views tend to be bound to clash with those of others who hold different political and sociopolitical convictions. Such clashes often take place outside the political arena, either in the form of online sociopolitical debates (e.g. Lewiński 2010; Egan 2016), or as face-to-face interactions as in the case study presented below. From a pragmatic point of view, it is relevant to consider cases in which ideological convictions occur in contexts of language aggression because the study of such scenarios provides first-hand insight into the social division triggered by politically and sociopolitically relevant convictions, as Haidt (2012) pointed out.

In the case study below, we use our speech act–anchored approach to the study of how ideological convictions emerge in the language use of social members in scenes of aggression involving sociopolitical activism. As scholars like Andersson (2021) and Bou-Franch (2022) have pointed out, aggression is always lurking in activist language use. Some form of conflict of varying degrees often emerges even when 'ordinary' – that is, non-activist – social members with

Ideological Convictions and Language Use 135

different ideological convictions interact with one another. This is because – as Haidt (2012: 366) pointed out – morality

> binds us into ideological teams that fight each other as though the fate of the world depended on our side winning each battle. It blinds us to the fact that each team is composed of good people who have something important to say.

Thus, as part of studying how politics and sociopolitics influence the language use of activists and other ordinary social members, it is particularly relevant to consider the role of morality in their language use. Following our contrastive view in this book, it is also relevant to consider how the morally loaded clashes in which ideological convictions relate to activism differ from more 'ordinary' ones in which no such convictions are present. We pursue particular interest in interactions in public where differences in ideological conviction may naturally lead to clashes.

8.2 Case Study

In the following case study, we investigate how 'moral order' comes into existence in a situation where a person with a politically relevant conviction – a radical animal rights protester – disturbs an event, and the politically relevant conviction is pitted against the convictions of ordinary social members.

We define moral order with Wuthnow (1987: 14), who argued that moral order involves 'what is proper to do and reasonable to expect' in terms of interpersonal behaviour in a particular context where the participants are aware of their rights and obligations and act accordingly. Moral order manifests itself in a cluster of unwritten social mores and conventions, which may be challenged in conflicts (Baumgartner 1989), and in the current study our goal is to identify such challenges with the aid of speech acts and interaction. Further, the moral orders (plural) of the participants can be disputed whenever the participants in a morally loaded conflict claim that the other behaves in an inappropriate way. In such conflicts, the participants tend to verbally pit **moral oughts** against one another (see Kádár and Marquez-Reiter 2016).[1] Since our goal is to capture such clashes through the lens of speech acts, we rely on our finite, replicable and interactional system of speech acts outlined in Chapter 2, since this system allows us to pin down a juxtaposition between moral orders in conflictive interactions in a replicable way.

8.2.1 Background

In pragmatics, moral order has been understood in two different ways. On the one hand the work of Garfinkel (1964) influenced researchers like Haugh (2013), who pinned down moral order through conversational notions like

---

[1] Moral oughts are often social oughts as well (see e.g. Horton 2011).

preference organisation. On the other hand, the sociological framework of Wuthnow (1987) and Douglas (1999) influenced researchers such as Spencer-Oatey and Kádár (2015), Kádár (2017), Parvaresh and Tayebi (2018) and Márquez-Reiter (2022), who interpreted moral order beyond a strictly conversational sense; that is, as unwritten social mores and conventions, which can manifest themselves in conflicting moral orders in a particular interaction. Along with the moral order itself, the study of morally loaded language use has gained momentum in politeness research (see e.g. Haugh 2013; Izadi 2015; Parvaresh and Tayebi 2018; Spencer-Oatey and Xing 2019; Haugh et al. 2023). Particular foci in this area include issues such as how moral norms and related moral oughts are pitted against each other in conflict, often centring on perceived violations of the moral order (e.g. Culpeper 2011; Kádár and Marquez-Reiter 2016), how taking offence relates to morality (Márquez-Reiter and Haugh 2019; Parvaresh 2022) and so on. The phenomenon of speech acts has been underrepresented in previous pragmatic inquiries on aggression: although scholars such as Harré (1987), Wahlström (2016) and House and Kádár (2021b) mentioned the role of speech acts in morally loaded interactions, particularly in conflicts, this area has been largely ignored in research on the interface between morality and pragmatics. We therefore believe that it is particularly important to identify replicable patterns of speech act realisation by interpreting the outcomes of a detailed analysis with the aid of both quantitative and qualitative evidence. We also believe that it is beneficial to integrate pragmatic research on morality, the moral order and aggression into the field of language and politics. While moral values have been discussed in CDA (see e.g. Chilton 2011), the approach we propose here is critically different from such CDA methodology, where often individual moral values are emphasised.

Research on language and (social) politics – particularly studies dedicated to the phenomena of **complex participation** and bystander intervention – is also relevant for the present study. The Goffmanian concept of complex participation has triggered significant interest in the study of political language use (e.g. Jacobs 2011; Chovanec and Dynel 2015; Murphy 2015). We hope to contribute to this area of research, by investigating the realisation patterns and morally loaded use of speech acts in the complex participatory setting of a public event in which activists clash with other members of the public, typically involving bystanders whose very presence makes participation complex (e.g. Hudson and Bruckman 2004; see also Chapter 9 below). We believe that complex participation is worth studying in the context of moral order and morality because the way in which morality is talked into being in such interactions tends to be influenced by the participants' awareness of the bystanders present. Conviction-fuelled public clashes are particularly interesting in this context because they often involve intrusion into the space of an organised group of participants and bystanders, and such intrusion is unavoidably a hotbed for moral appeals.

A relevant body of research to be mentioned here includes various CDA studies on activism and activist protests (e.g. Pask-Hughes 2013; Rosenfeld 2021; and many others), and a large body of sociological research dedicated to animal rights activism (see e.g. Munro 2012; Jacobsson and Lindblom 2017). Our approach differs from these areas of investigation simply because we follow our pragmatic approach.

Finally, the concept of alignment (Goffman 1981) is highly relevant for the present case study. We already discussed alignment in Chapter 7, and here we apply it in a more conventional multiple-source discourse-analytic sense. In pragmatics and conversation analysis, numerous studies have used this notion (e.g. Sidnell 2009; Lee and Tanaka 2016), and our case study explores how it can be intertwined with speech act research in the context of clashes involving ideological conviction(s). As already noted, according to Goffman (1981), alignment is an attitude whereby a participant in an interaction engages in a topic proposed by another interactant. Failure to align with the other means that a participant refuses to engage in this topic. In the realm of language and politics, in particular the context of ideology and ideological convictions, it is relevant to consider whether and how the lack of alignment correlates with two conflictive moral orders: our data feature a situation where one participant takes a certain argumentative line and makes related appeals to a moral ought, and the other participant takes a completely different line of argument and makes subsequent moral appeals. As part of this investigation, we devote special attention to how the lack of alignment can be pinned down through the realisation of speech acts. We will show that lack of alignment is a key feature of morally loaded conflicts involving convictions, and we investigate how it exacerbates the aggressivity of such conflicts.

8.2.2   Methodology and Data

In this case study, we investigate how our finite, replicable, interactionally defined and radically minimal system of speech acts can be used for the contrastive study of conflicts involving a clash between moral orders, and related conflicts of moral oughts, in discourse incidents centring on the ideological conviction of animal rights, and comparable incidents with no such conviction involved. We believe that the study of the relationship between speech acts and the moral order in such scenarios warrants in the first place a qualitative case study, which is then to be followed up by a quantitatively oriented corpus-based study.

As already noted in Chapter 2, our system of speech acts provides an interactionally based alternative to various speech act systems, starting from the seminal works of Austin and Searle (see also e.g. Geis 1995; Schiffrin 2005; Roberts 2018). Our typology operates with a replicable set of speech act categories and a broader interpretive framework through which illocution and interaction can be fruitfully combined. As also previously noted, as part of this system, we devote particular attention to how the units of illocution and interaction can be distinguished from one another, by arguing that many phenomena which are categorised by some as illocutions actually represent interactional categories. A typical example is 'refusal', which is in our sense an interactional move representing a case when the relationship between two speech acts is dispreferred. For instance, to present our system again, the speech act Invite ('Would you like to come to my party tonight?') may either be 'satisfied' ('Would love to, thanks'), or not ('Can't, I am afraid'). In our system, the second responsive speech act is not a 'refusal', which is an umbrella term – rather, it is a Resolve in illocutionary terms. Of course, refusal is not necessarily realised by the speech act Resolve: for example, 'I am really sorry, I have a commitment' is an Apologise which can fulfil the same refusing role as a Resolve here.

As part of our analysis, we also consider the prosodical features of our data because prosody is often relevant for the interpretation of morally loaded arguments (see e.g. Günthner's 1996 seminal study). Since in speech act analysis we refrain from using the more technical conversation-analytic annotation scheme, we use our own simple and easily intelligible discourse-analytic prosody annotation conventions.[2] In our case study, we devote particular attention to whether and how morally relevant notions mirroring convictions get stressed through prosody in a particular interaction.

Our main data consist of transcripts of ten anglophone animal rights protests where protesters disturb an event in public. In our qualitative analysis we focus on one particular incident, which in our view best represents the key pragmatic features of all the interactions in the corpus. This interaction consists of various pieces of footage of an incident which took place between the organisers of a children's party, an animal rights protester and the protester's like-minded boyfriend in Australia. The organisers of the children's party took two ponies dressed up as unicorns to the event under investigation. The footage includes the original video recordings made by the boyfriend of the animal rights protester,[3] and a news report which includes parts of the interaction.[4] We merged this footage in our transcript of the event. All the recordings are in the public domain and in our data no language use of participants below the age of eighteen is featured.

---

[2] Readers with interest in more intricate research on the relationship between prosody and politeness are advised to consult Brown and Prieto (2017).
[3] See https://bit.ly/4dUWn8d.   [4] See www.youtube.com/watch?v=UC3iiL1W9tk.

Our ancillary corpus consists of interactions drawn from the television show *Primetime: What Would You Do?*, a US programme dedicated to featuring cases of bystander intervention. The overarching theme of the show is that actors act out scenes in which some type of conflict or illegal activity occurs; hidden cameras record the event, and the focus is on whether bystanders intervene or not. Data from this show, which was also previously studied by Kádár (2017) and Kádár and Marquez-Reiter (2016), include 117 video recordings on average two minutes in length. This database of 117 recordings features cases of an intervener interfering in someone else's intimate relationship, thus infringing on their private space (Brown and Levinson 1987) as conventionally understood in US public settings (see, for example, Nelson 2002). We believe that this corpus qualifies as comparable with our main corpus because both corpora include complex (public) participatory settings, and also both represent conflicts where moral oughts are pitted against each other. Clearly, however, in the second data set no politically relevant ideological conviction is normally present.

As part of our analysis, we also compare the main outcome of our research in the two corpora from a quantitative point of view. As we will point out later, the pragmatic differences between the two corpora turned out to be relatively clear-cut.

8.2.3   Analysis

The following analysis is divided into two main sections, including the study of the main corpus and the ancillary investigation. In our main analysis, we outline recurrent speech act patterns, which we identified in the data and the main corpus. The interaction under investigation can be divided into two parts: at the beginning of the interaction a conflict occurs only between the animal rights protester and the organisers of the children's party. Later on, as the conviction-anchored conflict escalates, the animal rights protester tries to recruit bystanders and various of them become involved in the interaction. We therefore divide the analysis of the main corpus into two sections: first we analyse the interactionally simpler case when the conversation only includes the protester and the two organisers; later we examine the more complex second part of the interaction where bystanders are involved.

8.2.3.1   Our Main Data: Interactionally Simpler Cases

The pragmatically most salient feature of morally loaded ideological conviction-anchored aggression in our main data is lack of alignment, which pervades nearly the entire interaction, including interactionally simpler cases studied in this section. The following extract illustrates this phenomenon:

(8.1)

1. Protester: Yeah? What about these innocent beings that are slaves?
2. Organiser 1: I'm asking you to respect the children, please.
3. Protester: Well, I'm asking you to respect these innocent beings.

In turn 1, the animal rights Protester first uses the **gambit** or discourse marker 'yeah'. The rising intonation of this gambit is noteworthy: it can be argued that this 'yeah' adopts an accusatory tone, and as such it bolsters the Protester's appeal to a moral order. Next, the Protester realises the speech act Request (for information). Here again intonation is salient: she stresses the expressions 'innocent beings' and 'slaves', which are the central parts of her moral appeal. An aligned response to this speech act would most likely be an Informative speech act Tell, by means of which Organiser 1 would adjacently satisfy the Request. However, instead of such a Tell, the Organiser realises the speech act Request (to-do-x), asking the Protester to stop disturbing the party and upsetting the children. She stresses the expressions 'children' and 'please'. In our interpretation, once again there is a noteworthy emphasis on a morally relevant term in this debate, which is 'children' in turn 2, while stressing 'please' operates as an Upgrader for the Request (see Blum-Kulka et al. 1989). In terms of the moral order, we can reliably argue that here two moral oughts are pitted against each other: the welfare of children, which is the conviction of ordinary social members, versus the welfare of animals, which is the politically relevant ideological conviction involved in the clash.

The pragmatic effect of non-alignment in moral arguments like the one illustrated by extract (8.1) is to step up the verbal aggression hanging over the entire ideologically divided interaction: by failing to align with the other, the speaker unavoidably attacks the other's face because she completely ignores what the other has said. When the Protester attacks Organiser 1, she invokes a higher and more abstract moral principle, so the attack can even be said to be not strictly personal.

Another key feature of aggression exacerbation in our data also illustrated by extract (8.1) is **mimesis**. Normally, reciprocating mimesis is a tool of facework: by repeating the words of one's interactant, one can 'flatter' the other for being the originator of something that is significant and pertinent enough to deserve being repeated. However, the very opposite effect can be observed in extract (8.1): by mimetically repeating the words of Organiser 1 in turn 3, the animal rights Protester repositions her original Request in turn 1 as a moral ought through which she counters the moral ought that Organiser 1 pitted against her Request (for information).

Along with mimesis, another noteworthy interactional phenomenon in our main corpus is self-repetition. That is, on various occasions a particular speech act representing an appeal to a moral ought gets repeated by the same speaker, as illustrated by the following extract (8.2):

(8.2)

1. Organiser 1 (to the children): Girls, girls ...
2. Protester: Poor (inaudible) these animals deserve to live freely from harm.
3. Organiser 1: Um, there are children here, please. There are children here, please.
4. Protester: Yeah? What about these innocent beings that are slaves?

In turn 3, Organiser 1 uses the hesitation marker 'um', indicating that she is trying to gain time to launch her counterattack, and then she repeats the speech act Request (to-do-x) to give extra weight to it. In terms of intonation, she emphasises the expression 'children' in both utterances, hence reinforcing her moral appeal. In 'mainstream' speech act research, including Blum-Kulka et al. (1989), such a repeated use of a speech act has also been interpreted as an Upgrader through which more pragmatic weight is given to the speech act at hand.

The non-aligned nature of speech acts can also be captured from a quantitative point of view. Table 8.1 below illustrates the speech act sequences which we could observe in our data in cases where the interaction only takes place between the protester and the organisers. As part of our methodology we do not attempt to quantify the number of speech acts, considering that speech act quantification is a thorny issue (see Weisser 2014). In various cases, there is more than one realisation of the same speech act in the same turn, as we could see, for example, in the case of turn 3 in extract (8.2). In Table 8.1, the grey row highlights the non-aligned responses of the organisers which we could observe in all but one case in the transcribed interaction. We counted exchanges between the animal rights protester and the organisers by breaking them down into three-turn units. We applied this division partly because the phenomena of mimesis and self-repetition in non-alignment outlined above tend to emerge in three-turn sequences, as both the above extracts (8.1) and (8.2) have already shown. Furthermore, in our case study the attacks are one-sided in that they are always initiated by the animal rights protester, as the following example illustrates:

Table 8.1 Speech act sequences in the first part of our data

Participants and interactional turn	Non-aligned sequences					Aligned sequence		Participants and interactional turn
Protester (Turn 1)	Request (for information)	Request (for information)	Complain	Tell	Request (to-do-x)	Complain	Request (to-do-x)
Organiser 1/2 (Turn 2)	Request (to-do-x)	Request (to-do-x)	Thanks	Request (to-do-x)	Request (to-do-x)	Request (to-do-x)	Organiser (Turn 2)
Protester (Turn 3)	Request (to-do-x)	Request (for information)	Complain	Request (for information)/ Complain	Complain	Opine	Organiser (Turn 3)
Frequency of speech act exchange pattern	3	2	2	2	1	1	Frequency of speech act exchange pattern

Ideological Convictions and Language Use

(8.3)

Unit 1
- 1. Protester: Do you feel guilty? Is that your natural reaction to love because you're an animal abuser?
- 2. Organiser 1: There are children here. There are children here, please. There are children here, please.
- 3. Protester: Animal abusers!
- 4. Organiser 1: You can't ... I'd take a stop now, please. — Unit 2

...

Due to the one-sidedness of the attacks, we counted each third turn in our three-turn interactional unit both as a response to a defensive move or counterattack by one of the organisers and as an initiation of a new attack. For example, the speech act Complain in turn 3 above is both a non-aligned response to Organiser 1's Request and a Complain. As Bergmann (1998) pointed out, the speech act Complain – which is also upgraded through intonation in turn 3 above – is particularly apt to gain a strong accusative moral function, and as such is arguably useful for both realising a non-aligned response and launching a new attack.

Considering the brevity of our main case study (and all interactions in our two corpora), the numbers in Table 8.1 should be treated with caution. Yet it is noteworthy that in most of these dyadic exchanges (eight out of eleven), one of the organisers responds with a Request (to-do-x), appealing to the children's welfare by requesting that the wrongdoer the leave the scene. This ubiquity of Request (to-do-x) makes perfect sense if one considers that it is the protester who enters the other party's private space, and so she unavoidably infringes on both a moral and a social ought.

The only case when an organiser realises a speech act which is not a Request is the following:

(8.4)

1. Protester: Yeah, I just want to know who the slave owner is because this is disgusting. This is animal abuse.
2. Organiser 1: Okay, thank you.
3. Protester: This is animal abuse.

Here the speech act Thanks realised by Organiser 1 is just as non-aligned as a response as the Requests elsewhere in our data. Note that the interactionally embedded phenomenon we have here is what House and Kádár (2021a) defined elsewhere with the concept of **altered speech act realisation**; that is, when the original illocutionary force of the speech act is modified as it migrates to another illocution. More specifically, the Thanks transforms into a Resolve; that is, a speech act by means of which the speaker contradicts the other.

There is only one single exchange in our data, which we categorised as aligned. This exchange occurs at the beginning of the interaction:

(8.5)

1. Protester: This is animal abuse.
2. Organiser 3: Do you know what else is disgusting? Your arse hanging out of your shorts.
3. Organiser 1 to Organiser 3: No, no, no, no, no, no (inaudible).
4. Organiser 3 to Organiser 1: I'm sorry, but (inaudible).

While here Organiser 3 responds to the initiating Complain with a Request (for information) followed by the speech act Opine, instead of the ubiquitous Request (to-do-x), this response is clearly idiosyncratic in our data because here it is the Organiser who clearly infringes on the moral order by making the attack personal as she rudely comments on a physical attribute of the protester. Her intonation of the swear word makes the attack even more salient. It is not a coincidence that here our standard Protester→Organiser→Protester exchange scheme cannot be observed: in turn 3, Organiser 1 immediately intervenes with a Request (not to-do-x) consisting of a 'multiple saying' (see Stivers 2006), and, in turn 4, Organiser 3 realises a speech act Apologise (to Organiser 1), which indicates her awareness of the fact that she did indeed infringe on the moral order and was rude.

8.2.3.2 *Our Main Data: Cases of Complex Participation and Escalation*

As the interaction unfolds and an increasing number of non-aligned exchanges take place, an escalation of events can be observed in the following two respects:
1 The organisers begin to threaten the protester with the prospect of calling the police, and then they actually talk to the police on the phone, while the protester continues talking to them and, gradually, to the crowd observing the scene. The police arrive soon, which is the culmination of the escalation as they start to take action by talking to the participants.

2 The protester escalates the conflict by trying to recruit bystanders to participate in her protest (see here Drew and Couper-Kuhlen 2014). Various, but not all, of these bystanders are parents of the children participating in the party.

The following extracts illustrate the two elements outlined above through which escalation is manifested in our data:

(8.6)

1. Organiser 2:   Wait, we already know what you are saying.
2. Protester: Yeah, I'm trying to get the public to (inaudible),
                        no, I'm trying to create public awareness.
3. Organiser 1 (loud voice): And they won't leave and there are children
                        around. Please. Uh, they're abusing the two, uh,
                        handlers of the ponies, myself, and there are
                        children around. Erm … and she won't leave."

(8.7)

1. Protester (loud voice): Please stop this animal slavery! You have the right
                        to know the truth! Watch Dominion[5] on YouTube
                        for what happens in animal agriculture!
2. Woman in the crowd: What do you think of what you are doing to the
                        kid sitting here!

Extract (8.6) already represents a departure from the three-turn pattern outlined above where we could witness a protester→organiser→protester scheme of aggressive interaction. In extract (8.6), Organiser 2 realises the speech act Complain targeted at the protester, and in turn the protester realises the speech act Tell by referring to the point she wants to make. Organiser 1 apparently decides not to respond directly to the protester as she starts talking to the police in a loud voice on her phone, in order for the protester to overhear that a formal complaint is being made against her.

---

[5] *Dominion* is an Australian documentary film released in 2018 by animal rights activist Chris Delforce.

Extract (8.7) illustrates the second type of escalation outlined above. Here the animal rights protester realises a Request (to-do-x), a Tell and another Request in a loud voice, clearly addressing members of the public gathered around the scene. This attempt to recruit bystanders is evidenced by the fact that it is not an organiser but rather a bystander who responds to the protester. Note that this bystander appears not to be a parent but simply someone who is looking at the scene. Important for our analysis, the bystander's response is clearly non-aligned as a topic switch occurs: while the protester refers to animal welfare as a moral ought, the bystander switches the topic to the welfare of the children, who are supposed to be enjoying themselves. In other words, once again we can witness two conflicting and non-aligned moral oughts pitted against each other.

In the following, we examine how the realisation of speech acts and alignment (and its lack) helps us to capture the way in which aggression manifests itself in this part of the interaction where escalation unfolds. Extract (8.7) above has already shown that the protester's attempts to recruit bystanders often fail. The following extract illustrates a similar case:

(8.8)

1. Boyfriend:	So you're okay with this?
2. Bystander:	Huh?
3. Boyfriend:	Are you okay about this?
4. Bystander:	Why wouldn't I be?
5. Boyfriend:	Why would you be? How would you feel if a human was in this position?
6. Bystander:	D…Do they look stressed?
7. Boyfriend:	It's not about that. They're conditioned to be like this.
8. Bystander:	My kids are there, mate. I just really don't care.
9. Boyfriend:	So just because they're conditioned to be like this and objectified in this position. Look at them. They've been painted, they got flowers on them.
10. Bystander:	Mate, I don't want you videotaping my kids.

This interaction takes place between the boyfriend of the animal rights protester, who is having an argument with other members of the public, and a person in the crowd, who later identifies himself as a parent. In turn 1, the protester's boyfriend realises a morally loaded Request (for information) through which he aims to recruit the bystander. After the parent responds with a 'Huh' in turn 2, the boyfriend repeats the same morally loaded Request in turn 3 and the bystander responds with an aligned counter-Request. In turn 5, this counter-Request gets mimetically repeated, and then the boyfriend realises another morally loaded Request (for information). In turn 6, the bystander still responds with a counter-Request in an aligned way, which is answered with a satisfying Opine in turn 7. This is the point where conflict visibly emerges: in turn 8, the bystander identifies himself as a parent of one of the children in the party, by realising the speech act Disclose, which is clearly not aligned with the preceding Opine. Following this speech act, the parent utters a Resolve, which is a speech act referring to the speaker's imminent action. The boyfriend's attempt to recruit the bystander is explicitly refuted through this speech act. It is worth noting that the bystander stresses 'care' in 'I just don't care', which makes his non-alignment with the other even more salient. In turn 9 the boyfriend makes another attempt to recruit this bystander, by repeating his plea. However, in turn 10 the bystander yet again realises a non-aligned speech act, a Request (not-to-do-x). Here one can witness again the moral ought of children's welfare being pitted against animal welfare. In summary, extract (8.8) shows that occasionally non-alignment does not occur straightaway but emerges as the interaction unfolds in interactionally complex scenarios in our corpus.

8.2.3.3 Our Ancillary Data

Similarly to our main data, in our ancillary corpus one can also witness moral oughts pitted against each other. However, in this latter corpus we could very rarely detect the phenomenon of lack of alignment that we found in the main corpus. In our words, Haidt's (2012) observation about political causes dividing people clearly emerges – and can be pinned down with the aid of pragmatic evidence – once we contrast our activist data with ordinary public clashes.

The following extract (8.9) illustrates a typical interaction in our ancillary corpus:

(8.9) A couple is arguing in the park. Bystanders overhear the argument but seem conflicted over intervention. An elderly female bystander decides to intervene.

1. Boyfriend:	Stop crying. Shut up!
2. Elderly female:	Hey buddy! Cool it!
3. Boyfriend:	Ma'am, can you just let us do our own thing? It's my girlfriend. Can you just leave us alone?
4. Elderly female:	No. That's not how you treat someone. How about I call the cops?

In the interaction above, an elderly person intervenes with moral disgust as a male person (the 'boyfriend' in the transcript) physically threatens his girlfriend. In turn 1, the boyfriend of the abused person utters two heated Requests (to-do-x) to his girlfriend. He also pushes his girlfriend down to a bench. In turn 2, the elderly person, who is a bystander, and who – like all the bystanders in the corpus – is unaware of the fact that the scene is staged and secretly video-recorded, self-selects herself to intervene. First, she utters an Alerter and then a Request (to-do-x). In turn 3, the boyfriend responds with an aligned Complain ('Ma'am, can you just let us do our own thing?'), followed by a Grounder and a Request (to-do-x). His intonation adds a moral load to both the Request and the Complain, as he stresses 'own' and 'alone'. In turn 4, the intervening person responds with an aligned (and strongly emphasised) Resolve ('No'), followed by a Complain and a Resolve realised as an interrogative which upgrades the Resolve. It is worth noting that the intervening bystander stresses 'treat', hence giving a moral load to her Complain. Here the intervening bystander makes an appeal to the moral ought of appropriate treatment of others, whereas the boyfriend makes a counterappeal to the moral ought of not being disturbed (i.e. politeness). In other words, similarly to our main data, in the present interaction two moral oughts are pitted against one another, but no politically relevant ideological conviction is involved.

In the following, we provide another extract to illustrate that the difference between our two corpora outlined above applies also to other public interactions in the ancillary corpus:

(8.10) A dog has been left on the back seat of car on a very hot day and barks loudly as people pass by. It is illegal to leave a pet in a car in New Jersey.

1. Female: It's just so hot in there. […] But the police are coming right now.
2. Dog owner: You called the cops? How is any of that your concern?
3. Female: The dog is in there panting and could die. That's our concern. Not you.

Here again one can witness a clear alignment between the various speech acts constituting the subsequent turns of the interaction. In turn 1, the intervening person utters a Complain, stressing that it is very hot in the car, and then a menacing informative Tell. In response, the dog owner utters a Request (for information) loaded with indignation (he stresses 'cops'), doubting the justification of calling the police, and then a Request (for information) where he questions the other's right to intervene. Once again, here a moral conflict emerges where the utterances are aligned with each other. In turn 3, this sense of alignment continues as the intervening person justifies the reason for intervention.

As this brief analysis illustrates, while conflict and aggression tend to be present in different manifestations of morally loaded clashes, the lack of alignment is not automatic in such scenarios because no politically relevant ideological convictions are involved.

8.2.3.4 Contrastive Analysis

In the following, let us compare alignment and its lack in our two corpora from a quantitative point of view. Tables 8.2 and 8.3 summarise the presence/lack of alignment in three-turn units in our two corpora. Naturally, here we only quantified those parts of the interactions in our corpora where such three-turn units are identifiable.

The three-turn unit structure can also be observed in our ancillary corpus, as extracts (8.9) and (8.10) above illustrate, although here the participation structure is somewhat different in that these units follow an intervening bystander→wrongdoer→bystander structure. While, as we already noted, the two corpora differ in size, comparing them is still meaningful: while in our main corpus the ratio between non-aligned and aligned responses is 81.3 per cent versus 18.7 per cent, in the ancillary corpus we could only find three three-turn units where non-alignment occurs; that is, the ratio between non-aligned and aligned responses is 1.5 per cent versus 98.5 per cent. That is, while we cannot argue that the sociopolitically relevant interactions studied in this chapter are

Table 8.2 *Ratio of non-aligned to aligned responses in our main corpus*

Non-aligned speech acts (three-turn units)	Aligned speech acts (three-turn units)	Overall ratio
11 (92.6%)	1 (7.4%)	
8 (80%)	2 (2%)	
9 (69.2%)	4 (30.8%)	
15 (88%)	2 (12%)	
13 (92.8%)	1 (7.2%)	Non-aligned 81.3%
6 (50%)	6 (50%)	Aligned 18.7%
12 (85.7%)	2 (14.3%)	
9 (90%)	1 (10%)	
8 (72.7%)	3 (27.3%)	
12 (92.3%)	1 (7.7%)	

150 Language and Politics

Table 8.3 *Ratio of non-aligned to aligned responses in our ancillary corpus*

Non-aligned speech acts (three-turn units)	Aligned speech acts (three-turn units)	Overall ratio
3 (1.5%)	193 (98.5%)	Non-aligned 1.5% Aligned 98.5%

completely different from their non-activist counterparts because non-alignment occurs in both corpora, it is clear that non-alignment is much more prone to occur in the former than in the latter.

The difference between the main corpus and the ancillary corpus naturally leads us back to the main focus of this chapter – the influence of ideological convictions on language use. Our main corpus includes cases which can be regarded as a juxtaposition of (socio)political beliefs where at least one party – the activist – is holding a politically relevant ideological conviction. Although the interaction studied – and other interactions in this corpus – did not take place in an institutionalised political setting, it represents a clash between a person who had already staged similar protests,[6] and the organisers who are duty-bound to protect the children in their care. In other cases in our first corpus featuring activists, the other side was not bound by such duties but was nevertheless disturbed by the activist. Consequently, the interaction studied involves a moral clash and related aggression between participants holding different convictions formulated and held at least by one party well before the interaction. In other cases, the disturbed party may not engage in such a strong clash as the party organisers here, but even in such cases the activist often forces the disturbed party to formulate a conviction simply by being disturbed. The following extract illustrates this point:

(8.11)

Texan: Fuck off, fuck off mate.
Activist: This is fine, this is fine, no worry, I'm here to chat with you.
Texan: I've already been to jail, I don't give a fuck.

This interaction takes place between an activist and a customer in front of a burger bar. The activist disturbs a group of guests eating burgers by attempting to convince them to talk about the right of animals. As the above extract shows, one of the disturbed customers takes up an anti-animal rights conviction and interacts with the activist through non-aligned responses. In other words,

---

[6] Both various YouTube comments and the Facebook site of this person show that the demonstrator is a high-profile activist.

while this customer may have not had any conviction before the incident, by being forced into an interaction he naturally positions himself against the conviction held by the person who disturbs him.

In the ancillary corpus, on the other hand, the juxtaposition of (socio)political beliefs characterising the main corpus is absent, in that the convictions involved seem not to be held prior to the interaction. This is why the participants do not normally end up in parallel interactions.

In this chapter, we have investigated the effect of sociopolitically relevant ideological convictions on language use. Here we have adopted a different approach to ideology than in other parts of the present book. By default, in our pragmatic approach to language and politics we aim to *avoid* ideology as much as possible, by attempting to distance ourselves from pre-held ideologically motivated beliefs through our bottom-up approach. In this chapter, however, we considered ways in which ideology as a phenomenon influencing language behaviour can be incorporated into our framework. While ideology itself is a fundamental phenomenon in the study of language and politics, we have argued that it is particularly relevant to discuss ideological convictions in the pragmatics-anchored study of language and politics because they often manifest themselves in the language use of ordinary members and activists in public discourse, outside ritual language use in political institutions. Through the study of such convictions, it becomes possible to interconnect language and politics with the work of moral psychologists like Haidt (2012). While clashes are not the only important conviction-relevant phenomena worth considering – other conviction-relevant phenomena are, for example, in-group conversations between supporters of a cause are of equal relevance for the scholar – their study helps us to pin down the divisive effect of politics and sociopolitics on individual behaviour.

8.3 Recommended Readings

Katharyn A. Woolard. 2020. Language ideologies. In James M. Stanlaw (ed.), *The International Encyclopedia of Linguistic Anthropology*. London: Wiley. https://doi.org/10.1002/9781118786093.ie.

Woolard's study provides an accessible overview of the relationship between ideologies and language, and so we highly recommend this short article for readers with an interest in the role of ideology in language and politics. In the following section, Woolard defines the phenomenon of ideology from a linguistic point of view (references elided):

'Language ideologies', 'linguistic ideologies', and 'ideologies of language' are alternative labels for the same field of inquiry and are generally used interchangeably. Their focus is on ideologies that are in some crucial way about language itself, rather than all ideologies encoded in or through language. As most commonly understood now, ideologies of language are morally and politically loaded representations of the nature, structure, and use of languages in a social world... Societies of all kinds have language ideologies. In childrearing, everyday interaction, and interpersonal disputes as much as in ritual and political debates, small-scale traditional societies characterized by apparent cultural and linguistic homogeneity are as affected by language ideologies as are multilingual, multiethnic, late capitalist societies. Ideological representations of language(s) are enacted by ordinary community members as well as by official institutions and elites, including academic scholars.

> Teun A. van Dijk. 1998. *Ideology: A Multidisciplinary Approach.* Thousand Oaks, CA: Sage.

Perhaps the most important series of studies on language and ideology was provided by Van Dijk, from a CDA point of view. Although pragmatics and CDA differ in their approach to language and politics, including also the way in which scholars define their research objectives (see Chapter 1), when it comes to ideology as a concept, pragmatics has profited enormously from CDA. In the following excerpt, Van Dijk (1988: 1) discusses some basic issues relating to the study of ideology:

It's almost a routine. Studies of ideology often begin with a remark about the vagueness of the notion and the resulting theoretical confusion of its analysis, as I did in the Preface. Indeed, of all essentially contested and controversial concepts in the social sciences and the humanities, that of 'ideology' may well come out near the top of the list. One historical and political – and, yes, ideological – reason for this special status may be that 'ideology' is one of these notions that have divided Marxists and non-Marxists, as well as 'critical' scholars and 'uncritical' ones – obviously divisions that are themselves ideological.

Still, as a general concept, ideology is hardly more vague than similar Big Terms in the social sciences and the humanities. In many respects, the same holds for such notions as 'society', 'group', 'action', 'power', 'discourse', 'mind' and 'knowledge', among many others. These notions defy precise definition and seem to happily live the fuzzy life inherent in such catch-all terms that denote complex sets of phenomena and that are the preferred toys of philosophers and scholars in the humanities and the social sciences. Where 'ideology' differs from these other general notions, however, is that its commonsense usage is generally pejorative.

Definitions generally are hardly adequate to capture all the complexities of such notions. Indeed, such fundamental notions are the objects of inquiry for theories and whole disciplines. Definitions cannot be expected to summarize all the insights accumulated in such bodies of knowledge – even if there were no controversies over the meaning of the central concepts of such disciplines. In sum, as with many similar notions, and apart from its uses in everyday discourse, the various versions of the concept of ideology are simply the scholarly constructs of competing theories. That is, at least with this word, it is as Alice was told in Wonderland: we define what the word means. Of course, presuming that 'we' have the power to do so.

9 Aggression in Political Institutions

9.1 Introduction

In Chapter 8, we considered how aggression and sociopolitically relevant language use relate to one another. In the present chapter, we will examine a related area, namely 'disorderly' scenes in politically relevant events. In a sense, **disorder** is lurking in many scenes of politics where a conflict of interest and opposing ideologies and ideological convictions are present. This is exactly the reason why, in many political systems, institutionalised rituals have come into existence in order to keep aggression under control. For example, Bull et al. (2020) studied the British institution of Prime Minister's Questions, arguing as follows:

> In the United Kingdom, laws are passed by the House of Commons, which is supreme in legislative matters. The Prime Minister (PM) is answerable to the Commons and must maintain its support to stay in power. Every Wednesday at noon while Parliament is sitting, Members of Parliament (MPs) have the opportunity for at least the next half hour to pose questions to the PM on any topic of their choice in PMQs. From a theoretical point of view, what makes the discourse of PMQs relevant to pragmatics-based research on ritual is that it provides insight into the operation of communal and institutionalised ritual practices. On the one hand, PMQs operate within strict rights and obligations, and within an institutionalised veneer of public 'civility' ... On the other hand, PMQs is notorious for its adversarial language, variously described as a form of 'verbal pugilism' ... and even as a 'bear pit' ... For instance, in this paper we demonstrate that the phrase 'Mr. Speaker' is often deployed in attacks on the PM not to mitigate the face-threat but rather to indicate that a stronger face-threatening utterance is on the way. (Bull et al. 2020: 65, references elided)

Rituals, such as cloaking attacks on other MPs as 'civil' utterances to the Speaker of the House, keep aggression regulated in many scenes of politics, while at the same time they also *encourage* the participants to engage in aggressive behaviour. This aggression-triggering function of many political rituals is visible not only in ceremonial contexts such as the above-mentioned case of PMQs in the British Parliament, but also, for example, in televised presidential debates, which have been broadly studied in the field (e.g. Cienki 2004; Halmari 2008; Parvaresh 2018). In such debates, the mediator is ritually ratified to allocate timeslots for the participants, stop them if their behaviour trespasses the rules of the debate, and so on; that is, presidential debates represent a typically ritual situation with ratified rights and obligations. At the same time, participants in such debates must be aggressive in order to become winners in the ritual scenario.

We define such political rituals as **rites of anti-structure**. This term was borrowed from the seminal work the ritualist Victor Turner (1982: 44) who described such rituals as rites taking place in 'anti-structure':

> I have used the term 'anti-structure' ... [to describe] the liberation of human capacities of cognition, affect, volition, creativity, etc., from the normative constraints incumbent upon occupying a sequence of social statuses, enacting a multiplicity of social roles, and being acutely conscious of membership in some corporate group such as a family, lineage, clan, tribe, nation, etc., or of affiliation with some pervasive social category such as class, caste, sex or age-division.

As Turner argues, events which remove the individual from the expected flow of daily life are 'anti-structural' if they set in motion an alternative order that differs from the normally expected 'structural' order of 'civil' behaviour. Anti-structural events are often of a ritual scope for various reasons, as previous pragmatic research by Kádár and Robinson-Davies (2015) and Kádár (2017; 2024) has pointed out, and as such they tend to have various features in common:

a They are often public or at least unfold as if an audience were present, which accords with the communal orientation of interaction ritual in general.
b They are anchored in rights and obligations and related moral perceptions of 'acceptable' and 'unacceptable' behaviour in an aggressive context.
c They operate with conventionalised pragmatic features, even though these conventionalised features may be very different from what counts as 'conventional' in other domains of social interaction.
d Perhaps even more than other rituals, aggressive rites of anti-structure are also emotively invested (Collins 2004).
e They come into existence through an escalatory build-up, in the course of which the participants often insult each other as part of the drama of the ritual (see Turner 1979; 1982).

According to Turner, in anti-structural rituals the participants are not only allowed but are also encouraged to defy the norms holding for ordinary-life situations within certain boundaries, and such rites tend to create 'camps'. Thus the interactional frame of such rituals liminally prompts those who perform the ritual to display their 'toughness', while certain manifestations of behaviour which count as 'ordinary' and desirable in daily interaction may be evaluated as inappropriate. This is why the candidates of a televised presidential debate,

MPs in the British Parliament and any other political actors in scenes of mediatised political aggression are *expected* to be aggressive.

The reason why even those who are not part of the camps of the antagonists of such anti-structural rituals accept such behaviour as somehow 'normal' is that it is often institutionalised and as such represents a standard situation for the participants. Our concept of **'standard situation'**, originating in Hoppe-Graff et al.'s (1985) work, was first applied in cross-cultural pragmatic research by House (1989: 115), as follows:

> The notion of a standard situation involves participants' rather fixed expectations and perceptions of social role. Role relations are transparent and predetermined, the requester has a right, the requestee an obligation, the degree of imposition involved in the request is low, as is the perceived degree of difficulty in realizing it. In a nutshell, the participants know where and who they are. Clearly, the distinction between a standard and a nonstandard situation is not clear-cut. For example, in an interaction where a policeman is reprimanding a car owner, when, for instance, the policeman utters a request to move the car, it is evident that the expression please takes place in a standard situation and thus has been formulated with the goal of indicating this situation.

The standardness of many political scenes of aggression implies that even those situations which are seemingly ad hoc and confusing may be standard for their participants and many observers. So while such situations may not be **institutionalised** in the conventional sense of the word, they nevertheless often operate with clear conventions and related rights and obligations, and with the aid of a bottom-up pragmatic approach it is possible to describe their conventions on a par with those of political institutions. As Thornborrow (2002) pointed out, the concept of 'institutionalised' in fact covers a wide range of situations in which power is present, and following this train of thought it is reasonable to argue that standard political situations with no clearly defined or schematic language use also represent institutionalised contexts, often with anti-structural ritual features. In the case study presented in this chapter, we examine one such situation, namely heckling in the US in various contexts. More specifically, following our contrastive view, we examine different contexts of heckling – not only political events but also sports heckling and so on. We believe that studying such scenes of aggression is particularly important in language and politics not only because pragmatics helps us to capture the dynamics of aggression, but also because the study of contexts of aggression shows that political institutions influence language behaviour far beyond what one would normally think.

9.2   Case Study

In this study, we examine heckling in US, UK and Hungarian contexts. Heckling is a form of aggressive behaviour by means of which a person or group interrupt a person who speaks or performs onstage, in order 'to harass and try to disconcert [him or her] with questions, challenges, or jibes'.[1] This interruption, by means of which an audience member attempts to become an unratified participant (Goffman 1967), often occurs in political settings, the performing arts and other public events.

We are interested in heckling for two interrelated reasons. First, we aim to consider whether scenarios in which heckling occurs and forms of speaker and heckler behaviour are essentially comparable; that is, whether political heckling can be related to other forms of heckling. If heckling has conventionalised contextual and behavioural features, it can then be argued that heckling represents a rite of anti-structure and a related standard situation, with recognisable features for the participants. Also, if the participants in heckling scenarios behave in conventionalised ways, we have first-hand evidence for the fact that politically relevant institutions influence many interactional scenes well beyond the realm of institutionalised politics. Second, an interesting feature of heckling is that it is heavily ideologised, similarly to many other politically relevant forms of aggression. For example, Fiss (1986) argues that the heckler 'is an obstructionist, who is not so much conveying an idea as preventing someone else from doing so'. Jordan (2011: 118), on the other hand, refers to the heckler as follows:

Let's upend the conformist definition of the heckle as anti-social and instead think of the heckler as heroic, a kind of public speech super hero, with the ability to suspend rhetoric, preserving the right to speak out of turn. The violence, awkwardness and embarrassment of the heckle are signs of its political courage, fearlessness and agency. The heckler's interruption opens up a space for public discourse. Deprived of the heckler we would have one less method of turning passers-by into assembled publics.

Such definitions seem to reflect different world views: Fiss's description seems to reflect the perspective of those who are interested in the maintenance of the order of public speeches, while Jordan's description shows her neo-Marxist stance.[2] The concept of 'heckling' also has an interesting history. For example, associating the heckler's activity with potential heroism and democracy – and the spread of the word 'heckling' and variants such as 'barracking' – is a post-industrial development (Chapman 1948), while some forms of heckling have arguably existed in the context of entertainment since ancient times. For example, Smith (2006) notes in an article on ancient Rome that the verb *explodere* was used in the context of entertainment, to describe the actions of 'driving out by clapping', and 'hissing (a player) off the stage'. Another thought-provoking example of heckling in antiquity, in the context

---

[1] See Merriam-Webster Online dictionary (www.merriam-webster.com/dictionary/heckle).
[2] We are grateful to Mel for pointing this out. Neo-Marxist works in general (e.g. Bruff 2013) tend to represent heckling as an essentially positive phenomenon.

of political discourse, can be found in a passage in Cicero's letters to Atticus (I.16.1), where Cicero reports an episode of heckling in the Roman Senate. That is, on 15 May, 61 BC, Clodius insulted Cicero ad hominem during his talk, and this heckle culminated in a verbal fight, which ended with Cicero managing to silence Clodius (at least, as Cicero claims). In sum, the phenomenon of heckling existed well before the word 'heckling' came into existence.[3] We therefore believe that by defining heckling as a rite of anti-structure and by looking at the typological features of this anti-structural ritual, we can more reliably pin down this phenomenon than if we approach it by using more popular ideologised definitions.

The phenomenon of heckling has been examined in various areas, including, for example, conversation analysis (e.g. McIlvenny 1996), pragmatics (Rao 2011; Stopfner 2013), rhetoric (e.g. Jacobs 1982; Jacobs and Jackson 1993), gender and language (e.g. Baxter 2002) and interaction and social psychology (e.g. Silverthorne and Mazmanian 1975; Bull and Fetzer 2010), as well as in other disciplines, such as psychology and cognitive research (e.g. Ware and Tucker 1974), the arts (e.g. Zeman 1984; Jordan 2011) and law (e.g. Korey Lefteroff 2005). In many of these previous discussions, the political relevance of heckling has been emphasised.

9.2.1 Methodology and Data

Following our interest in capturing politically relevant institutionalised aggressive behaviour as anti-structural rituals, we approach manifestations of heckling and various situations of clashes between speaker and heckler. These settings include both political and non-political data, and we attempt to elaborate a pragmatics-anchored typology of such settings in which heckling emerges. We aim to consider how the behaviour of the participants is influenced by the constraints and affordances of these settings. Capturing pragmatic behaviour in these standard situations of heckling allows us to systematise seemingly ad hoc aggression in scenes of heckling.

Our study is based on a corpus of 112 video-recorded interactions in English and Hungarian, retrieved from community websites such as YouTube (see more in Kádár 2015). Along with video-recorded interactions, we also examined thirty-seven narrated cases of heckling, including two interactions which Kádár encountered in person. The heckling incidents studied occurred in the following four settings:
• Political speeches
• Sport events

---

[3] On the other hand, as Kádár and Ran (2016) pointed out, Chinese and Japanese equivalents of 'heckling' have a very different history from this Western concept.

158 Language and Politics

- Public talks
- Stand-up comedies

In studying heckling in these situations, categorising different heckling behaviours and relying on data drawn from different political linguacultures, we follow our contrastive take outlined in Chapter 2. In terms of our analytic units, here we conduct a mainly discourse-analytic approach. Following our contrastive take, we compare political heckling with other heckling types.

Out transcription symbols in the case study are the following:

(.)	noticeable pause
(1.0)	timed pause
=	interruption
(())	transcriber's explanation

9.2.2   Analysis

9.2.2.1   Categories of Heckling

In attempting to categorise types of heckling, we set out from the context rather than the content of the scenarios: we distinguish two fundamentally different settings in which heckling takes place, namely *interactional* and *presentational* settings, which provide different affordances and constraints for the public speaker. 'Interactional' scenes encompass situations in which the public speaker has an opportunity to interact directly with the heckler and the audience, while 'presentational' scenes are settings in which the speaker acts as a presenter without the possibility of directly reacting to heckling. The following extracts, drawn from non-political settings for the sake of preparing the ground to discuss politically relevant data later on, illustrate the operation of heckling in interactional and presentational settings:

(9.1)

EC = Eliot Chang (American Asian comedian)
H = heckler
AUD = audience

1. EC: I was in DC
2. H: Huuuu (screams)
3. EC: (1.0) True! All right ...
4. AUD: ((laughter))
...
5. EC: No, I'm saying she [i.e. the heckler] is a singer! Oh f***
6. AUD: ((laughter))
7. H: My baby is a singer!

> EC: raises his fist as a mock gesture of support, then smiles

> EC: grasps the microphone and mockingly imitates the heckler, who in the manner of a 'singer' interrupted her with screams

(Retrieved from www.youtube.com/watch?v=NXJgmCsZQsM)

(9.2)   CR = Colby Rasmus (US professional baseball center fielder)
         H = heckler
         AUD = audience

   1. H: Get a haircut, hippie!
   2. AUD: ((laughter))
   3. CR: ((does not visibly react))
               (Retrieved from www.youtube.com/watch?v=nPm6WwE5vVg)

Extract (9.1) is drawn from a stand-up comedy performance: a woman from the audience heckles the comedian Eliot Chang several times, first by interrupting him as she screams in a high-pitched voice, and then through a verbal exchange. This interactional situation allows Chang to respond to the challenge, and he handles the situation successfully; for example, in turn 3 he mocks the heckler vis-à-vis an ostensible act of agreement. In contrast to (9.1), the presentational setting of extract (9.2) constrains the public 'speaker', the baseball player Colby Rasmus, who is mocked for his notably long hair, to shout back at the heckler. It can be argued that many politically relevant situations represent the interactional scene. However, as we will show in our case study, this is not always the case; that is, this contextual typology helps us to describe political heckling as an anti-structural ritual, on a par with other heckling scenes, with different hidden sacred rights and obligations involved.

In interactional settings, such as public political speeches and stand-up comedy, the speaker is in a physically *elevated* position and has the institutional right not only to deliver a presentation but also to directly *interact with the audience*. In interactional settings the heckler may prepare for the act of heckling. Presentational settings afford a fundamentally different conventional pragmatic pattern for the participants. In such settings the speaker is not elevated but rather *exposed*; being 'exposed' implies that the speaker does not have an institutional right to interact directly with the audience, although there are indirect means for the speaker to counter a heckler.[4] This setting allows heckling to become a more elaborate performance because the heckler can not only prepare for the act of disruption but also make use of the speaker's exposed condition. Presentational settings can be transformed into interactional ones, if a speaker who is institutionally not supposed to directly interact with the heckler decides to temporarily deviate from ritual conventions and makes the decision to go 'off script' clear to the participants (see extract 9.4).

Interactional–elevated and presentational–exposed settings tend to trigger different heckling behaviours. In interactional–elevated settings, heckling is often *competing* and potentially *emergent*, as the heckler can 'get a voice' and affiliate with the participants through the (potentially symbolic) attempt to halt

---

[4] On the problem of directly responding to certain forms of heckling see also a brief empirical description in Eisenstadt (1958).

the speech/performance of the speaker, hence 'competing' with him. For example, in extract (9.1) the long silence in turn 3 indicates that the heckler manages to halt the presentation for a certain period of time – that is, her performance 'competes' with that of Chang in a certain respect – the emergent nature of the heckle becomes clear as the interaction unfolds between the speaker and the heckler. As the speaker has an institutionalised right to counteract, the disruptive act of heckling tends to motivate him to react to the repeated attacks. In presentational settings, heckling is usually *concurrent* and potentially *predesigned*, as the heckler can acquire a voice and affiliate with the audience by continuously disturbing the speaker's ongoing speech/performance, and the speaker has no right to react directly to the disruption. This can be illustrated by extract (9.2), in which the actions of the speaker and the heckler take place in a simultaneous 'concurrent' way.

The interrelation between interactional–elevated settings and competing–emergent heckling, on the one hand, and presentational–exposed settings and concurrent–predesigned heckling on the other, is a tendency afforded by the pragmatic dynamics of these settings. Yet, while in interactional–elevated settings, concurrent–predesigned behaviour can take place (e.g. when a politician is being booed off by hecklers), it is significantly rarer for competing–emergent heckling to appear in presentational–exposed settings. This is because such settings do not usually afford this interactional type of heckling; for example, a sports heckler's or a traditional theatre performance audience's disruptive shouting is not interactional, if one understands 'interaction' as a form of interdependent action (e.g. Baker 1999), in the sense that institutional norms prevent the speaker from directly reacting to it.

Consequently, it is also rare in our data for the two types of heckling to transform one into the other. A simpler question is why interactional (competing–emergent) heckling behaviour is not usually replaced with the concurrent–predesigned type: once a heckler manages to affiliate himself with the audience through interacting with the speaker, it is not logical for him to 'withdraw' from this interactional participation status. But in fact it is unusual even for concurrent–predesigned heckling behaviour to transform into competing–emergent heckling. This is partly due to the following two factors:

- Physical constraints in those interactional–elevated settings which accidentally trigger concurrent–predesigned heckling: e.g. in a political speech it can be difficult for the heckler who holds up a sign or tries to boo off the speaker (concurrent–predesigned heckling) to obtain the microphone and compete with the speaker.[5]

---

[5] This reality has been described by an online documentary (www.youtube.com/watch?v=8GXskjzQnvo) as follows: 'But the balance of power is rarely in the heckler's favor. The politician has a podium and a security detail; it's not really a fair fight. The politician also has a microphone, meaning that the heckler has to scream at the top of their lungs just to be heard.'

- The interactional constraints of such settings: if a setting, such as a parliament debate, necessitates concurrent–predesigned forms of heckling, the speaker also tends to have the institutional affordances to counter the heckler's attempts to switch to an interactional mode.

The operation of such constraints and affordances is illustrated by the following case of political heckling in the Hungarian Parliament. In 2013, members of the far-right radical party Jobbik interrupted a debate on the so-called Act of Land, by standing behind the pulpit of the acting head of the debate, János Latorcai, and holding up the following large sign:

A magyar föld átjátszása idegeneknek: HAZAÁRULÁS!
Giving Hungarian land to foreigners is: TREASON!

The sign – which can be interpreted as a form of ritual performance, as it is meant to display the message of a group of people in a dramatic mediatised way to a wide audience – also displayed two shaking hands, symbolising the European Union and the governing party, Fidesz, and flags of countries which, the radicals claimed, profited from the Act of Land, including Germany, Israel and Russia. As the following transcript illustrates, the leader of the radicals who stood right behind the acting president could not transform his group's concurrent–predesigned heckling into a competing–emergent type. That is, although he managed to disrupt the work of the Parliament, his group could not effectively take the floor in the course of the interaction.

(9.3)
JL = János Latorcai (acting head)
GV = Gábor Vona (leader of the radical party)

1. JL: a (1.0) Házba hogy (1.0) alávetik magukat
2. GV: ((inaudible)) ((inaudible))
3. JL: az Országgyűlés honlapján (.)
4. GV: ((inaudible)) ((inaudible))
5. JL: az elnök úr által megjelent (1.0) rendnek (.)
6. GV: rendszabályoknak melyek az ülést
...
7. JL: önöknek nincs lehetőségük
8. JL: vélemény nyilvánításra
9. VG: ((inaudible))
10. JL: amennyire (.) bocsánat frakcióvezető
11. VG: ((inaudible))
12. JL: úr most egyelőre (.) a (1.0) vendégeikhez
13. JL: szólok
...
1. JL: the (1.0) Parliament that (1.0) you oblige
2. GV: ((inaudible)) ((inaudible))
3. JL: the Parliament's (.) webpage
4. GV: ((inaudible)) ((inaudible))

JL: looks on the crowd and clearly ignores GV;
GV: gesticulates and, standing behind JL's chair, moves closer to JL

5. JL: regulations (1.0) published by the president (.)
6. GV: these rules are meant to make discussions
...
7. JL: you <u>are not</u> allowed
8. JL: to express your opinion   ⸺ GV: gesticulates and moves slightly closer to JL;
9. GV: ((inaudible))
10. JL: and if (.) excuse me mr. faction
11. GV: ((inaudible))   ⸺ JL: raises his arm and points towards the audience; continuously avoids looking at GV
12. JL: leader but right now (.) I (1.0) communicate with
13. JL:the guests [reference to participants brought in by the radical parliament faction]
(Retrieved from www.youtube.com/watch?feature=player_embedded&v=Og_4yg_Y5D4#at=26)

Although JL makes several emphatic pauses (Wood and Kroger 2000), without a microphone GV is not able to utilise these pauses to get the floor through interruption (see e.g. Bennett 1981). JL also ignores GV's attempts to converse directly by not acknowledging his interruptions until turn 10. This behaviour of ignoring the heckler is also reinforced on the non-linguistic level: JL ignores GV, who initiates interaction through gestures, by looking at the crowd and not changing his bodily posture. Although in turns 10–13 JL finally acknowledges GV's interruption, this acknowledgement functions as a rebuke – JL does not allow GV to take the floor – and on the non-linguistic level he continues to ignore GV's presence by avoiding looking at him or even turning his body towards him.

The lack of transition between the two types of heckling is also due to the fact that these heckling types are associated with ritual roles. While heckling is a form of disruption by means of which the heckler can 'acquire a voice' for his opinion (see Jordan 2011), getting a voice does not inherently imply that the heckler wants to interrupt in an *interactional way* and to give up his role as a disruptive heckler via an onstage 'competing' performance. This situation is illustrated by the following extract, which represents the heckling of a video-recorded political speech. While a transition occurs here between the presentational–exposed and interactional–elevated types – the speaker and his supporters aim to transform this presentational setting into an interactional one in order to cope with the heckler's challenge – the heckler refuses to switch to an interactional mode, even though the change of setting would allow this:

(9.4)

BK = Ben Konop
H = heckler
SUP = group of supporters around the SPEAKER

[An extended period of heckling occurs before the start of the transcript]
1. BK: we are here again to   ((laughs))
2. H: boooo booo liar booo   ⸺ BK: smiles and looks towards the ground, then he turns his head towards the heckler, and finally he turns back to the camera
3. BK: (10.0)
4. BK: all right
5. HL   booo Ben Konop liar booo

6. SUP: why don't you come on down and tell all our
7. SUP: TV cameras what your problem is (.) there
8. BK: yeah
9. SUP: ((inaudible))
10. BK: let's just get (.) let's get it out of the way
11. BK: and then I can say my piece and you can say your piece
[…]
12. BK: no you are not coming down here (.) okay well then
13. BK: let me speak my piece and maybe they'll come interview you afterwards
14. BK: and you can present your argument okay
15. BK: that's fair (4.0)
16. BK: all right (2.0) stage four
17. SUP: ((giggle))
18. BK: OK we're here at Parkway for a very serious issue
19. H: booo liar

BK: smiles, then turns head towards the heckler; the camera then shows H, who smiles and then shakes his head

(Retrieved from www.youtube.com/watch?v=s9dNdIV6eg8)

This interaction takes place after Ben Konop, a US politician, is interrupted several times by a heckler on the street, while he tries to deliver his video-recorded speech. In each case of interruption Konop stops and looks towards the ground – this body language seems to symbolise disaffiliation with the heckler's behaviour – and then he turns back to the camera. In the excerpt analysed here, the heckler gets the invitation to present his argument when in turns 6 and 7 one of Konop's supporters invites him to come down from the terrace of his home. Konop takes up this idea: he not only repeats his supporter's invitation, but in this case he also turns his head and upper body towards the heckler and repeats the invitation, hence giving emphasis to the act (Norrick 1987). However, the heckler refuses both the invitation and the request to let Konop finish what he wants to say ('that's fair'), and he again heckles Konop, who then attempts to affiliate with the participants and lay observers through humour (uttering 'stage four').

In summary, transitioning from concurrent–predesigned to competing–emergent heckling is difficult, although it is possible and in certain interactions the heckler can even *take over* the speaker's role. Such a case can be illustrated by an incident of the stand-up comedian Jamie Kennedy, who was first heckled in a concurrent–predesigned way (the heckler screamed swear words in a large hall and was not able to interact with Kennedy), but after Kennedy angrily left the podium the heckler occupied the stage.[6] The typological relationship between interactional settings and forms of heckling is illustrated by Figure 9.1.

The left-hand side of the figure represents the interaction between the speaker and the heckler:

- the two-sided arrows indicate the default relationship between context types and heckling types;

---

[6] See a clip of this interaction at www.youtube.com/watch?v=0AJm-iwxRug.

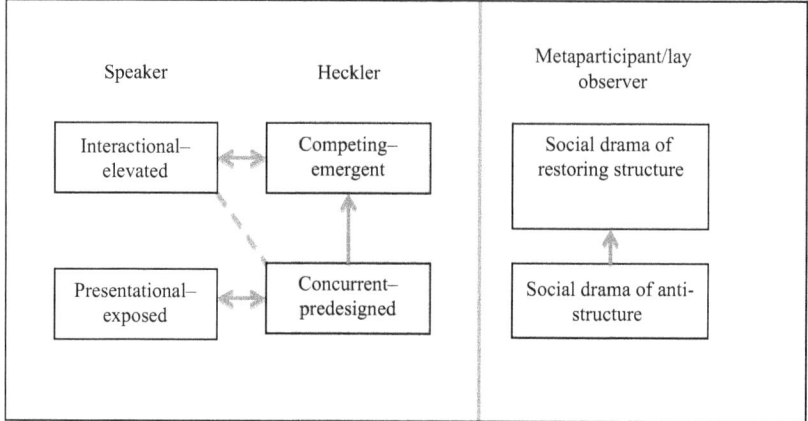

Figure 9.1 Types of heckling

- the dotted line denotes that concurrent–predesigned heckling may, occasionally, occur in interactional–elevated settings;
- the one-sided arrow indicates that concurrent–predesigned heckling can, potentially, transform into competing–emergent heckling, but this does not tend to happen the other way around.

The right-hand side of the figure represents the relationship between heckling and the attitudes/feelings of the participants/lay observers, by drawing on Turner's (1982) concept of anti-structure. The pragmatic dynamics that the interactional–elevated and the presentational–exposed settings afford seem to trigger different expectations. These different expectations influence evaluations of the heckler's and the speaker's behaviours, and they are also present in micro-level interactional features.

In the case of competing–emergent heckling, the audience seems, typically, to expect the speaker to restore structure from anti-structure. Such a ritual counterperformance is expected as the speaker has the right and capability to do so. In the case of concurrent–predesigned heckling there seems to be less pressure on the speaker, because the institutional setting triggers the anticipation that the heckled one has little opportunity to directly counteract (see e.g. extract 9.2). Thus, referring again to Turner's (1982) terminology, concurrent–predesigned heckling is expected to become a social drama of anti-structure by default, even though it can transform into a drama of restoring structure through successful counterperformance.

Let us here refer to an experiment we undertook, which supports this model of the participants' anticipatory expectations towards the ritual standard situations outlined above. In the video-recorded data studied, we measured

	Time range of focus on the speaker	Time range of focus on the heckler
Interactional–elevated	72–91%	9–28%
Presentational–exposed	54–85%	15–46%

Figure 9.2 The camera's focus on the speaker and the heckler

the length of time the camera focused on the speaker and the heckler. As the length of every interaction in our corpus differs, we calculated focus proportionally. For example, if, in a recording one minute and forty-eight seconds long, the camera's focus is on the speaker for sixty seconds, on the heckler for forty-four seconds, and moving between the two persons for the remaining four seconds, we took the 'dead time' of four seconds off and calculated proportions as follows:

Full length = 104 sec (100%)
Speaker = 60 sec (57.7%)
Heckler = 44 sec (42.3%)

The rounded results of this experiment are given in Figure 9.2.

The camera's focus does not necessarily represent the observers' focus, and also the time devoted to the speaker versus the heckler may depend on the video-recording person's relationship with one or both of them. However, one can reliably argue that the cameraman presents an audience perspective. The significant focus difference between interactional–elevated and presentational–exposed settings shows that in the former type more attention is devoted to the speaker, which indicates raised expectations for him to counterperform, while in the latter setting the heckler gets relatively more attention.

In what follows, let us illustrate how forms of heckling operate in interactional–elevated and presentational–exposed settings.

9.2.2.2 Interactional–Elevated Settings

The interaction studied here took place between the showman Jamie Kennedy and a female heckler who felt that Kennedy's use of the word 'waitress' was 'politically incorrect'.

(9.5)
JK = Jamie Kennedy
H = Heckler
AUD = audience

1. JK: and I had a really interesting erhm (.) waitress service here (1.5)
2.   that woman took my order at this diner and how
3.   much =this has (inaudible)

> JK: looks at audience; bodily posture is that of the public speaker

166　Language and Politics

4. H: =server (1.0) they are called server (2.0) 5. AUD: ((laughing/booing)) (5.0) 6. JK: wow a a woman is proud to be a	JK: looks at the heckler's direction, his mouth slightly opens and he gulps; H: nods and smiles
7. JK: waitress (0.5) 8. AUD: ((laughter))	JK: looks at audience, his face shows surprise and scorn
9. JK: it's a (7.0) it's weird when 10. AUD: ((laughter))	JK: looks at audience, massages his eyebrows (sign of tiredness)
11. JK: I see them I just say hey bitch um hi 12. AUD: ((laughter))	JK: smiles at audience (acknowledgement of laughter);
	JK: performs a parody of waitress by first raising his hand and then shaking his bottom towards the audience

(Retrieved from www.youtube.com/watch?v=ITBfwhp8XMY)

The speaker's counterperformance comes into operation after the act of competing–emergent heckling occurs in turns 3–4. Kennedy – who speaks in a conventional presentational mode before his talk is disrupted (he looks in different directions and he has what one would describe as the typical bodily posture of a public speaker) – suddenly stares in the heckler's direction, opens his mouth and gulps, which seems to be a potential sign of surprise and preparation for countering the heckler. The audience's reaction also reveals that this is a transition point in the interaction, as the heckler's interruption triggers laughter and booing.

If one analyses Kennedy's behaviour, it becomes evident that his 'answer' to the heckler is actually a dramatic performance. On the level of non-linguistic behaviour, there are various signs which show that Kennedy aims to align with his audience – by restoring the normative order of the interaction – rather than to interact with the heckler:

- In turn 5, after getting through the initial surprise, Kennedy redirects his gaze to the audience, and he disaffiliates with the heckler through facial expressions (his face shows surprise and scorn) and gestures (he massages his eyebrows, which seems to be a sign of 'annoyance').
- When the participants reward the counterperformance with laughter, Kennedy smiles at them.
- Finally, Kennedy performs a parody of a waitress (first by raising his hand and then shaking his bottom towards the audience in a feminine way).

In terms of language use, it is clear that Kennedy undertakes something more than directly responding to the heckler:

- He first utters a mock acknowledgement of the interruption's appropriateness ('wow') and then refers to the heckler in the third person ('a woman').
- Following this, in turns 9 and 11, he begins to narrate a mock ordering ('it's weird when ... I just'); through this performance he completely regains the floor to speak.

Aggression in Political Institutions 167

The audience's reaction in turns 8, 10 and 12 illustrates that in interactional–elevated settings the participants expect the speaker to counterperform and restore the interactional structure. In these turns laughter arguably is a supportive move, considering that Kennedy is a comedian, and such 'supportive laughter' (Björkman 2011) reflects indirect encouragement for the speaker to proceed with the counterperformance.

The heckler's competing–emergent interruption can also be interpreted as a sort of performance, although this performance is much simpler than that of the speaker. In extract (9.5) the woman not only interrupts Kennedy, but also uses the silence that the interruption creates to rearticulate (Hoffman 1991) her utterance; that is, she realises a 'non-spontaneous' repetition (Clark 2006: 379). The fact that she refers to 'servers' in the third person gives her utterance a potentially theatrical shape, as this rhetorical technique animates the voice of a group that, it is claimed, is ignored. On the non-linguistic level, the heckler nods and smiles, supposedly in order to affiliate herself with the audience in the social drama. The performance scope of the heckler's utterance is best illustrated by the audience's reaction: the participants react to her words with laughter/booing; that is, they frame (Goffman 1974) the interruption as an onstage part of the comedy.

In the case of stand-up comedy, the speaker's counteraction is naturally associated with 'performance', and it tends to be evaluated accordingly (e.g. Kennedy receives supportive laughter). Yet the speaker's and the heckler's *roles* – and basic expectations of these roles – are relatively similar across different contexts, all the more so because any public speech is inherently theatrical. The following excerpt illustrates this point; this interaction took place when the US first lady Michelle Obama was heckled by gay rights activist Ellen Sturtz (June 2013). A noteworthy element in the conversation is that Obama actually refuses to counterperform, but this is a symbolic refusal which defeats the heckler:

(9.6)
MO = Michelle Obama
ES = Ellen Sturz
AUD = audience

1. MO: and I don't care what you believe
2. MO: and we don't
3. ES: ((inaudible))
4. MO: wait wait wait
5. ES: ((inaudible)) executive order
6. MO: (.) one of the things I
7. ES: ((inaudible))
8. MO: one of the things I don't do (1.0) well (1.5) is this
9. AUD: ((enthusiastic laughter/clapping))
[…]
10. MO: [listen to me or] you can take the mike   MO: walks off the podium, faces the heckler

168   Language and Politics

11. MO:	but I'm leaving (.) so you all decide		MO: begins to dramatically walk out, then interacts with other members of the audience, with body language which suggests appeal; following the audience's request to stay she smiles and makes her way back to the podium
12. AUD:	no no I'm sure noooo ((various voices))		
13. ES:		I need your husband to	
14. MO:	you have one choice		
15. AUD:	((various voices))	no please don't leave	

(Retrieved from www.youtube.com/watch?v=aE09MScupks)

Turns 1–9 are only available in an audio-recorded form, and so this part does not allow studying facial expressions and gestures. Linguistic analysis of this section illustrates that Obama restores interactional order by refusing to counterperform ('one of the things I don't do, well, is this [i.e. answering hecklers]'); notably, long pauses in this utterance are supposedly meant to emphasise the refusal. The theatrical nature of Obama's behaviour is illustrated by the audience's reaction: the participants applaud her, which shows that her symbolic non-performance is actually interpreted and framed as a successful (counter)performance.

The following video-recorded part further illustrates the theatrical nature of Obama's linguistic and non-linguistic actions. She first ritually showcases her 'toughness' by walking off the podium and facing the heckler, and then by symbolically giving the audience a fait accompli as she makes the audience decide whether they want her or the heckler to leave. The noteworthy element in this action, which shows its theatrical–ritual nature, is that it takes place only *after* Obama clearly manages to affiliate herself with the audience (the participants' reaction in turn 9 reveals that they take her side). Obama puts further dramatic 'pressure' on the audience as she begins to leave the place of the event, in spite of the fact that various participants request her to stay. She then exchanges sympathetic words with the audience, and 'lets herself be convinced' to return to the podium, while the audience applauds her.

Similarly to the previous extract (9.5), the audience seems to expect Obama to 'do something' (counterperform). This is illustrated by the aforementioned fact that they reward Obama's symbolic refusal to counterperform with laughter and clapping.

9.2.2.3   *Presentational–Exposed Settings*

Presentational–exposed settings provide more affordances for the heckler to perform the social drama of anti-structure, as such settings trigger concurrent–predesigned forms of heckling. Such forms of heckling also include written forms of heckling. For example, in the case of sports heckling, which is a representative case of concurrent–predesigned heckling, hecklers often use carefully designed signs to draw attention, and in many cases artistic performance plays an important role in the operation of such signs, as the case of a heckled hockey referee illustrates (Figure 9.3):

Aggression in Political Institutions 169

Figure 9.3 A heckling sign for a hockey referee
(See www.youtube.com/watch?v=MeZm9S1yzSo)

This sign was displayed behind the plastic fence which separates the players from the audience. The message in the cartoon thought bubble can function properly only if it is displayed close to the public figure's head in a way that those who sit on the opposite side of the stadium see it as if the referee himself had such 'thoughts'. Signs like this not only illustrate the artistic element and preparation work involved in certain concurrent–predesigned forms of heckling, but they also show that heckling can operate in complex ways.

As already noted, in presentational–exposed settings the speaker/public figure is not supposed to directly counteract. Although the speaker can attempt to transform such settings into interactional–elevated ones, as extract (9.4) has shown, if the context does not afford such a transformation and the speaker fails to continue his performance, he is likely to lose his 'professional face' (Planken 2005). This is also the case when it comes to politically relevant data. This is illustrated by the following case of the British journalist Nick Robinson, who was heckled by peace protesters who held up a two-sided sign during his reporting on Britain's participation in the Afghan war:

(9.7)

NR = Nick Robinson
H = Heckler(s)

1. NR: overseas aid for example
2. NR: and he's doing it by classic welfare (.)
3. NR: but he will not write the next chapters
4. NR: in this story (.) that will be written as
5. NR: councils decide what to cut (.) as others decide
6. NR: what to cut he says the title for this saga is back

H: holds up the sign with the text 'CUT THE WAR NOT THE POOR'; then the sign is turned, and it reads 'Bring Our Troops Home Now' (first four words in black, 'Now' in red, supposedly with the goal of emphasis); the sign is moved towards the centre of the stage, right next to NR

170   Language and Politics

7. NR: from the brink (.) others may say (1.0)
8. NR: it's over the edge (10.0)
9. NR: ((grasps the sign and breaks it to pieces))
10. H: ((clasp/cheering))
11. H: you should be ashamed of yourself, mate
12. H: you should be ashamed (.) shame on you, mate
((NR leaves the podium, H approaches him, and a debate begins))

NR: looks at the camera, then smiles and slowly turns round; half way through he uses a handkerchief to rub his mouth (potential sign of embarrassment/anger) and then turns towards H

H: holds up another sign

(Retrieved from www.youtube.com/watch?v=5rU8YU3loeQ)

The hecklers' concurrent–predesigned action shows similarity with Figure 9.3, in that it is a performance – that is, it displays the hecklers' values/beliefs to the public. In fact, the performance here is not clearly targeted *at* the speaker: instead of humiliating the speaker, as in the case of Figure 9.3, the hecklers want to display a message about their peace protest. Yet, in terms of physical action, the hecklers act identically to the sport heckler in the hockey stadium: they move the sign slowly towards the speaker and then keep it close to him, supposedly anticipating that the sign will be recorded by the camera (and a side camera operated by another protester). As they move the sign, they also turn it, which is part of the performance as such a move has the potential to draw attention. In turn 8, Robinson keeps a long silence and smiles, which technically signals the end of the report. However, at this point Robinson seems to realise that something has gone wrong, supposedly from the facial expression of his colleague who is standing opposite him. As he slowly turns round, he displays a potential sign of embarrassment or anger as he rubs his mouth with a handkerchief, and then he loses his temper as he grasps the sign. The hecklers mockingly clap and cheer him, hence acknowledging this outrage. This mocking behaviour is supposedly generated by Robinson's failure to keep his role as a presentational–exposed speaker. Note that while, at this point, the interview is formally over, the speaker is still supposed to 'follow' his role, which is ongoing as long as he is on the stage. Also, technically speaking, the interactional event remains staged, as one of the protesters films it, and both the speaker (who can see this camera even though he is talking to another camera) and the hecklers are supposed to be aware of this fact.

The negative evaluation of the speaker's failure becomes clear in two respects:

- Within the actual interaction, the hecklers reflect on Robinson's outburst by switching to a competing–emergent mode of heckling.
- In his blog, Robinson expressed regret for losing his temper, as he wrote, 'I have a confession. After the news was over, I grabbed the sign and ripped it up – apparently you can watch video of my sign rage in full glorious technicolour on the web. I lost my temper and I regret that.'[7] As Robinson is the offended one, the rationale behind this apology seems to be the conflict between his role as a speaker in a presentational–exposed setting and his direct reaction to the heckling.

[7] See https://bit.ly/4ehAgsr.

In presentational–exposed settings the speaker can defeat the heckler either by avoiding reacting or by reacting indirectly; that is, through managing to counterperform while the 'scripted' show continues according to the presentational–exposed role. This latter technique is illustrated by the following extract, which represents an interaction between the baseball player Tony Gwynn Jr and a sport heckler:

(9.8)
TG = Tony Gwynn Jr
H = heckler
M = participants, including peers of the heckler and other members of the audience

1. H: hey don't act like you're playing
2. M: ((mixed voices))
3. TG: ((changes bodily posture and puts his glove behind his bottom))
4. M: ((laughter))
5. M: ((in altered tone of parody)) and I'm gonna (1.0) shut up
6. M: ((laughter))

TG: avoids turning towards the heckler but changes his posture

TG: uses his glove to imitate speech; someone in the audience utters the words in turn 5 with some delay, following the movement of TG's fingers

(Retrieved from www.youtube.com/watch?v=YTGnh0rcQsc)

In this interaction the public figure manages to counterperform in an indirect way, and as comments on the YouTube page in which this video was found made it clear, through his performance he even managed to turn fans of the other camp to his side.[8] Throughout this whole interaction Gwynn avoids turning towards the heckler and so he keeps his presentational–exposed performance. Furthermore, he skilfully manages to affiliate with the participants when he puts his gloves behind his bottom; this move seems to symbolise the heckler's insignificance (the heckler's imagined mouth is moved close to Gwynn's bottom). The audience rewards Gwynn's counterperformance with laughter, and this seems to motivate Gwynn to continue his counterperformance as he moves his fingers in the glove to imitate speech. A member of the audience interprets this act as an invitation, and he *counterheckles the heckler* by animating the heckler's voice in an altered tone of parody, uttering 'and I'm gonna shut up'. The audience rewards this act of heckling the heckler with laughter.

To sum up, in presentational–exposed settings the speaker can utilise an ad hoc counterperformance, which is not part of the ongoing event. This ad hoc counterperformance protects the flow of the event onstage, and it is *symbolically* indirect, as it operates like 'aside' utterances in theatre. However, in the realm of politics such a counterperformance is rare as far as our data are concerned;

---

[8] There are various comments on this point on YouTube on which this interaction was found. For example, a poster notes, 'He [the heckler] got owned because TG Jr was able to get the Rockies fans on his side. The guy as you can plainly tell became the joke ... Ranter.'

that is, political actors mostly display their toughness in this context by continuing their performance and waiting for the heckler to be removed.

In this chapter, we have examined the role of aggression in politically relevant institutions. We have argued that many political institutions encourage aggression to emerge, not only in the case of covert forms that we could observe in high-level politics in previous chapters, but also in overt ways. However, as with any political institution, even scenes of overt aggression unfold in a 'regulated' way; that is, as far as a politically relevant setting is institutionalised to a certain degree it imposes a ritual frame on the participants with clear rights and obligations through which aggression is kept under control in interactions. We have used Victor Turner's concept of the rite of anti-structure to define a cluster of politically relevant institutions in which aggression lurks. As a case study we have focused on heckling, showing that although behaviour in such scenes is often seemingly ad hoc, the behaviours of the public speaker and the heckler are constrained by ritual rights and obligations, and so scenes of heckling represent standard situations for the participants. The study of scenes of heckling has also helped us to show that the boundaries of politics are often far wider than one would normally think.

9.3 Recommended Readings

Victor Turner. 1969. *The Ritual Process: Structure and Anti-structure*. New Brunswick and London: Transactions.

Victor Turner's classic is a must-read for the study of rites of anti-structure: Turner not only established a groundbreaking framework through which such rituals can be studied, but also described his framework in a very reader-friendly way, making it accessible not only for anthropologists but also for linguists and experts in other fields. In the following section, Turner discusses the concept of liminality:

The attributes of liminality or of liminal personae ('threshold people') are necessarily ambiguous, since this condition and these persons elude or slip through the network of classifications that normally locate states and positions in cultural space. Liminal entities are neither here nor there; they are betwixt and between the positions assigned and arrayed by law, custom, convention, and ceremonial. As such, their ambiguous and indeterminate attributes are expressed by a rich variety of symbols in the many societies that ritualize social and cultural transitions. Thus, liminality is frequently likened to death, to being in the womb, to invisibility, to darkness, to bisexuality, to the wilderness, and to an eclipse of the sun or moon.

Liminal entities, such as neophytes in initiation or puberty rites, may be represented as possessing nothing. They may be disguised as monsters, wear only a strip of clothing, or even go naked, to demonstrate that as liminal beings they have no status, property, insignia, secular clothing indicating rank or role, position in a kinship system – in short, nothing that may distinguish them from their fellow neophytes or initiands. Their behavior is normally passive or humble; they must obey their instructors implicitly, and accept arbitrary punishment without complaint. It is as though they are being reduced or ground down to a uniform condition to be fashioned anew and endowed with additional powers to enable them to cope with their new station in life. Among themselves, neophytes tend to develop an intense comradeship and egalitarianism. Secular distinctions of rank and status disappear or are homogenized. (Turner 1969: 95–96)

Peter Bull, Anita Fetzer and Dániel Z. Kádár. 2020. Calling Mr Speaker 'Mr Speaker': The strategic use of ritual references to the Speaker of the UK House of Commons. *Pragmatics* 30(1): 64–87.

In this chapter, we examined heckling, which transpires to be institutionalised only after we examine such data in a bottom-up way. Some other anti-structural data, such as PMQs in the British Parliament studied by Bull et al., are more clearly institutionalised. In the following section, Bull et al. discuss the anti-structural ritual nature of their PMQs data:

PMQs: A ritual practice

In the House of Commons, the presiding officer is known as the Speaker, who chairs the debates, maintains order, and determines which members may speak. The continuous history of the office is held to date back to 1376, to the reign of the medieval English king Edward III ... At that time, the Speaker was the MP chosen by the other MPs to quite literally speak on their behalf, in particular, to communicate their decisions to the reigning monarch. This was a dangerous business. Between 1399 and 1535 no less than seven Speakers had their heads chopped off. In modern times, this grisly history is reflected in a ritual whereby the MP newly elected to the office shows reluctance to accept it and is forcibly dragged to the chair by other MPs. Thus, the role of the Speaker is not only institutionalised, but may also be seen in a Durkheimian sense as sacred ... as a semi-religious figure initiated into the role through a distinctive rite of passage ... thereby endowed with particular rights and privileges, as well as with particular obligations. In the context of PMQs, the Speaker has in certain respects powers even greater than that of the PM, for example, rebuking noisy MPs from either government or opposition benches for excessive interruptions, barracking, and general rambunctiousness. Importantly, it is the Speaker who decides who gets to question the PM, and how long the session lasts (recent controversies concerning Speaker Bercow indicate how important is this power). While the PM has the ability to rebuke MPs who are being disorderly, it is only the Speaker who is empowered to actually 'do' anything about this.

One of the Speaker's tasks is to preside over PMQs, the central British parliamentary institution and its highest profile parliamentary event. PMQs always begin with the same tabled question to the PM, asking if s/he will list his/her official engagements for the day; thus, like any institutionalised ritual, PMQs are to a certain degree 'scripted' or 'demarcated' ... The Speaker's response to this question is also scripted, i.e. PMQs depart with a ritual sequential chain ... This initial ritual continues, as the called Member can then pose a supplementary question (termed a 'supplementary') on almost anything that relates to the PM's general responsibilities or to some aspect of government policy. The MP is limited to this one supplementary and cannot follow up the PM's response with any further utterance ... However, this is permissible for the Leader of the Opposition, who is allowed up to six questions. Often, only the initial question regarding the PM's engagements is tabled, although MPs can table 'Questions for oral answer on a future day' which the PM would have notice of. (Bull et al. 2019: 65–66, references elided)

10   Politics and Translation

10.1   Introduction

In this final chapter of Part 2, we examine a key phenomenon in the field of politics and translation, by looking at the **difficulty of translating** certain politically relevant terms. This issue of translation difficulty is particularly relevant for the framework proposed in this book because by considering this difficulty we can further elaborate the conceptual issue leading to pitfalls, which we outlined in Chapter 3. More specifically, by considering why certain politically relevant terms are very difficult to translate, we again revisit the pitfall of ethnocentrism always lurking in the study of language and politics and propose a translation-based approach through which this pitfall can be avoided. In order to position the area which we discuss in this chapter, let us here refer to three main bodies of research dedicated to translation and politics.

First, in discussing the role of politics in translation, scholars have often used the concept of 'politics' in a broad sense. For example, Almanna and House (2023: 1) argue as follows: 'Politics . . . refers to those strategies and techniques which are utilised by all those involved in the process of translation at its macro level to achieve their aim.' In accordance with this broad interpretation of politics in translation studies, the sociopolitical embeddedness of practices of translation has also been discussed in translation as a politically relevant issue. Let us here refer to the study of Gal (2015: 227), who provided the following overview of the study of the influence of sociopolitics on translation practices:

Current interest in translation centers on particular kinds of ethnographic sites: global or cross-regional capitalisms, transnational political movements or migrations, and the work of universalizing projects such as Christian missionizing, scientific research, humanitarian aid, biomedicine, and (neo)liberal governance. Many of these create or manage marginalized, subordinated populations.

In such inquiries, a particularly important topic is the study of the relationship between translation and globalisation (see Pym 2006 for an overview; see also House and Kádár 2020).

Second, various scholars have approached translation from the point of view of language and politics, in particular CDA. In CDA-driven inquiries, scholars showed less interest in the degree of success of translation and other technical issues relating to translation, and rather used translation to capture broader sociopolitical issues, such as the effect of ideology on language use (see Munday 2012). In this body of research, translation has also often been presented as a practice of political discourse. For instance, Schäffner (2004: 144) argues as follows:

> I refer to four strategic functions (coercion; resistance, opposition, protest; dissimulation; legitimation and delegitimation) with which to link political situations and processes to discourse types and levels of discourse organisation. These functions can also be applied to translation, both at a macro-level and at a micro-level.

Third, in the pragmatics-based study of translation and politics, scholars have examined technical issues emerging in the translation of politically relevant single-source discourse, in particular the problem of the difficulty of translating many politically relevant notions. Following Derrida's (1998) discussion of hospitality and ethnocentrism, scholars like Beck (2006) and Delanty (2009) assumed the possibility of transcending ethnocentrism through translation. Bielsa and Aguilera (2017: 5) took a more critical stance on this issue, arguing as follows:

> To respect the other, to do justice to the difference of the foreign text, means to resist to the highest possible degree the ethnocentric demand of intelligibility, the violence inherent in translation. However, this resistance also implies subjecting the translator's language to the strangeness of a different tongue and can lead to the production of a text that threatens to become unintelligible.

We also believe that ethnocentrism cannot be easily transcended, and this is why in this book we present ethnocentrism as one of the most important pitfall types in the field of language and politics. In the following case study, we present a model based on House's translation framework, which allows us to capture the difficulty of translation by introducing the notion of **cultural filtering** and its lack (see e.g. House 2024). Through cultural filtering, the translator takes into account differences in discourse norms and consequently the expectation norms on the part of the reader of the translated text.

In terms of our methodology, translation provides an example par excellence of the necessity of empirical contrastive analysis. This is because the study of translation unavoidably involves a comparative analysis through which the original and the translated texts are compared on different linguistic levels. Also, in the study of politically relevant terms like **policy expressions** studied here, the analyst unavoidably brings together the units of expression and discourse.

10.2 Case Study

In the present study, we examine why it is difficult to translate Chinese expressions that are frequently used for communicating policies to the public. We focus on the expression *wenming* 文明. While *wenming* has a cluster of complex meanings and uses in Chinese, it often ends up being conveyed in English simply as 'civilised'. Not only does such a translation narrow down the manifold uses of *wenming*, but also 'civilised' occurs in many collocations which turn out to be rather alien to Western audiences.

We adopt a multi-method approach based on multiple corpora. This approach to policy-related expressions such as *wenming* is bottom-up, similar to other approaches proposed in this book. More specifically, when one examines expressions assumed to be frequent in the communication of policies in a particular linguaculture, one first needs to 'innocently' investigate whether they are in fact frequent in policy communication, and, if so, how. We believe that our contrastive approach is particularly useful for unearthing the relationship between expressions and policy communication because there is significant linguacultural variation in the salience of certain comparable expressions in the communication of policies. For instance, while *wenming* is a policy-related expression, the English 'civilised' is not. It is also important to explore the impact of such linguacultural differences on translation, especially from our main point of view here – the goal of avoiding ethnocentrism in the study of language and politics.

Chinese policy-related expressions are not only used by the media, but also on public signs and notices. For example, *wenming-xiaoyuan* 文明校园 (lit. 'civilised campus') – describing a university's policy to maintain orderly traffic, cleanliness nd so on on campus – not only appears in printed and online materials but also may be displayed in the form of public banners. Following Stein (2005: v), we believe that policy and politics are always related because 'implementing public policy occurs in political systems'.

10.2.1 *Background*

10.2.1.1 *The Origin and Historical Development of* Wenming

Wenming is a loanword borrowed from Japanese during China's colonisation in the late nineteenth and early twentieth centuries (He 2019). Following Japan's rapid modernisation after the Meiji Restoration (1867), Japanese scholars translated many Western expressions into Japanese by using Chinese characters (*kanji*). It was the Japanese philologist Fukuzawa Yukichi 福沢諭吉 who coined the expression *bunmei* 文明 (*wenming* in Chinese) in 1877, by combining the characters *bun* 文 (lit. 'literature', 'writing' and 'literacy') and *mei* 明 (lit. 'light' and 'enlightenment').

In response to the colonisation of China by Western powers, Chinese intellectuals attempted to modernise the country, and in the process several Western expressions gained prominence in policymaking (Pan and Kádár 2011). 'Civilised' was one such expression imported into Chinese. A representative *wenming* collocation of the colonial period is *wenminggun* 文明棍 (lit. 'civilised stick', i.e. a Western-style walking stick). This collocation typically illustrates that, following its adoption, the notion of *wenming* was a locally interpreted concept, implying something desirable that could only be achieved by the country's radical modernisation.

While in our bottom-up approach we do not initially assume that *wenming* is inherently policy-related, previous research has argued that *wenming* has frequently been used in Chinese policymaking (Xu 2003). Although we distance ourselves from such an automatic ascription of the use of *wenming*, historical evidence validates such a claim: *Wenming* became particularly important during the leadership of Deng Xiaoping, who initiated major economic and social reform in 1978. As part of this reform, Chinese policymakers launched the so-called *Liangge-Wenming* 两个文明 (Two Wenming) movement. This movement relied on the principles of *Jingshen Wenming* 精神文明 (Spiritual *Wenming*) and *Wuzhi Wenming* 物质文明 (Material *Wenming*) – with the former referring to the principle of improving public manners, and the latter describing the principle of improving the efficiency and quality of industrial production (see Marinelli's authoritative 2018 study on this subject). This dual use of *wenming* highlights a fact which is of central importance to our study: the uses of *wenming* vary substantially and clearly go beyond good manners, even though various pragmaticians have previously associated *wenming* with politeness (e.g. Chen 1989; Lee-Wong 2009).

The *Wenming* movements are still alive today in China. Between the year 2000 and 2010, Chinese policymakers launched the *Sange Wenming* 三个文明 ('Three Wenming') movement, by reinvigorating the two aforementioned principles of the *Liangge-Wenming* movement and adding *Zhengzhi Wenming* 政治文明 ('Political *Wenming*') as a new principle. Also, recently *Shengtai Wenming* 生态文明 ('Ecological *Wenming*') has become frequent in Chinese political discourse.

10.2.1.2 Translation Theoretical Background

Since we are studying the problems associated with the translation of culturally embedded expressions, it is worth revisiting the classic writings of Roman Jakobson (1959) and Eugene Nida (1964; see also Nida and Taber 1969). As Jakobson (1959: 234) famously stated, 'All cognitive experience and its classification is conveyable in any existing language. Whenever there is deficiency, terminology may be qualified and amplified by loanwords, neologisms or semantic shifts, and finally by circumlocutions.'

Notwithstanding this 'law of universal translatability', we should nevertheless not forget that certain real translatability limits *do* exist (see House 1971;

1973; 1997; 2018; 2024). Jakobson recognises this problem by explicitly referring to 'all *cognitive* experience'; that is, the possibility that translation will be severely restricted if we take connotations into account (see also Chafe's (2000) notion of 'shadow meanings'). Connotations defy explicit definitions: they even vary in one individual's mind as a person's moods and experiences change. Also, connotations cannot be delimited from denotative meanings. So connotative meanings are far too elusive to be captured in translation. Translatability is also limited whenever the form of a linguistic unit takes on a special importance. Connotations and the special importance of the form of a linguistic unit relate to the translational issue that we will study in this chapter by considering the case of *wenming*. We must qualify Jakobson's dictum of universal translatability, as Nida and Taber (1969: 4) have done: 'Anything that can be said in one language can be said in another, unless the form is an essential element of the message.'

This is why translation-related research like our study benefits from departing from an essentially contrastive pragmatic approach, instead of relying on the dictionary meanings of the expressions being studied (see also House 2015).

Another classic work discussing the limits of translatability is Catford (1964):

Source language texts and items are *more* or *less* translatable, rather than absolutely translatable and untranslatable. For translational equivalence to occur, both source language and target language text must be relatable to the *functionally* relevant features of the situation. A decision, in any particular case, as to what is functionally relevant must ... remain to some extent a matter of opinion. (Catford 1964: 93–94, original emphasis)

This means that when judging the appropriateness of any translation there will always be a remnant of subjectivity. House (1977; 1997; 2015) tried to minimise this subjectivity by providing a systematic framework of categories to assess the quality of a certain translation. Figure 10.1 displays the essence of this framework. Our repertoire of translational terms is rooted in this model.

In House's model, translation needs to be regarded as an act of **re-contextualisation** in a new situational context. The 'context of situation' (Malinowski 1935) is opened up through the register categories of 'Field', 'Tenor' and 'Mode', as in the Hallidayan tradition (see e.g. Halliday 2004). While we do not use all the fine details of this model, it provides a framework which can be used to find out why the translations of certain uses of *wenming* into English are problematic. Further, we believe that this model can also be used when it comes to the translation of any other politically relevant expression. The corpus part of the research – indicated by the lower right-hand box and arrow in Figure 10.1 – allows us to avoid speculating about the significance of idiosyncratic translations.

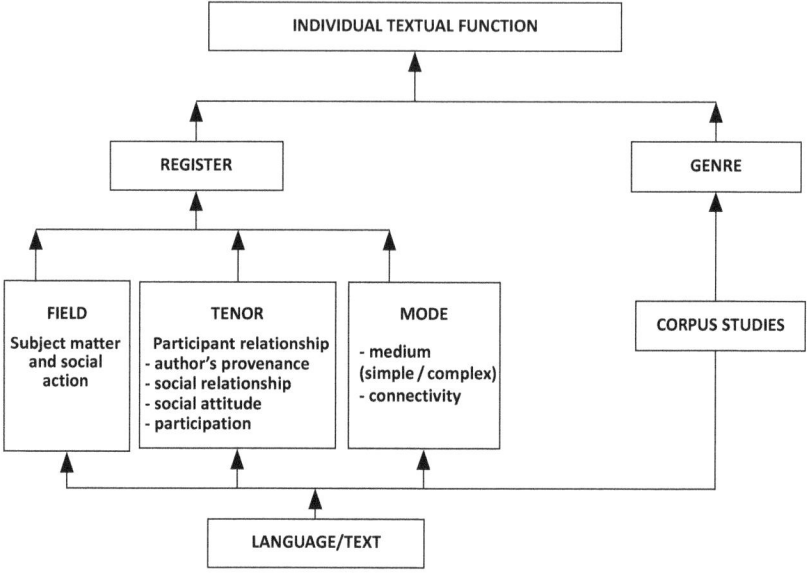

Figure 10.1 House's system of comparative text analysis and evaluation

In the process of re-contextualisation, the categories of **overt** and **covert translation** need to be emphasised in particular (see also House 2018; 2024). Briefly, an overt translation is a translation in which the original text is left intact as far as possible – for example when *wenming* is translated as 'civilised' in any context – whereas a covert translation takes into account the needs of a new audience, with the translator making changes to the original text by applying a cultural filter. We pay particular attention to whether *wenming* collocations are overt or covert in scope, and in our mixed-methods approach we rely on the system outlined in Figure 10.1.

10.2.1.3 Wenming-*Related Research*
Various sinologists have explored *wenming* from sociological and political perspectives. However, they have not tackled the translational issues of this expression, nor have they systematically considered how *wenming* collocations indicate policymaking, including, for example, Boutonnet (2011) and Nguyen (2012). Another relevant area of research includes sociological explorations of *wenming* as a concept denoting civil behaviour (e.g. De Seta 2018). Such

research on civility has not considered translational issues, nor has it explored the use of *wenming* collocations in corpora.

In domestic Chinese research, one witnesses a surge of interest in *wenming*, including studies on the translational issues surrounding this expression. For example, Deng et al. (2014) compared *wenming* as a noun with the English word *civilisation*, by arguing that these two expressions are radically different. He (2019) argued that although *wenming* as a polysyllabic word existed in Classical Chinese texts before this expression was borrowed from the West through Japanese, the Classical Chinese *wenming* expression should be strictly distinguished from its modern Chinese counterpart. Liang (2020) argued that both proper nominal and common nominal translations of *wenming* (*Wenming* versus *wenming*) and singular and plural uses of *wenming* translations should be distinguished from one another. Another key study is Huang (2007), which explores the complexity of *wenming* in late imperial Chinese texts.

Several more essentialist studies should also be mentioned here. Sun (2006) set up some sweeping generalisations about *wenming* by relying on dictionary definitions of the nominal *wenming* and its English counterpart *civilisation*. Liu (2010) conducted essentially ideologically driven research on *wenming* by assuming an East–West dichotomy. He (2007) approached *wenming* primarily as a concept describing etiquette and using it in a moralising manner. Such overgeneralisations show that pitfalls lurking in the study of *wenming* – and, arguably, other politically relevant terms – include not only ethnocentrism, but also the other pitfall types we outlined in Chapters 3, 4 and 5.

10.2.2 *Methodology and Data*

Our case study uses a multi-method approach to examine *wenming*, which we believe can also be used when it comes to similar politically relevant studies. The approach is data-driven in nature, in the following respects:

a Instead of considering ready-made dictionary meanings of *wenming* and *civilised*, or relying on any other a priori assumptions, we contrastively investigate how *wenming* and *civilised* are used in our corpora (see below).
b Instead of pre-assuming that *wenming* is inherently related to policymaking, we approach *wenming* 'innocently', by investigating (1) how it collocates with other linguistic units and (2) which collocations indicate policies.

10.2.2.1 *Methodology*

We focus on the adjectival uses of *wenming* and compare them with those of the English adjective *civilised*. In Chinese, an adjective can either modify a noun directly, implying a strong relationship between the modifying adjective and the noun, or with the aid of the particle *de* 的, indicating a weaker adjective–noun relationship. We only examine *wenming*–noun phrases because we are assuming that the context of policymaking implies a strong relationship between *wenming* and the noun it modifies. Indeed, as our corpus-based research will illustrate, a typical policy-related expression is *wenming-shenghuo* 文明生活 (lit. 'civilised life', i.e. 'progressive lifestyle'), while *wenming-de-shenghuo* 文明的生活 ('progressive-*DE*-lifestyle') is never used in policy communication.

We apply a tripartite approach, involving the following phases:

1 We first conduct an individual corpus search of the adjectival uses of *wenming* and *civilised*. This individual analysis is followed by a contrastive pragmatic analysis of these uses and collocations. The corpora (see more below) that we use in this phase allow us to consider the broader context of the uses and collocations of *civilised* and *wenming*: both corpora provide links to longer stretches of the texts in which these critical tokens occur. We sampled a representative set of 200 examples in each language, by manually excluding invalid examples (e.g. when *civilised* is used as the past participle of a verb). Initially, we do not assume any linguacultural differences between the uses and collocations of *wenming* and *civilised*, given our bottom-up procedure, and we investigate how these tokens are used in the individual corpora. This investigation reveals that the uses of *civilised* and *wenming* can be differentiated according to the following criteria:

   a whether they relate to the behaviour of an individual or a group,

   b whether they describe a state already achieved or a state to be achieved.

We adopt these two criteria as focal points in our corpus-based annotation of the uses and collocations of *civilised* and *wenming*. Our teams involved both Chinese members and ourselves representing linguaculture outsiders, and as part of our bottom-up procedure our Chinese team worked exclusively on the Chinese corpus and we ourselves on the English corpus, without initially discussing the outcomes of the annotation. Our aim was not to create hard and fast annotation categories; rather, our goal was to obtain an empirically grounded set of categories that would be useful and manageable in the ensuing contrastive analysis of the uses and collocations of *wenming* and *civilised*. The two teams then convened to harmonise the annotation. For example, the Chinese team annotated certain uses of *wenming* as 'polite', whereas we labelled the comparable annotation category as 'well-mannered'. We ultimately zeroed in on the annotation category 'well-mannered', simply because 'politeness' has a specific academic meaning. We also harmonised the number of categories, by keeping the number of use-type categories of *wenming* and *civilised* below the threshold of five in each linguaculture, and by merging less frequent categories into more frequent ones. The ultimate goal of this contrastive research is to identify problem sources for translators.

Politics and Translation 183

2 During the second phase, we study how *wenming* is rendered in the English version of Chinese news outlets. We first categorise *wenming* translations in our corpus of bilingual media texts according to the *wenming* annotation categories obtained during the first phase. We then examine whether *wenming* in the bilingual texts really turned out to be problematic to translate into English, by relying on our model of translation (Figure 10.1). In other words, we consider whether *wenming* is translated overtly or covertly in our corpus, and we analyse overt solutions with no cultural filtering through the lens of register concepts, in particular Tenor.

3 The third phase of our research consists of a translation task and follow-up interviews, conducted with a panel of ten expert translators in China. The aim of this follow-up approach is to triangulate our research (see more in House and Kádár 2021b); that is, we aim to test whether the translational tendencies (overt versus covert translation) in phase two can also be observed in the translational solutions provided by our experts. This is an intriguing question because we expect that Chinese public media sources follow preset conventions when it comes to translating policy-related expressions due to the importance and general validity of such policies – we want to find out whether translational tendencies can be interconnected with the Mode involved (see Figure 10.1). The task we provide for our participants consists of short examples drawn from our Chinese corpus (cf. phase one), reflecting the uses of *wenming* according to the outcomes of phase one. Following the test, we interviewed our participants regarding their translational choices.

Figure 10.2 provides a brief summary of our tripartite approach.

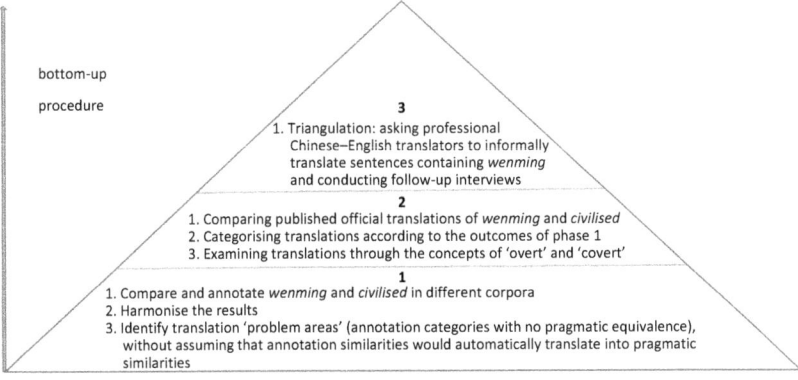

Figure 10.2 Our methodological procedure

Table 10.1 *Our corpus of media texts (Chinese texts only)*

Wenming	Number of tokens	Number of news items featuring *wenming*	Size of the Chinese corpus (Chinese characters)
China Daily (in Chinese)	140	124	50,375
Huanqiu shibao	49	41	16,665
Total	189	165	67,040

10.2.2.2 Data

The corpora used during the first phase of our study include the Balanced Chinese Corpus (BCC, at http://corpus.zhonghuayuwen.org/CnCindex.aspx) and the British National Corpus (BNC). As already noted in this book, we agree with Sharoff et al. (2013) that no corpus is perfect or representative. In our case, this imperfection includes differences in the size of the two corpora, as well as certain differences in the genres featured in them. As mentioned above, the results of our Chinese and English corpus search include 200 valid examples per linguaculture.

The second phase of our research involves Chinese–English bilingual news outlets that feature the expression *wenming* in Chinese, and its English translations. We only included reports on domestic Chinese events to ensure that bilingual news featured the 'native' uses of *wenming* and their English translations. We drew our corpus from the following two news outlets:

1 *China Daily*, at https://language.chinadaily.com.cn and
2 *Global Times*, at www.huanqiu.com; www.globaltimes.cn.

We chose these sources because they are well known. Table 10.1 summarises the frequency of occurrence of the expression *wenming* in our corpus of source texts.

The third phase of our research (translational task) involved occurrences of *wenming* in utterances drawn from the BCC, and consequent interviews with our participants. The overall length of these interviews was approximately 100 minutes. We removed all personal information from the data set.

10.2.3 Analysis

10.2.3.1 Phase One: Corpus-Based Examination of Civilised *and* Wenming

In this section, we first examine the use of *civilised* and *wenming* in our English and Chinese corpora, and then conduct a contrastive analysis.

Uses of *Civilised* Extracted from the BNC

Table 10.2 provides a summary of our annotation categories for *civilised* and their frequency in our sample of 200 examples drawn from the BNC.

Table 10.2 *Annotation categories for* civilised *and their frequency in our sample of 200 examples (BNC)*

Annotation category	Frequency
1 Cultured and developed	97 (48.5%)
2 Governed by law and regulations	49 (24.5%)
3 Sophisticated and refined	23 (11.5%)
4 Well-mannered	21 (10.5%)
5 Well-looked-after and well-cared-for	10 (5%)

In the following, we provide examples to illustrate these five annotation categories.

Cultured and Developed

(10.1) In these civilised times, husbands are no longer given the right to beat their wives.

(10.2) It has often been noted that while barbarians fight with hatchets, civilised men fight with gossip.

Here, *civilised* indicates a sense of advancement, which distinguishes members of one society from those of another more 'primitive' one. In terms of our focal points outlined above, this adjectival use refers to the behaviour of a group and a state which the given group has already achieved.

Governed by Law and Regulations

(10.3) Our lawyers and judges will never turn off this mad process which, for them, is a fountain of dollars and a source of power: it is up to the Press to publicise civilised European libel procedures and insist that we get them too.

(10.4) The Intifada, now two years old, has brought the first chance for a civilised end to the Arab–Israeli conflict.

In this category, *civilised* is used in reference to supra-individual norms to describe the characteristics of a group and an already achieved state.

Sophisticated and Refined

(10.5) MR DAVID MELLOR, the Home Office Minister handling the Broadcasting Bill, is a civilised chap, the sort of Government minister you will find on a Friday night addressing the Putney Music Club ...

(10.6) Where the Healey is a fairly civilised blend of high-speed tourer and sporting pedigree, comfortable enough for long-distance Continental holidays as well as for Sunday afternoon thrashes through the countryside, the Cobra is just a beast.

As opposed to the previous categories, such use of *civilised* tends to refer to an individual entity and a state already achieved.

Well-Mannered

(10.7)   Lady Julie observes ... the extraordinarily civilised behaviour of the Eritreans; their exemplary treatment of prisoners ('We will insult you with our compassion') ...

(10.8)   Other plus-points are civilised lift queues ...

In this category, *civilised* refers to the characteristics of an individual's behaviour and a state already achieved.

Well-looked-after and cared-for

(10.9)   Her civilised paw curves round a glass.

(10.10)   It sounded a pleasant, civilised household to settle in until he had time to look around him ...

In this case, *civilised* denotes the very opposite of neglect, referring to the behaviour of an individual and a state already achieved.

Table 10.3 summarises the uses of *civilised* in our corpus through the two categories of 'Relation to individual versus group' and 'State achieved versus state to be achieved'.

Uses of *Wenming* Extracted from the BCC

Table 10.4 provides a summary of our annotation categories for *wenming* and their frequency in our sample of 200 examples drawn from the BCC.

Table 10.4 shows that, in keeping with our English corpus, the most frequent use of *wenming* relates to 'cultured and developed'. However, this similarity does not imply translational equivalence (see more below), and not surprisingly our category of 'Cultured, developed and well-mannered' was labelled differently by our Chinese team than the English category 'Cultured and developed' even after the harmonisation process. This is because this use of *wenming* tends to be

Table 10.3 *Characteristics of the uses of* civilised *(in order of frequency)*

Annotation category	Relation to individual versus group	State achieved versus state to be achieved
1 Cultured and developed	Group reference	State achieved
2 Governed by law and regulations	Group reference	State achieved
3 Sophisticated and refined	Individual reference	State achieved
4 Well-mannered	Individual reference	State achieved
5 Well-looked-after and well-cared-for	Individual reference	State achieved

Table 10.4 *Frequency and annotation categories for* wenming *in our sample of 200 examples (BCC)*

Annotation category	Frequency
1 Cultured, developed and well-mannered	131 (65.5%)
2 Modernised	33 (16.5%)
3 Accountable, responsible and environmentally friendly	28 (14%)
4 Civilised	8 (4%)

associated with good manners (see more below), unlike the comparable English category ('Well-mannered' is a different category for *civilised*; see Table 10.3).

Cultured, Developed and Well-Mannered

(10.11)　这个县开展争创'十星级文明户'活动,以家庭为单位,通过"自我申报,群众评议,支部审定,三榜定星"的方式进行。

This county initiated the '*Ten Star Wenming Household*' movement, taking households as units, by means of 'individual applications, public evaluations, Party branch approval, and a threefold approval system'.

(10.12)　站在校门口,那块市委和市政府授予的'文明学校'的有机玻璃牌子...

At the school gate there is a plexiglass plaquette which indicates that the municipal government has bestowed the title of 'Wenming School' on this organisation...

In this case, *wenming* not only refers to the public domain, but also describes states which are to be achieved by members of the public. This highlights the fact that *wenming* has a policy-related characteristic here, and this is further reinforced by the fact that, in this category, *wenming* frequently appears in slogans as a modifying adjective, as in extracts (10.11) and (10.12). In such collocations, *wenming* is often used in four- and six-character combinations (*sizi/liuzi-shuyu* 四字、六字熟语) (see Kádár 2007), which is a typical Chinese layout for routine formulae (see Coulmas 1979).

Such *wenming* uses are often interrelated with good manners, and in some cases in our corpus *wenming* is used with the expression *limao* 礼貌 ('politeness'), as in the following example:

(10.13)　在今年全国文明礼貌月活动中,解放军某部干部战士奋战三天,才把垃圾清除

During this year's National Wenming Limao Month, it took three days for the soldiers of the People's Liberation Army to remove the rubbish

Here, one can witness a near-tautology, in that it is very difficult to distinguish between the meanings of *wenming* and *limao* in the title 'National Wenming Limao Month'.

Not all uses of *wenming* in this category are found in titles, as the following example demonstrates:

(10.14) 同时,我也期盼广大市民'与文明同行,做文明乘客',相互尊重,平等友善地对待出租车驾驶员,理解和支持我们的工作。

At the same time, I also expect most citizens to 'proceed in a *wenming*ly way, and become a *wenming* passenger', respect each other mutually, be nice to taxi drivers, and understand and support our work.

Modernised

This category is close to the previous category of 'Cultured, developed and well-mannered', but *wenming* is often used here in the context of governmental modernisation policies, as the following examples illustrate:

(10.15) 石狮市永宁镇山边村为推进新农村建设,构建和谐社会,树立文明乡风,建立了村读书室 . . .

Shishi City, Yongning Township, Shanbian Village, to promote new countryside, well-structured and harmonious society and to encourage creating a *wenming* countryside atmosphere, created a village reading room . . .

(10.16) 第五个问题:电子书品种贫乏。面对如此的文明变革,传统出版社下一步应该怎么去做?

The fifth question: the lack of different varieties of ebooks. Faced with such *Wenming* Reform, what should traditional publishing houses do next?

In this category, *wenming* is used in routine formulae that describe future states to be achieved by the public.

Accountable, Responsible and Environmentally Friendly

Since Deng Xiaoping's reforms in the 1980s, China has undergone significant modernisation, particularly in the building and industrial sectors. As part of this modernisation programme, governmental organisations often initiated policies to reduce the negative impact that modernisation had on the public's welfare. As the following examples illustrate, *wenming* is often used to communicate such policies:

(10.17) 企业要将文明生产、文明施工作为科技进步和技术创新的重要条件和内容,

The key condition and content for the enterprise is to operate according to *wenming* production and *wenming* construction to achieve scientific progress and innovation.

(10.18) 北京中铁公司在打造企业品牌中,把文明施工、树立良好形象和信誉,作为重要内容。

Beijing China Zhongtie Corporation, in creating its industrial brand, made *wenming* construction and good image and social credit the most important requirements for promotion.

Here, *wenming* is used in routine formulae that refer to future states to be achieved by the public.

Civilised

The final category of *wenming* includes cases where it denotes 'civilised' in a historical sense:

(10.19)   胡锦涛说,中国和印度都是<u>文明古国</u>,也是发展中大国。

> Hu Jintao said, both China and India are <u>*wenming* ancient countries</u>, and both are large countries in development.

(10.20)   长城作为<u>文明古迹</u>

> The Great Wall is a <u>*wenming* landmark</u>

It is only this use of *wenming* which does not refer to a state to be achieved.

Table 10.5 summarises the uses of *wenming* in our corpus through the two categories of 'Relation to individual versus group' and 'State achieved versus state to be achieved'.

Contrastive Analysis

Table 10.6 summarises the differences and similarities between the uses of *civilised* and *wenming*. Table 10.6 is divided into two different parts: part 1 considers the uses that exist in both linguacultures, while part 2 considers the uses which exist in only one of the two linguacultures.

Wenming and *civilised* have two comparable uses (part 1 of Table 10.6), with the first being the most frequently employed in both linguacultures. While in this use both *wenming* and *civilised* refer to the state of groups, it is only *wenming* which refers to a state to be achieved, a fact which stems from the policy-related nature of this expression. The second comparable use of *wenming* is the least frequently employed in the Chinese corpus (see Table 10.4). This use is listed second in Table 10.6 because, to a certain degree, it is comparable to that of *civilised*. While in this case *wenming* still refers to

Table 10.5 *Characteristics of the uses of* wenming *(in order of frequency)*

Annotation category	Relation to individual versus group	State achieved versus state to be achieved
1 Cultured, developed and well-mannered	Group reference	State to be achieved
2 Modernised	Group reference	State to be achieved
3 Accountable, responsible and environmentally friendly	Group reference	State to be achieved
4 Civilised	Group reference	State achieved

Table 10.6 *Similarities and differences between the uses of* civilised *and* wenming

Civilised: Annotation category	Relation to individual versus group	State achieved versus state to be achieved	wenming: Annotation category	
Cultured and developed	Group reference	*Wenming*: state to be achieved *civilised*: state achieved	Cultured, developed and well-mannered	Part 1
Sophisticated and refined	*wenming*: group reference *civilised*: individual reference	State achieved	Civilised	
NIL: no equivalent use of *civilised*	Group reference	State to be achieved	Accountable, responsible and environmentally friendly	
NIL: no equivalent use of *civilised*	Group reference	State to be achieved	Modernised	
Well-mannered	Individual reference	State achieved	NIL: no equivalent use of *wenming*	Part 2
Well-looked-after and cared-for	Individual reference	State achieved	NIL: no equivalent use of *wenming*	
Governed by law and regulations	Group reference	State achieved	NIL: no equivalent use of *wenming*	

groups, whereas *civilised* refers to individuals, these uses are essentially comparable because both describe a state that has already been achieved. The examination of such uses of *wenming* has revealed that this category is the only non-policy-related one in Chinese, and this is why it does not relate to a future state of affairs. In summary, part 1 of Table 10.6 consists of two comparable uses of *wenming* and *civilised*, with the first of these uses being the most frequently employed in both linguacultures. However, these uses differ significantly and, as such, might lead to translational difficulties.

The uses detailed in part 2 of Table 10.6 might imply different translational difficulties than those in part 1 because they have no linguacultural equivalent. At this point, we hypothesise that this lack of linguacultural equivalence might trigger a preference for covert translation and cultural filtering, in comparison with the first use in part 1.

In the following discussion, we will only consider the first use in part 1 and those uses of *wenming* in part 2 for which there are no equivalent uses of *civilised*; that is, the first two rows in part 2. These uses of *wenming* are all group-related and indicate states to be achieved; that is, they are typically policy-related expressions.

Table 10.7 *Translations of* wenming

Wenming (Chinese original)	Category	Translation	Frequency	Percentage	
	Cultured, developed and well-mannered	*Civilised*	116	61.4%	Part 1
		Best	3	1.6%	
		Civility	2	1.1%	
		[Omission]	4	2.1%	
	Civilised	*Civilisation*	10	5.3%	
		[Omission]	5	2.6%	
	Accountable, responsible and environmentally friendly	*Civilised*	11	5.8%	Part 2
		Appropriately	4	2.1%	
	Modernised	*Civilised*	31	16.4%	
		Positive	3	1.6%	
Total			189	100%	

10.2.3.2 Phase Two: The English Translations of Wenming

Table 10.7 provides a summary of the *wenming* translations in our Chinese–English corpus of media texts. Table 10.7 has been aligned with Table 10.6: we divide the translational categories into two parts, as outlined above. We highlight those uses which, according to the research outcomes of phase one, may be particularly problematic for translators. As Table 10.7 shows, by far the most frequent translational solution in our corpus of Chinese–English translations includes instances of overt translation and the related lack of cultural filtering: in 158 cases, representing 83.6 per cent of the translations, *wenming* is translated according to its 'civilised' dictionary meaning. This tendency can be explained by referring to the category of Tenor in our translation model (Figure 10.1): since *wenming* tends to be used in communicating policies, both the source texts and the translated texts are characterised by a social relationship between an authoritative power (the government) and its citizens, who have to form alignment with the creator of the discourse in Goffman's (1981) sense.

In the following, we first examine translations of the 'Cultured, developed and well-mannered' use of *wenming*, representing part 1 in Table 10.7. We then examine the other two uses of *wenming* in part 2.

Cultured, Developed and Well-Mannered

Example (10.21) represents a typical overt translation of *wenming* in this category – here the translation relies on the dictionary meaning of 'civilised':

(10.21)　在仪式上,福州、西藏道路交叉口、黄皮公路、淮海路被列为'十大文明路口',70条、49条公交线路被评为'十大文明公交线路'。

> At the ceremony, the intersections at Fuzhou and Xizang roads, and Huangpi and Huaihai roads, were on the list of the Top 10 Civilised Intersections, and bus lines 70 and 49 were ranked among the Top 10 Civilised Bus Lines.

This is the standard translation when it comes to this most frequent use of *wenming*. As Table 10.7 shows, there are also a small number of covert translations in our corpus:

(10.22)　'星级文明户' 评选、寻找'最美家庭'等活动,社会主义核心价值观广泛传播,贫困地区文明程度显著提升。

> Activities, such as competition for best households and families, have been organised to carry forward cherished family traditions, spread core socialist values, and enhance social etiquette and civility.

In the Chinese original, *wenming* occurs as a qualifying adjective in the proper noun expression *Xingji-wenming-hu* 星级文明户 (lit. 'Wenming Household of Star-Award Level'). The translation resolves the difficulty of conveying the original message by using cultural filtering and converting the original proper noun into a common noun in English. This is clearly different from example (10.21), in which the translated text keeps intact the original Chinese proper noun.

Accountable, Responsible and Environmentally Friendly

When it comes to the categories 'Accountable, responsible and environmentally friendly' and 'Modernised', one witnesses a similar preference for overt translation and the consequent lack of cultural filtering, as in the case of the 'Cultured, developed and well-mannered' category. Thus our hypothesis that the lack of equivalence of use between Chinese and English could translate into cultural filtering turned out to be invalid. The following examples illustrate overt and covert translations of these uses of *wenming*:

Overt Translations

(10.23)　铁道部要求,要引导风景名胜区、宾馆饭店等履行社会责任,加强自律,倡导文明旅游。

> The ministry called for efforts to guide scenic spots, hotels and restaurants, among others, to fulfil their social responsibilities, strengthen self-discipline and advocate civilised tourism.

(10.24)　大力开展宣传教育活动,增强爱粮节粮意识,抑制不合理消费需求,减少'餐桌上的浪费',形成科学消费、健康消费、文明消费的良好风尚。

China will launch publicity and education activities to enhance public awareness of food conservation, contain unnecessary consumption, reduce food waste and foster rational, healthy and <u>civilised consumption</u>.

Covert Translations

(10.25) 办法要求寄递企业规范操作和<u>文明</u>作业,避免抛扔、踩踏等行为。

The guideline also requires companies to deliver parcels <u>appropriately</u>, banning behaviour such as tossing and stamping on parcels.

(10.26) 坚持预防为主,深入开展爱国卫生运动,倡导健康<u>文明生活</u>方式,预防控制重大疾病。

We will, with emphasis on prevention, carry out extensive patriotic health campaigns, promote healthy and <u>positive lifestyles</u>, and prevent and control major diseases.

While the foreign reader of examples (10.23) and (10.24) may find the *civilised* collocations distinctly odd and culturally alien, this problem is resolved in examples (10.25) and (10.26) by cultural filtering. However, once again such cultural filtering is rare in our data because of the Tenor of the texts, which appears to preclude the creative adaptation of the Chinese text for a foreign, English-speaking audience.

10.2.3.3 Phase Three: Translation Task and Follow-Up Interviews

During the third phase of our research, we asked ten professional Chinese translators to translate eight utterances including *wenming* drawn from the BCC. We chose eight examples because phase one had revealed that *wenming* affords four different uses; that is, we provided two examples for each use. Our goal was to test whether translational tendencies (in particular, overt versus covert translation) can also be observed in our subjects' translations. We were particularly interested in finding out whether the fact that the task was unofficial – allowing for 'private' solutions – influences translational preferences. Table 10.8 shows our subjects' translational choices. As Table 10.8 shows, while the translators occasionally applied a cultural filter, such as by translating *wenming* in its 'Cultured, developed and well-mannered' use as 'model' and 'harmonious', they still mostly zeroed in on the overt translation 'civilised'. This outcome surprised our team because our subjects were expert translators. We can explain this phenomenon by referring to the category of Tenor: despite the private nature of the task, the official character of the text and the close connection between *wenming* and policy communication turned out to be dominant. Here we provide one example each of overt and covert translations of the use 'Cultured, developed and well-mannered':

Table 10.8 *Translations of* wenming *by Chinese translators*

Category	Translation	Number of translations	Frequency
Cultured, developed and well-mannered	*Civilised*	14	70%
	Model	3	15%
	Harmonious	1	5%
	Right	1	5%
	[Omission]	1	5%
Modernised	*Civilised*	15	75%
	Orderly	3	15%
	Courteous	1	5%
	Polite	1	5%
Accountable, responsible and environmentally friendly	*Civilised*	14	70%
	Good	6	30%
Civilised	*Civilised*	20	100%
Total		80	

(10.27) Translator 2's overt translation
Task sentence:
统计数据是在上海电视台的颁奖典礼上宣布的。在仪式上,福州、西藏道路交叉口、黄皮公路、淮海路被列为'十大文明路口',70条、49条公交线路被评为'十大文明公交线路'。

Translation:
The statistics were announced at the award ceremony of Shanghai TV. At the ceremony, Fuzhou, Xizang Road intersections, Huangpi Highway and Huaihai Road were listed as the 'top ten civilised intersections', and 70 and 49 bus lines were rated as the 'top ten civilised bus routes'.

(10.28) Translator 10's covert translation
Task sentence:
'星级文明户'评选、寻找'最美家庭' 等活动,促进社会主义核心价值观广泛传播,贫困地区文明程度显著提升。

Translation:
Activities such as the selection of 'Model Households' and the search for 'the most beautiful family' have promoted the wide dissemination of socialist core values and significantly improved the degree of civilisation in underdeveloped areas.

The following are excerpts from the interviews conducted with the translators of the above examples (10.27) and (10.28):

Translator 2 (overt translation of extract 10.27)
'这个十大文明路口' … 我就觉得既然人家都这么使用了呢(.),我就也这么使了。

Regarding this 'top ten civilised intersections' ... since others use this form (.) all the time, I opted for it as well.

Translator 10 (covert translation of extract 10.28)
我觉得外国人会不理解文明指的是什么。

I feel that foreigners may not understand the meaning of *wenming* in this context.

As the second excerpt shows, translators who applied covert solutions and cultural filtering usually referred to the fact that translating *wenming* as 'civilised' when announcing domestic Chinese policies may sound alien to foreigners. For us, this was a particularly important outcome: while in the case of our previous corpus of bilingual texts we did not want to speculate about the reasons why a small number of translators chose covert translation, the translators involved in the translation task revealed that their awareness of the difficulty that foreign readers might have in understanding the overt translation of *wenming* may be responsible for their choices. We will revisit this point below.

Some translators revealed their awareness of the complex meanings of *wenming*, which they argued they themselves do not always fully understand:

Translator 9
其实我也不太明白'星级文明户'到底指的是什么。

In fact, I myself do not understand exactly what 'star-level *wenming* household' describes.

10.2.4 Discussion

In this case study, we have used a bottom-up approach to the study of expressions associated with Chinese policies, such as *wenming*. That is, we did not assume that the expression *wenming* is inherently related to communicating policies, but rather we examined and categorised a number of its uses by applying a contrastive approach to fully understand exactly which of these uses occur in communicating policies. Our tripartite approach brought together this contrastive take and translation studies. It also helped us to venture beyond ethnocentric and overgeneralising views. For example, while we could have simply looked at Chinese policy expressions by using 'civilised' as a technical term and without considering deep-seated differences between *wenming* and *civilised*, such an approach would have unavoidably been ethnocentric.

The category of Tenor in our translation model (Figure 10.1), which relates to the relationship between the writer of the text and the potential addressee, proved useful for explaining the overriding frequency of overt translations of *wenming*. Since our corpus-based contrastive examination has revealed that most uses of *wenming* relate to communicating policies, it is obvious that in the Chinese linguacultural context translators tend to shy away from 'tampering' with the officially decreed meaning of *wenming*, and supposedly other similar expressions, because of the authority of the government. This is in line with the fact that many bilingual Chinese news outlets are designed essentially for domestic audiences (Kádár and Zhang 2019); that is, the main goal of these texts is to trigger alignment between the government and the local audience. It may be awareness of the international relevance of certain news items that led translators to opt for using covert translation and cultural filtering. While we cannot prove this point based on our bilingual media corpus, the interviews conducted with the translators following the translation task appear to confirm this hypothesis.

The complexities surrounding Chinese policy expressions, such as *wenming*, demonstrate why studying the translation of these expressions is fundamental for going beyond essentialist generalisations about Chinese language and politics, and language and politics in general. It is also important to rely on language-based translation models, such as the one presented in this chapter, when it comes to translational issues in language and politics, if our goal is to avoid the pitfalls outlined at the beginning of this book. We argued that in language and politics issues such as 'hospitable translation' are more important than more ideologised notions, such as 'empowering' certain groups through translation. We therefore believe that in the future study of translation in language and politics more bottom-up research needs to be dedicated to actual issues, such as how certain deeply culturally entrenched politically relevant notions can be appropriately translated to other linguacultures, instead of speculating about non-linguistic issues, such as the identity of the translator.

In this chapter, we have examined a key phenomenon in the field of politics and translation, by looking at the difficulty of translating a politically relevant term. Having covered key topics in the field of language and politics with the aid of our framework, in the following final chapter we summarise the contents of this book and propose vistas for future research.

10.3   Recommended Readings

Juliane House. 2024. *Translation: The Basics. 2nd Edition.* London: Routledge.

In this chapter, we applied House's model for the study of politically relevant data. Readers with interest in pragmatics-based translation in a more general sense are recommended to consult the book cited above, which provides a more comprehensive introduction to House's framework. In the following section, House (2024: 9–10) provides an overview of how the phenomenon of translation can be captured:

Translation is a procedure where an original text, often called 'the source text', is replaced by another text in a different language, often called the 'the target text' . . . Over the centuries, translation has been regarded both positively and negatively.

Positively, because translation can provide access to new ideas and new experiences that stem from a different language community, opening horizons that would otherwise remain unknown behind the barrier of another language. Negatively, because translated texts can never be 'the real thing': they remain something second-hand, a kind of inferior substitute for the original. From the positive perspective, translation has often been compared to an act of building bridges or extending horizons. Translators are valued because their act of mediating between different languages, cultures and societies provides an important service for people who only speak their mother tongue.

Seen from a negative perspective, any translation clearly lacks originality: it merely gives people access to a message that already exists in another language. So translation is, of its nature, a type of secondary communication. In the process of translating, an original communicative event is repeated in order to enable persons to understand and appreciate the original event, from which they would otherwise be excluded.

In translation, there is always both an orientation backwards to the original's message and an orientation forwards towards the communicative conditions of the intended readers, and towards how similar, 'equivalent' texts are written in the target language. This basic 'in-betweenness' of a translation can be called a 'double-blind relationship', which is a defining characteristic of translation.

Backwards orientation means that generally the content of the original text needs to be kept equivalent in the translated text. This type of equivalence is called semantic equivalence.

Esperança Bielsa and Antonio Aguilera. 2017. Politics of translation: A cosmopolitan approach. *European Journal of Cultural and Political Sociology* 4(1): 7–24.

It is important to consider the difficulty of translating certain political terms because this self-reflexive exercise helps us to avoid ethnocentrism and other pitfall types in the study of language and politics. Readers who have interest in how translation can help us to avoid ethnocentrism are recommended to consult the study of Bielsa and Aguilera, who explore a wide variety of issues relating to the relationship between translation and ethnocentrism. In the following section, Bielsa and Aguilera (2017: 14) outline what they call 'hospitable translation':

A politics of hospitable translation insists on the materiality of language, beyond any reduction of the linguistic to a set of ideas that are transferred from a source to a receiver, a reductionism of language to signification or discursivity, to mere communication. It is very close to the artistic processes that are capable of taking that hospitality to other means of expression, always around the senses, movements, and drives of human intelligence capable of establishing the means and the ends for everything that is human desire, in all its variety and multiplicity. Such a conception of language is placed before a linguistic idealism that emphasises signification or discursivity, believing that the signifying means are only instruments of information or communication, which leads to underrating not only the aesthetic aspect of language, but also those languages and cultures that are apparently distant from certain lines of progressive development. It is also placed before an idealist cosmopolitanism, which minimises or does not take seriously enough the real difficulties that exist for adopting the perspective of the other in one's own culture, ignoring the cultural resistances that emerge when one embarks on a translation that does not falsify, which attempts to offer hospitality to what is translated.

11 Conclusion

11.1 Retrospect

In the following, we provide short synopses of the contents of the chapters of this book.
- Chapter 1: We positioned our approach to language and politics and outlined the contents the present book.
- Chapter 2: We presented our analytic framework and discussed what we regard as the three major pitfalls in the field of language and politics: (1) following an ethnocentric view of one's data, (2) uncritically associating values with political actors and entities and (3) using one's research to prove a pre-held conviction.
- Chapters 3, 4, 5: We illustrated how our methodology can be used to avoid the pitfalls. We examined case studies drawn from different contexts, including Chinese and US news, interaction between representatives of former Yugoslavian states and the EU, and historical diplomatic exchange between Chinese and US politicians.
- Chapter 6: We considered how sensitive data can be analysed in a bottom-up, non-prejudiced way, by focusing on war crime apologies realised by representatives of Japan and Germany.
- Chapter 7: We discussed how it is possible to capture the interactional dynamics of single-source news reports, with the aid of a case study featuring public announcements in Chinese newspapers.
- Chapter 8: We examined how sociopolitical ideological convictions emerge in language use outside professional politics; that is, in interactions between ordinary social members. This study allowed us to capture the fundamental issue of how politics divides social members from a pragmatic point of view.
- Chapter 9: We studied disorderly events in political scenarios in English and Hungarian, by arguing that such scenarios are often ritual in nature, and so language use in them follows ritualised pragmatic patterns. As a case study, we looked at heckling in various contexts, including both the political and the non-political.

- Chapter 10: We examined a key topic in politics and translation, focusing on the difficulty of translating politically and sociopolitically relevant terms. In particular, we looked at translations of the Chinese policy-related expression *wenming* into English.

11.2 Prospect

In this book, we have argued that pragmatics represents an important line of inquiry in the field of language and politics which can neatly complement other bodies of research, in particular CDA. Pragmatics also provides a better alternative for the study of language and politics than many overgeneralising areas of inquiry, such as cultural discourse analysis. This is particularly the case if one adopts a bottom-up approach to political language use, like that proposed in this book. In a sense, the present book is only the beginning of a longer journey, and we believe that there are many areas in the field of language and politics which need further investigation, and in the following we outline some of these areas.

We have shown that sensitive topics such as war crimes can be 'safely' discussed with the *instrumentarium* provided by cross-cultural contrastive pragmatics. There are many sensitive topics worth studying, representing academic 'beehives' for scholars, provided that scholars do not set out to prove what they already know at the very outset. Many such issues centre on colonialist exploitations, on the racist treatment of minorities and on genocides. We believe that a current issue with such sensitive issues and related phenomena is that what someone is about to find out in their study is often proscribed; that is, the analysis of these phenomena is imprisoned by a dominant line of discourse. Linguists do not need to challenge such dominant lines of discourse but rather *venture beyond them*, by looking at exactly *how* language is used in a sensitive context. For example, following what we proposed about colonialism in this book, it would be fruitful to look at colonialism in many geopolitical contexts to tease out the language dynamics of how Western powers suppressed the indigenous population, and to consider whether such mechanisms are comparable to what we observed in the East Asian context. Such research would also allow us to avoid many futile discussions about the 'singularity' of a certain sensitive historical experience. For example, instead of speculating about whether it was Black People, Native Americans or Asians who suffered 'more' from colonialism, it would be more productive and less arrogant to compare corpora featuring particular contexts and acts of suppression involving members of these ethnic groups. By so doing, we would of course not challenge the dominant discourse that colonialism per se is evil – rather, we would go beyond this generally accepted notion and would not waste academic effort on confirming it again and again.

Another area which deserves further pragmatics-based academic attention involves activism. In this book, we only touched on activism in the context of animal rights. Surely, there are many other current areas of activism which emerge in daily clashes both online and offline. For example, the environment, abortion, wars, gender, migration and many other burning issues continue to divide social members worldwide, often triggering activism and leading to violent eruptions of emotions and subsequent altercation and violence. Haidt's (2012) findings therefore remain accurate because certain issues in politics and sociopolitics remain globally divisive and can be fruitfully studied through pragmatic analysis.

The translatability of political notions is also an area which should be further explored. We are surrounded by a whole network of expressions which seem to be 'neutral' but are in actual fact linguaculturally specific. Considering that the East–West dichotomy and other wild generalisations cannot serve as useful notions for the study of politically relevant data, a particular difficulty for the scholar of language and politics is that it is counterproductive to use such seeming 'universal' concepts for capturing political language use in whole blocks of linguacultures. For example, while 'democracy' is often described as a universally desirable notion, its use tends to be heavily influenced by local conventions. Also, 'democracy' can be used as an interactional resource both to gain the upper hand over countries whose government is understood to be 'non-democratic' and to camouflage non-democratic acts. A key area for future research would be to consider how cross-cultural pragmatic discrepancies among the uses of concepts such as 'democracy' manifest themselves in translation.

In summary, in this book we hope to have shown that language and politics is a vibrant and fascinating area, which is worth studying from a cross-cultural contrastive pragmatic point of view and through a bottom-up lens.

References

Aichholzer, Julian and Johanna Willmann. 2020. Desired personality traits in politicians: Similar to me but more of a leader. *Journal of Research in Personality* 88, 103990. https://doi.org/10.1016/j.jrp.2020.103990.

Aijmer, Karin. 2004. Pragmatic markers in spoken interlanguage. *Nordic Journal of English Studies* 3(1): 173–190. https://doi.org/10.35360/njes.29.

Almanna, Ali, and Juliane House. eds. 2023. *Translation Politicised and Politics Translated*. Berne: Peter Lang.

Anderson, Marta. 2021. The climate of climate change: Impoliteness as a hallmark of homophily in YouTube comment threads on Greta Thunberg's environmental activism. *Journal of Pragmatics* 178: 93–107. https://doi.org/10.1016/j.pragma.2021.03.003.

Archer, Dawn. 2008. Verbal aggression and impoliteness: Related or synonymous? In Derek Bousfield and Miriam Locher (eds.), *Impoliteness in Language: Studies on Its Interplay with Power in Theory and Practice*. Berlin: Mouton de Gruyter, 181–208. https://doi.org/10.1515/9783110208344.3.181.

Assmann, Alida, and Anja Schwarz. 2012. Memory, migration and guilt. *Crossings: Journal of Migration & Culture* 4(1): 51–65. https://doi.org/10.1386/cjmc.4.1.51_1.

Austin, John. 1962. *How to Do Things with Words*. Oxford: Oxford University Press.

Awwad, Mona. 2023. The failure of diplomatic mediations in the Syrian conflict: A comparative analysis. *Queios*. www.qeios.com/read/CLCHV3.

Ayyad, Ahmad. 2012. Uncovering ideology in translation: A case study of Arabic and Hebrew translations of the 'Roadmap Plan'. *Journal of Language and Politics* 11(2): 250–272. https://doi.org/10.1075/jlp.11.2.05ayy.

Baker, Michael J. 1999. Argumentation and constructive interaction. In Pierre Coirier and Jerry Andriessen (eds.), *Foundations of Argumentative Text Processing*. Amsterdam: University of Amsterdam Press, 179–202.

Barbé, Esther, Anna Herranz-Surrallés and Michał Natorski. 2015. Contending metaphors of the European Union as a global actor. *Journal of Language and Politics* 14(1): 18–40. https://doi.org/10.1075/jlp.14.1.02bar.

Barsalou, Lawrence. 1992. Frames, concepts and conceptual fields. In Adrienne Lehrer and Eva Feder Kittay (eds.), *Frames, Fields and Contrasts*. Hillsdale, NJ: Erlbaum, 21–74.

Baumgartner, M. C. 1989. *The Moral Order of a Suburb*. Cambridge: Cambridge University Press.

Baxter, Judith. 2002. Competing discourses in the classroom: A post-structuralist discourse analysis of girls' and boys' speech in public contexts. *Language in Society* 13(6): 827–842. https://doi.org/10.1177/0957926502013006760.

Beard, Adrian. 2000. *The Language of Politics*. London and New York: Routledge.

Beardsley, Kyle, David Cunningham and Peter White. 2018. Mediation, peacekeeping, and the severity of civil war. *Journal of Conflict Resolution* 63(7): 1682–1709. https://doi.org/10.1177/0022002718817092.
Beck, Ulrich. 2006. *The Cosmopolitan Vision*. Cambridge: Polity Press.
Bednarek, Monika. 2005. Frames revisited: The coherence-inducing function of frames. *Journal of Pragmatics* 37: 685–705. https://doi.org/10.1016/j.pragma.2004.09.007.
Bednarek, Monika 2011. Approaching the data of pragmatics. In Wolfram Bublitz and Neal R. Norrick (eds.), *Foundations of Pragmatics*. Berlin: Mouton, 537–560. https://doi.org/10.1515/9783110214260.537.
Bednarek, Monika and Helen Caple. 2012. *News Discourse*. London: Continuum.
Bendazzoli, Claudio. 2023. Breaching protocol and flouting norms on the European Parliament floor: Reactions from a micro- and macro-context perspective in 22 languages. *Contrastive Pragmatics* 4(1): 64–87. https://doi.org/10.1163/26660393-bja10072.
Benedict, Ruth. 1946. *The Chrysanthemum and the Sword: Patterns of Japanese Culture*. Boston MA: Mariner.
Bennett, Adrian. 1981. Interruptions and the interpretation of conversation. *Discourse Processes* 4(2): 171–188. https://doi.org/10.1080/01638538109544513.
Benoit, William L. 1995. *Accounts, Excuses and Apologies: A Theory of Image Restoration Strategies*. New York: State University of New York Press.
Bercovitch, Jacob and Jeffrey Rubin (eds.) 1994. *Mediation in International Relations: Multiple Approaches to Conflict Management*. Basingstoke: Palgrave Macmillan.
Bercovitch, Jacob and Scott Gartner. 2007. Is there method in the madness of mediation? Some lessons for mediators from quantitative studies of mediation. *International Interactions: Empirical and Theoretical Research in International Relations* 32(4): 329–354. https://doi.org/10.1080/03050620601011024.
Beres, Louis. 2015. Defending Israel against Iranian nuclear aggression: War, genocide, and international law. *Israel Journal of Foreign Affairs* 9(2): 179–188. https://doi.org/10.1080/23739770.2015.1049400.
Bergmann, Jörg R. 1998. Introduction: Morality in discourse. *Research on Language & Social Interaction* 31(3/4): 279–294, DOI: 10.1080/08351813.1998.9683594.
Bergman, Marc L. and Gabriele Kasper. 1991. The interlanguage of apologizing: Cross-cultural evidence. *University of Hawai'i Working Papers in ESL* 10(2): 139–176.
Bielsa, Esperança and Antonio Aguilera. 2017. Politics of translation: A cosmopolitan approach. *European Journal of Cultural and Political Sociology* 4(1): 7–24. https://doi.org/10.1080/23254823.2016.1272428.
Björkman, Beyza. 2011. Pragmatic strategies in English as an academic lingua franca: Ways of achieving communicative effectiveness? *Journal of Pragmatics* 43(4): 950–964. https://doi.org/10.1016/j.pragma.2010.07.033.
Blakemore, Scott. 2019. *Faith-Based Diplomacy and Interfaith Dialogue*. Leiden: Brill.
Blanchard, Robert, Vincent O'Donnell and Caroline Blanchard. 1979. Attack and defensive behaviors in the albino mouse. *Aggressive Behavior* 5(4): 341–352. https://doi.org/10.1002/1098-2337(1979)5:4<341::AID-AB2480050403
Blommaert, Jan and Jef Verschueren. 1991. The pragmatics of minority politics in Belgium. *Language in Society* 20(4): 503–531. https://doi.org/10.1017/S0047404500016705.

Blum-Kulka, Shoshana, Juliane House and Gabriele Kasper. eds. 1989. *Cross-cultural Pragmatics: Requests and Apologies*. Norwood, NJ: Ablex.

Boese, Vanessa A. 2019. How (not) to measure democracy. *International Area Studies Review* 22(2): 95–127. https://doi.org/10.1177/2233865918815571.

Bolsover, Gillian. 2018. Slacktivist USA and authoritarian China? Comparing two political public spheres with a random sample of social media users. *Policy and Internet* 10(4): 454–482. https://doi.org/10.1002/poi3.186.

Bou-Franch, Patricia. 2022. Morality, aggression, and social activism in a transmedia sports controversy. *Language and Communication* 84: 33–45. https://doi.org/10.10 16/j.langcom.2022.02.001.

Boutonnet, Thomas. 2011. From local control to globalised citizenship: The civilising concept of wenming in official Chinese rhetoric. In Corrado Neri and Florent Villard (eds.), *Global Fences: Literatures, Limits, Borders*. Lyon: Université Jean Moulin-Lyon, 79–103.

Brady, William, Julian Wills, Dominic Burkart, John Jost and Jay van Bavel. 2019. An ideological asymmetry in the diffusion of moralized content on social media among political leaders. *Journal of Experimental Psychology: General* 148(10): 1802–1813. https://doi.org/10.1037/xge0000532.

Braithwaite, John 2000. Repentance rituals and restorative justice. *Journal of Political Philosophy* 8(1): 115–131. https://doi.org/10.1111/1467-9760.00095.

Breeze, Ruth. 2016. Negotiating alignment in newspaper editorials: The role of concur-counter patterns. *Pragmatics* 26(1): 1–19. https://doi.org/10.1075/prag.26.1.01bre.

Breeze, Ruth. 2020. Exploring populist styles of political discourse in Twitter. *World Englishes* 39(4): 550–567. https://doi.org/10.1111/weng.12496.

Brooks, Roy. 1999. *When Sorry Isn't Enough: The Controversy over Apologies and Reparations for Human Injustice*. New York: New York University Press.

Brown, Lucien and Pilar Prieto. 2017. (Im)politeness: Prosody and gesture. In Jonathan Culpeper, Michael Haugh and Dániel Z. Kádár (eds.), *The Palgrave Handbook of Linguistic (Im)Politeness*. London: Palgrave Macmillan. https://doi.or g/10.1057/978-1-137-37508-7_14.

Brown, Penelope and Stephen C. Levinson. 1987. *Politeness: Some Universals of Language Usage*. Cambridge: Cambridge University Press.

Bruff, Ian. 2013. The materiality of the body and the viscerality of protest. *Keynote talk presented at the Heckler Symposium*, Nottingham, July 2013.

Bull, Peter. 2013. The role of adversarial discourse in political opposition: Prime Minister's questions and the British phone-hacking scandal. *Language and Dialogue* 3(2): 254–272. https://doi.org/10.1075/ld.3.2.06bul.

Bull, Peter. 2017. Collectivism and individualism in political speeches from the UK, Japan and the USA: A cross-cultural analysis. *Politics, Culture and Socialisation* 1(2): 71–84. https://doi.org/10.3224/pcs.v6i1-2.06.

Bull, Peter and Anita Fetzer. 2010. Face, facework and political discourse. *Revue internationale de psychologie sociale* 23(2/3): 155–183. www.cairn.info/revue-internationale-de-psychologie-sociale-2010-2-page-155.htm.

Bull, Peter, Anita Fetzer and Dániel Z. Kádár. 2020. Calling Mr Speaker 'Mr Speaker': The strategic use of ritual references to the Speaker of the UK House of Commons. *Pragmatics* 30(1): 64–87. https://doi.org/10.1075/prag.19020.bul.

Cameron, Deborah. 2006. Ideology and language. *Journal of Political Ideologies* 11(2): 141–152. https://doi.org/10.1080/13569310600687916.

Carbaugh, Donal. 2007. Cultural discourse analysis: Communication practices and intercultural encounters. *Journal of Intercultural Communication Research* 36(3): 167–182. https://doi.org/10.1080/17475750701737090.

Carvalhaes, Claudio. 2011. 'Gimme de kneebone bent': liturgics, dance, resistance and a hermeneutics of the knees. *Studies in World Christianity* 14(1): 1–18. https://doi.org/10.1353/swc.0.0008.

Catford, J. C. 1964. *A Linguistic Theory of Translation: An Essay in Applied Linguistics*. Oxford: Oxford University Press.

Celermajer, Danielle. 2009. *The Sins of the Nation and the Ritual of Apologies*. Cambridge: Cambridge University Press.

Chafe, Wallace. 1994. *Discourse, Consciousness and Time*. Chicago: University of Chicago Press.

Chafe, Wallace. 2000. Loci in diversity and convergence in thought and language. In Martin Pütz and Marjolijn Verspoor (eds.), *Explorations in Linguistic Relativity*. Amsterdam: Benjamins, 101–124. https://doi.org/10.1075/cilt.199.08cha.

Chapman, Dennis. 1948. The combination of hecklers in the East of Scotland 1822 and 1827. *Scottish Historical Review* 27(104): 156–164. www.jstor.org/stable/25525959.

Chen, Songcen. 1989. *Politeness and Language*. Beijing: Commercial Press [in Chinese].

Chilton, Paul. 1990. Politeness, politics and diplomacy. *Discourse and Society* 1(2): 201–224. https://doi.org/10.1177/0957926590001002005.

Chilton, Paul. 2004. *Analysing Political Discourse: Theory and Practice*. London and New York: Routledge.

Chilton, Paul. 2011. Still something missing in CDA. *Discourse Studies* 13(6): 769–781. https://doi.org/10.1177/1461445611421360a.

Chilton, Paul and Christina Schäffner. eds. 2002. *Politics as Text and Talk: Analytic Approaches to Political Discourse*. Amsterdam: John Benjamins.

Chomsky, Noam. 1988. *Language and Politics*. Oxford: AK Press.

Chovanec, Jan. 2014. *Pragmatics of Tense and Time in News: From Canonical Headlines to Online News Texts*. Amsterdam: John Benjamins.

Chovanec, Jan and Marta Dynel. 2015. Researching interactional forms and participant structures in public and social media. In Marta Dynel and Jan Chovanec (eds.), *Participation in Public and Social Media Interactions*. Amsterdam: John Benjamins, 1–23. https://doi.org/10.1075/pbns.256.01cho.

Cienki, Alan. 2004. Bush's and Gore's language and gestures in the 2000 US presidential debates: A test case for two models of metaphors. *Journal of Language and Politics* 3(3): 409–440. https://doi.org/10.1075/jlp.3.3.04cie.

Ciftci, Hilal. 2022. Mediation as a diplomatic tool in Ottoman capitulations. *Codrul Cosminului* 28(1): 29–54. https://doi.org/10.4316/CC.2022.01.02.

Clark, Herbert H. 2006. Pragmatics of language performance. In Laurence L. Horn and Gregory Ward (eds.), *The Handbook of Pragmatics*. Oxford, Blackwell, 365–382. https://doi.org/10.1002/9780470756959.ch16.

Coetzee, Wayne Stephen. 2020. Doing research on 'sensitive topics': Studying the Sweden–South Africa arms deal. *Scientia Militaria: South African Journal of Military Studies* 48(2). https://doi:10.5787/48-2-1278.

Collins, Randall. 2004. *Interaction Ritual Chains*. Princeton: Princeton University Press
Cornejo, Marcela, Gabriela Rubilar and Pamela Zapata-Sepúlveda. 2019. Researching sensitive topics in sensitive zones: Exploring silences, 'the normal', and tolerance in Chile. *International Journal of Qualitative Methods* 18. https://doi.org/10.1177/1609406919849355.
Coulmas, Florian. 1979. On the sociolinguistic relevance of routine formulae. *Journal of Pragmatics* 3(3/4): 239–266. https://doi.org/10.1016/0378-2166(79)90033-X.
Cui, Zhihai. 2004. Liang Qichao and Japan: On the eastern study background of Liang Qichao's enlightenment thought. *Modern History Research* 4: 179–206.
Culpeper, Jonathan. 2011. *Impoliteness: Using Language to Cause Offence*. Cambridge: Cambridge University Press.
Culpeper, Jonathan, Derek Bousfield and Anne Wichmann. 2002. Impoliteness revisited: With special reference to dynamic and prosodic aspects. *Journal of Pragmatics* 35: 1545–1579. https://doi.org/10.1016/S0378-2166(02)00118-2.
Cunningham, William, John Nezlek and Mahzarin Banaji. 2004. Implicit and explicit ethnocentrism: Revisiting the ideologies of prejudice. *Personality and Social Psychology Bulletin* 30(10): 1332–1346. https://doi.org/10.1177/0146167204264654.
Dagtas, Banu. 2020. At the crossroads of the New Silk Road: News discourses in the Turkish press. *Communication and the Public* 4(4): 276–290. https://doi.org/10.1177/2057047319896214.
Delanty, Gerard. 2009. *The Cosmopolitan Imagination*. Cambridge: Cambridge University Press.
Deng, Fei, Li Zhang and Xu Wen. 2014. Exploring the non-symmetry of word derivation in Chinese–English translation: 'Wenming' for 'Civilization'. *Open Journal of Modern Linguistics* 4(3): 65–73. https://doi.org/10.4236/ojml.2014.43034.
Derrida, Jacques. 1998. *Monolingualism of the Other*. Stanford, CA: Stanford University Press.
De Seta, Gabriele. 2018. (Un)civil society in digital China, Wenming Bu Wenming: The socialization of incivility in postdigital China. International Journal of Communication 12: 21–30. https://ijoc.org/index.php/ijoc/article/view/6219/2344.
Diermeier, Daniel, Jean-François Godbout, Bei Yu and Stefan Kaufmann. 2012. Language and ideology in Congress. *British Journal of Political Science* 42: 31–55. https://doi.org/10.1017/S0007123411000160.
Ding, Xiaochang and Zhixiang Mao. 2000. *Study of Official Documents in Ancient China*. Hefei: Anhui Literature and Art Publishing House.
Dou, Weilin and Xiaoying Zhang. 2007. Cross-cultural pragmatic analysis of evasion strategy at Chinese and American regular press conferences – with special reference to the North Korean nuclear issue. *Caligrama (São Paulo. Online)* 3(2). https://doi.org/10.11606/issn.1808-0820.cali.2007.65490.
Douglas, Mary. 1999. *Implicit Meanings: Selected Essays in Anthropology*. London: Routledge.
Drew, Paul and Elizabeth Couper-Kuhlen. 2014. Requesting: From speech act to recruitment. In Paul Drew and Elizabeth Couper-Kuhlen (eds.), *Requesting in Social Interaction*. Amsterdam: John Benjamins, 1–34. https://doi.org/10.1075/slsi.26.01dre.

Dunmire, Patricia L. 2012. Political discourse analysis: Exploring the language of politics and the politics of language. *Language and Linguistic Compass* 6(11): 735–751. https://doi.org/10.1002/lnc3.365.
Edmondson, Willis. 1981. *Spoken Discourse: A Model for Analysis*. London: Longman.
Edmondson, Willis and Juliane House. 1981. *Let's Talk and Talk About: A Pedagogic Interactional Grammar of English*. München: Urban and Schwarzenberg.
Edmondson, Willis and Juliane House. 2011 (4th ed). *Einführung in die Sprachlehrforschung*. Tübingen: Narr.
Edmondson, Willis Juliane House and Dániel Z. Kádár. 2023. *Expressions, Speech Acts and Discourse: A Pedagogic Interactional Grammar of English*. Cambridge: Cambridge University Press. https://doi.org/10.1017/9781108954662.
Eelen, Gino. 2001. *A Critique of Politeness Theories*. Manchester: St. Jerome.
Egan, Charlie, Advaith Siddharthan and Adam Wyner. 2016. Summarising the points made in online political debates. In *Proceedings of the 3rd Workshop on Argument Mining, the 54th Annual Meeting of the Association for Computational Linguistics, Association for Computational Linguistics (ACL)*. Stroudsburg, PA, 134–143. www.aclweb.org/anthology/W16-2816.
Eisenstadt, Arthur A. 1958. Speech blocks: How to deal with them. *Today's Speech* 6(3): 13–15.
Fairbank, John K. 1982. *The Cambridge History of China. Volume 12, Republican China 1912–1949*. Cambridge: Cambridge University Press.
Fairclough, Isabela and Normal Fairclough. 2012. Argument, deliberation, dialectic and the nature of the political: A CDA perspective. *Political Studies Review* 11: 336–344. https://doi.org/10.1111/1478-9302.12025.
Fairclough, Norman. 1992. Discourse and text: Linguistic and intertextual analysis within discourse analysis. *Discourse & Society* 3(2): 193–217. https://doi.org/10.1177/0957926592003002004.
Fairclough, Norman. 1996. A reply to Henry Widdowson's discourse analysis: A critical view. *Language and Literature* 5(1): 49–56. https://doi.org/10.1177/096394709600500105.
Fairclough, Norman. 2003. 'Political correctness': The politics of culture and language. *Discourse & Society* 14(1): 17–28. https://doi.org/10.1177/0957926503014001.
Fairclough, Norman. 2010. Language and ideology. In Norman Fairclough (ed.), *Critical Discourse Analysis*. London: Routledge, 9–27.
Fauconnier, Gilles and Mark Turner. 2008. Rethinking metaphor. In Raymond W. Gibbs Jr (ed.), *The Cambridge Handbook of Metaphor and Thought*. Cambridge: Cambridge University Press, 53–66. https://doi.org/10.1017/CBO9780511816802.005.
Fetzer, Anita ed. 2013. *The Pragmatics of Political Discourse*. Amsterdam: John Benjamins.
Fetzer, Anita and Gerda Lauerbach. (eds.). 2007. *Political Discourse in the Media: Cross-cultural Perspectives*. Amsterdam: John Benjamins.
Field, Norma. 1995. The difficulty of apology: Japan's struggle with memory and guilt. *Japan Quarterly* 42(4): 405–418.
Fillmore, Charles. 1982. Frame semantics. In Linguistic Society of Korea (ed.), *Linguistics in the Morning Calm*. Seoul: Hanshin, 111–137.

Fiss, Owen M. 1986. Free speech and social structure. *Faculty Scholarship Series* (online). http://digitalcommons.law.yale.edu/fss_papers/1210.

Fitzmaurice, Andrew. 2003. *Humanism and America: An Intellectual History of English Colonisation, 1500–1625*. Cambridge: Cambridge University Press. https://doi.org/10.1017/CBO9780511490521.

Flowerdew, John. 2018. Critical discourse studies and context. In John Flowerdew and John E. Richardson (eds.), *The Routledge Handbook of Critical Discourse Studies*. New York: Routledge, 165–178.

Fousek, John. 2000. *To Lead the Free World: American Nationalism and the Cultural Roots of the Cold War*. Chapel Hill and London: University North Carolina Press.

Fendrick, Reed J. 2012. Diplomacy as an instrument for national power. In J. Boone Bartholomees (ed.), U.S. Army War College Guide to National Security Policy and Strategy. Retrieved from www.jstor.org/stable/pdf/resrep12115.16.pdf.

Fetzer, Anita. 2008. The expression of non-alignment in British and German political interviews: Preferred and dispreferred variants. *Functions of Language* 15(1): 35–63. https://doi.org/10.1075/fol.15.1.04fet.

Friedman, Elie. 2017. Evasion strategies in international documents: When 'constructive ambiguity' leads to oppositional interpretation. *Critical Discourse Studies* 14(4): 385–401. https://doi.org/10.1080/17405904.2017.1292932.

Friedman, Elie, Zohar Kampf and Meital Balmas. 2017. Exploring message targeting at home and abroad: The role of political and media considerations in the rhetorical dynamics of conflict resolution. *International Journal of Communication* 11: 1597–1617. https://ijoc.org/index.php/ijoc/article/view/4658.

Furko, Peter. 2017. Manipulative uses of pragmatic markers in political discourse. *Palgrave Communications* 3, 17054. https://doi.org/10.1057/palcomms.2017.54.

Gal, Susan. 1989. Language and political economy. *Annual Review of Anthropology* 18: 345–367.

Gal, Susan. 2015. Politics of translation. *Annual Review of Anthropology* 44: 225–240.

Geis, Michael L. 1987. *The Language of Politics*. New York: Springer.

Geis, Michael L. 1995. *Speech Acts and Conversational Interaction*. Cambridge: Cambridge University Press. https://doi.org/10.1017/CBO9780511554452.

Garfinkel, Harold. 1964. Studies of the routine grounds of everyday activities. *Social Problems* 11(3): 225–250. https://doi.org/10.2307/798722.

George, Alexander L. 1991. *Forceful Persuasion: Diplomacy as an Alternative to War*. Washington, DC: United States Institute of Peace Press.

Gibney, Mark, Rhoda E. Howerd-Hassmann, Jean-Mark Coicaud and Niklaus Steiner. eds. 2008. *The Age of Apology*. Philadelphia: Pennsylvania University Press.

Gilboa, Eytan. 2001. Diplomacy in the media age: Three models of uses and effects. *Diplomacy and Statecraft* 12(2): 1–28. https://doi.org/10.1080/09592290108406201.

Glaurdic, Josip. 2013. The owl of Minerva flies only at dusk? British diplomacy on the eve of Yugoslav wars. *East European Politics & Societies* 27(3): 545–563. https://doi.org/10.1177/0888325413484

Goffman, Erving. 1956. *The Presentation of Self in Everyday Life*. New York: Doubleday.

Goffman, Erving. 1967. *Interaction Ritual. Essays on Face-to-Face Behavior*. Garden City, NY: Doubleday.

Goffman, Erving. 1971. *Relations in Public: Microstudies of the Public Order.* London: Harper & Row.

Goffman, Erving. 1974. *Frame Analysis: An Essay on the Organization of Experience.* Cambridge, MA: Harvard University Press.

Goffman, Erving. 1979. Footing. *Semiotica* 25(1–2): 1–30. https://doi.org/10.1515/semi.1979.25.1-2.1.

Goffman, Erving. 1981. *Forms of Talk.* Philadelphia: University of Pennsylvania Press.

Grainger, Karen. 2002. Politeness or impoliteness? Verbal play on the hospital ward. Retrieved from https://extra.shu.ac.uk/wpw/politeness/grainger.htm.

Gu, Chonglong. 2018. Mediating 'face' in triadic political communication: A CDA analysis of press conference interpreters' discursive (re)construction of Chinese government's image (1998–2017). *Critical Discourse Studies* 16(2): 201–221. https://doi.org/10.1080/17405904.2018.1538890.

Gu, Ming Dong. 2012. *Sinologism: An Alternative to Orientalism and Postcolonialism.* London: Routledge.

Guan, Shilin. 2017. Wan Qing Yingguo zhuHua waijiao daibiao jiguan yinxin, gongwen-de 'Zhongguo-hua' 晚清英國駐華外交代表機關印信、公文的'中國化' [The sinicization of official seals and papers of British diplomatic establishments in China in late Qing]. *Journal of National Museum of China* 166(5): 124–139.

Günthner, Susanne. 1996. The prosodic contextualization of moral work: An analysis of reproaches in 'why'-formats. In Elizabeth Couper-Kuhlen, Margaret Selting and Paul Drew (eds.), *Prosody in Conversation: Interactional Studies.* Cambridge: Cambridge University Press, 271–302.

Guo, Weidong. 2003. 'Zhaohui' yi Zhongguo waijiao wenshu jindai fanshi de chugou '照會'與中國外交文書近代範式的初構 [The 'diplomatic note' and the initial format of modern diplomatic documents in China]. *Historical Research* 3: 92–102.

Gürkan, Emrah. 2015. Mediating boundaries: Mediterranean go-betweens and cross-confessional diplomacy in Constantinople, 1560–1600. *Journal of Early Modern History* 19(2–3): 107–128. https://doi.org/10.1163/15700658-12342453.

Habermas, Jürgen. 1979. *Communication and the Evolution of Society* (trans. T. McCarthy). New York: Beacon.

Haidt, Jonathan. 2012. *The Righteous Mind: Why Good People Are Divided by Politics and Religion.* London: Penguin.

Halliday, Michael A. K. (revised by C. Matthiessen). 2004. *An Introduction to Functional Grammar.* London: Arnold.

Halmari, Helena. 2008. On the language of the Clinton–Dole presidential campaign debates: General tendencies and successful strategies. *Journal of Language and Politics* 7(2): 247–270. https://doi.org/10.1075/jlp.7.2.04hal.

Hao, Shiyuan. 2004. The origin of the Chinese word 'nationality'. *Ethnic Study* 6: 60–69 (in Chinese).

Harré, Rom. 1987. Enlarging the paradigm. *New Ideas in Psychology* 5 (1): 3–12. https://doi.org/10.1016/0732-118X(87)90039-0.

Harris, Sandra. 1991. Evasive action: How politicians respond to questions in political interviews. In Peter Scannell (ed.), *Broadcast Talk.* London: Sage, 76–79.

Harris, Sandra. 2001. Being politically impolite: Extending politeness theory to adversarial political discourse. *Discourse & Society* 12(4): 451–472. https://doi.org/10.1177/0957926501012004003.

Harris, Sandra, Karen Grainger and Louise Mullany. 2006. The pragmatics of political apologies. *Discourse and Society* 17(6): 715–737. https://doi.org/10.1177/0957926506068429.

Haugh, Michael. 2013. Im/politeness, social practice and the participation order. *Journal of Pragmatics* 58, 52–72. https://doi.org/10.1016/j.pragma.2013.07.003.

Haugh, Michael, Dániel Z. Kádár and Rosina Márquez Reiter. Eds. 2023. *Offence and Morality*, special issue, *Language & Communication* 87.

Hayes, Carlton J. 1931. *The Historical Evolution of Nationalism*. New York: Macmillan.

He, Ping. 2007. The concept and enlightenment of civilization: China and Europe. *Research on Historical Theory* 4: 22–33 (in Chinese).

He, Qian. 2019. On wenming. *Forum of Political Science and Law* 1: 17–30 (in Chinese).

He, Yinan. 2007. Remembering and forgetting the war: Elite mythmaking, mass reaction, and Sino-Japanese relations, 1950–2006. *History and Memory* 19(2): 43–74. https://doi.org/10.2979/his.2007.19.2.43.

Hein, Patrick. 2010. Patterns of war reconciliation in Japan and Germany: A comparison. *East Asia* 27(2): 145–164. https://doi.org/10.1007/s12140-010-9106-z.

Hepple, Chris. 2003. The politics of speech act theory. *Journal of Language Culture and Communication* 5(2): 1–10.

Herring, Susan. ed. 1996. *Computer-Mediated Communication: Linguistic, Social and Cross-cultural Perspectives*. Amsterdam: John Benjamins.

Hills, Matt. 2015. Location, location, location: Citizen-fan journalists' 'set reporting' and info-war in the digital age. In Lincold Geraghty (ed.), *Popular Media Cultures*. London: Palgrave Macmillan. https://doi.org/10.1057/9781137350374_9.

Hinkel, Eli. 1997. Appropriateness of advice: DCT and multiple choice data. *Applied Linguistics* 28(1): 1–26. https://doi.org/10.1093/applin/18.1.1.

Hirata, Keiko and Mark Warschauer. 2014. *Japan: The Paradox of Harmony*. New Haven: Yale University Press.

Hodge, Bob and Louie Kam. 1998. *The Politics of Chinese Language and Culture: The Art of Reading Dragons*. London: Routledge.

Hoffman, Mark. 1991. Restructuring, reconstruction, reinscription, rearticulation: Four voices in critical interaction theory. *Millenium* 20(2): 169–185. https://doi.org/10.1093/oso/9780190463427.003.0005.

Hooghe, Marc. 2008. Ethnocentrism. In William A. Darity (ed.), *International Encyclopedia of the Social Sciences*. 2nd Edition. New York, McMillan, 11–12.

Hoppe-Graff, Siegfried, Theo Herrmann, Peter Winterhoff-Spurk and Roland Mangold. 1985. Speech and situation: A general model for the process of speech production. In Joseph P. Forgas (ed.), *Language and Social Situations*. New York: Springer, 81–95.

Horelt, Michel-Andre von. 2019. *Dramas of Reconciliation: A Performance Approach to the Analysis of Political Apologies in International Relations*. Berlin: Nomos.

Horton, Paul. 2011. School bullying and social and moral orders. *Children & Society* 25 (4): 268–277. https://doi.org/10.1111/j.1099-0860.2011.00377.x.

House, Juliane. 1971. *Theoretical Aspects of Translation*. MA thesis, University of Toronto.

House, Juliane. 1973. Of the limits of translatability. *Babel* 19: 166–167. https://doi.org/10.1075/babel.19.4.06hou.

House, Juliane. 1977. A model of assessing translation quality. *Meta* 22: 103–109. https://doi.org/10.7202/003140ar.
House, Juliane. 1986. Acquiring translational competence in interaction. In Juliane House and Shoshana Blum-Kulka (eds.), *Interlingual and Intercultural Communication: Discourse and Cognition in Translation and Second Language Acquisition Studies*. Tübingnen: Narr, 179–192.
House, Juliane. 1989. Politeness in English and German: The functions of please and bitte. In Shoshana Blum-Kulka, Juliane House and Gabriele Kasper (eds.), *Cross-Cultural Pragmatics: Requests and Apologies*. Norwood, NJ: Ablex, 96–119.
House, Juliane. 1996. Contrastive discourse analysis and misunderstanding. In Marlis Hellinger and Ulrich Ammon (eds.), *Contrastive Sociolinguistics*. Berlin: Mouton de Gruyter, 345–361.
House, Juliane. 1997. *Translation Quality Assessment: A Model Revisited*. Berlin: Narr.
House, Juliane. 2006. Communicative styles in English and German. *European Journal of English Studies* 10(3): 249–267. https://doi.org/10.1080/13825570600967721.
House, Juliane. 2015. *Translation Quality Assessment: Past and Present*. London: Routledge.
House, Juliane. 2018. *Translation: The Basics*. London: Routledge.
House, Juliane. 2024. *Translation: The Basics*. 2nd Edition. London and New York: Routledge.
House, Juliane and Dániel Z. Kádár. 2020. T/V pronouns in global communication practices: The case of IKEA catalogues across linguacultures. *Journal of Pragmatics* 161: 1–15. https://doi.org/10.1016/j.pragma.2020.03.001.
House, Juliane and Dániel Z. Kádár. 2021a. Altered speech act indication: A contrastive pragmatic study of English and Chinese Thank and Greet expressions. *Lingua* 264: 103162. https://doi.org/10.1016/j.lingua.2021.103162.
House, Juliane and Dániel Z. Kádár. 2021b. *Cross-Cultural Pragmatics*. Cambridge: Cambridge University Press. https://doi.org/10.1017/9781108954587.
House Juliane and Dániel Z. Kádár. 2023. Speech acts and interaction in second language pragmatics: A position paper. Language Teaching. https://doi.org/10.1017/S0261444822000477.
House, Juliane and Dániel Z. Kádár, Fengguang Liu and Yulong Song. 2023. Aggression in diplomatic notes: A pragmatic analysis of a Chinese–American conflict in times of colonisation. *Text & Talk* 43(6): 755–776. https://doi.org/10.1515/text-2021-0036.
Huang, Xingtao. 2007. The formation and historical practice of modern concepts of 'civilization' and 'culture' in the late Qing Dynasty and the early Republic of China. *Knowledge of Literature and History* 3: 153–160 (in Chinese).
Hudson, James and Amy Bruckman. 2004. The bystander effect: A lens for understanding patterns of participation. *Journal of the Learning Sciences* 13(2): 165–195. www.jstor.org/stable/1466904.
Ide, Sachiko. 1989. Formal forms and discernment: Two neglected aspects of universals of linguistic politeness. *Multilingua* 8(2–3): 223–248. https://doi.org/10.1515/mult.1989.8.2-3.223.
Ihalainen, Pasi. 2006. Between historical semantics and pragmatics: Reconstructing past political thought through conceptual history. *Journal of Historical Pragmatics* 7(1): 115–143. https://doi.org/10.1075/jhp.7.1.06iha.

Ilie, Cornelia. 2003. Discourse and metadiscourse in parliamentary debates. *Journal of Language and Politics* 2(1): 71–92. https://doi.org/10.1075/jlp.2.1.05ili.

Izadi, Ahmad. 2015. Persian honorifics and im/politeness as social practice. *Journal of Pragmatics* 85: 81–91. https://doi.org/10.1016/j.pragma.2015.06.002.

Jacobs, Geert. 2011. Press conferences on the internet: Technology, mediation and access in the news. *Journal of Pragmatics* 43(7): 1900–1911. https://doi.org/10.1016/j.pragma.2010.09.019.

Jacobs, Geert, Henk Pander Maat and Tom van Hout. 2008. The discourse of news management. *Pragmatics* 18(1): 1–8. https://doi.org/10.1075/prag.18.1.01jac.

Jacobs, Scott. 1982. The Rhetoric of Witnessing and Heckling: A Case Study in Ethnorhetoric. PhD Dissertation, University of Illinois at Urbana–Champaign.

Jacobs, Scott. 2002. Maintaining neutrality in dispute mediation: Managing disagreement while managing not to disagree. *Journal of Pragmatics* 34(10–11): 1403–1426. https://doi.org/10.1016/S0378-2166(02)00071-1.

Jacobs, Scott and Sally Jackson. 1993. Failures in higher order conditions in the organization of witnessing and heckling episodes. In: Frans H. van Eemeren, Scott Jacobs and Sally Jackson (eds.), *Reconstructing Argumentative Discourse*. Tuscaloosa, AL: University of Alabama Press, 140–169.

Jakobsen, Peter Vigo. 2011. Pushing the limits of military coercion theory. *International Studies Perspectives* 12(2): 153–170. https://doi.org/10.1111/j.1528-3585.2011.00425.x.

Jakobson, Roman. 1959. On linguistic aspects of translation. In Reuben A. Brower (ed.), *On Translation*. Cambridge, MA: Harvard University Press, 233–239.

Jacobsson, Kerstin and Jonas Lindblom. 2017. *Animal Rights Activism*. Amsterdam: Amsterdam University Press.

Jaworski, Adam and Nicholas Coupland. Eds. 1999. *The Discourse Reader*. London: Routledge.

Jiang, Xiangying. 2006. Cross-cultural pragmatic differences in US and Chinese press conferences: The case of the North Korea Nuclear crisis. *Discourse & Society* 17(2): 237–257. https://doi.org/10.1177/0957926506060249.

Jordan, Mel. 2011. Heckle, hiss, howl and holler. *Arts & the Public Sphere* 1(2): 117–119. https://doi.org/10.1386/aps.1.2.117_2.

Joseph, John. 2006. *Language and Politics*. Edinburgh: Edinburgh University Press.

Jucker, Andreas. 2005. Mass media communication from the seventeenth to the twenty-first century. In Anne Skaffari, Matti Peikola, Ruth Carroll, Risto Hiltunen and Brita Wårvik (eds.), *Opening Windows on Texts and Discourses of the Past*. Amsterdam: John Benjamins, 7–21. https://doi.org/10.1075/pbns.134.04juc.

Jucker, Andreas and Irma Taavitsainen. 2008. Apologies in the history of English: Routinized and lexicalized expressions of responsibility and regret. In Andreas Jucker and Irma Taavitsainen (eds.), *Speech Acts in the History of English*. Amsterdam: John Benjamins, 195–228.

Kádár, Dániel Z. 2007. *Terms of (Im)Politeness: On the Communicational Properties of Historical Chinese Terms of Address*. Budapest: Eotvos Lorand University Press.

Kádár, Dániel Z. 2012. Historical Chinese politeness and rhetoric. A case study of epistolary refusals. *Journal of Politeness Research* 8(1): 93–110. https://doi.org/10.1515/pr-2012-0006.

Kádár, Dániel Z. 2017. *Politeness, Impoliteness and Ritual: Maintaining the Moral Order in Interpersonal Interaction*. Cambridge: Cambridge University Press. https://doi.org/10.1017/9781107280465.

Kádár, Dániel Z. 2024. *Ritual and Language*. Cambridge: Cambridge University Press. https://doi.org/10.1017/9781108624909.

Kádár, Dániel Z. and Juliane House. 2019. Ritual frames: A contrastive pragmatic approach. *Pragmatics* 30(1): 142–168. https://doi.org/10.1075/prag.19018.kad.

Kádár, Dániel Z. and Rosina Marquez-Reiter. 2016. (Im)politeness and (im)morality: Insights from intervention. *Journal of Politeness Research* 11(2): 239–260. https://doi.org/10.1515/pr-2015-0010.

Kádár, Dániel Z., Vahid Parvaresh and Puyu Ning. 2019. Morality, moral order, and language conflict and aggression: A position paper. *Journal of Language Aggression and Conflict* 7(1): 6–31. https://doi.org/10.1075/jlac.00017.kad.

Kádár, Dániel Z. and Yongping Ran. 2015. Ritual in intercultural contact: A metapragmatic case study of heckling. *Journal of Pragmatics* 77: 41–55. https://doi.org/10.1016/j.pragma.2014.12.011.

Kádár, Dániel Z. and Sen Zhang. 2019. Alignment, 'politeness' and implicitness in Chinese political discourse: A case study of the 2018 vaccine scandal. *Journal of Language and Politics* 18(5): 698–717. https://doi.org/10.1075/jlp.18053.kad.

Kampf, Zohar. 2008. The pragmatics of forgiveness: Judgments of apologies in the Israeli political arena. *Discourse & Society* 19(5): 577–598. https://doi.org/10.1177/0957926508092244.

Kampf, Zohar. 2009. Public (non-)apologies: The discourse of minimizing responsibility. *Journal of Pragmatics* 41(11): 2257–2270. https://doi.org/10.1016/j.pragma.2008.11.007.

Kampf, Zohar. 2012. From 'There are no Palestinian people' to 'Sorry for their suffering': Israeli discourse of recognition of the Palestinians. *Journal of Language and Politics* 11(3): 427–447. https://doi.org/10.1075/jlp.11.3.06kam.

Kampf, Zohar. 2015. Political discourse analysis. In Karen Tracy (ed.), *The International Encyclopaedia of Language and Social Interaction*. New York: Wiley, 1–17.

Kampf, Zohar, Lee Aldar, Roni Danziger and Mia Schreiber. 2019. The pragmatics of amicable interstate communication. *Intercultural Pragmatics* 16(2): 123–151. https://doi.org/10.1515/ip-2019-0007.

Kampf, Zohar and Nava Löwenheim. 2012. Rituals of apology in the global arena. *Security Dialogue* 43(1): 43–60. https://doi.org/10.1177/0967010611431095.

KhosraviNik, Majid. 2010. The representation of refugees, asylum seekers and immigrants in British newspapers: A critical discourse analysis. *Journal of Language and Politics* 9(1): 1–28. https://doi.org/10.1075/jlp.9.1.01kho.

KhosraviNik, Majid and Mahrou Zia. 2014. Persian nationalism, identity and anti-Arab sentiments in Iranian Facebook discourses: Critical discourse analysis and social media communication. *Journal of Language and Politics* 13(4): 755–780. https://doi.org/10.1075/jlp.13.4.08kho.

Kim, Dam Hee and Nojin Kwak. 2022. When does incidental exposure prompt political participation? Cross-national research on the importance of individualism and collectivism. *International Journal of Communication* 16: 1737–1758. https://ijoc.org/index.php/ijoc/article/view/17479/3735.

Kirsch, Helen and Christian Welzel. 2019. Democracy misunderstood: Authoritarian notions of democracy around the globe. *Social Forces* 98(1): 59–92. https://doi.org/10.1093/sf/soy114.

Kissine, Mikhail. 2013. *From Utterances to Speech Acts*. Cambridge: Cambridge University Press.

Kohn, Hans. 2005. *The Idea of Nationalism: A Study in Its Origins and Background*. New Brunswick: Transaction Publishers.

Korey Lefteroff, Lindsay. 2005. Excessive heckling and violent behaviour at sporting events: A legal solution? *University of Miami Business Law Review* 119: 134–135. https://repository.law.miami.edu/umblr/vol14/iss1/4.

Körner, Robert, Jennifer Overbeck, Erik Körner and Astrid Schütz. 2022. How the linguistic styles of Donald Trump and Joe Biden reflect different forms of power. *Journal of Language and Social Psychology* 41(6): 631–658. https://doi.org/10.1177/0261927X221085309.

Krzyżanowski, Michal and Joshua Tucker. 2018. Re/constructing politics through social & online media: Discourses, ideologies, and mediated political practices. *Journal of Language and Politics* 17(6): 1–14. https://doi.org/10.1075/jlp.18007.krz.

Laineste, Liisi. 2011. Politics of state in a post-socialist state: A case study. In Villy Tsakona and Diana Elena Popa (eds.), *Studies in Political Humour: In between Political Critique and Public Entertainment*. Amsterdam: John Benjamins, 217–242.

Lakoff, George. 1995. Metaphor, morality, and politics, or, why conservatives have left liberals in the dust. *Social Research* 62(2): 177–213. www.degruyter.com/database/COGBIB/entry/cogbib.7062/html.

Lange, Deborah. 2010. Examples of diplomatic behavior: Backroom-bargaining and negotiations. In Deborah Lange (ed.), *Power and Influence*. London: Palgrave Macmillan, 121–135 .

László, Ervin. 2013. *Individualism, Collectivism, and Political Power: A Relational Analysis of Ideological Conflict*. New York: Springer.

Ledoux, Sarah and Peter Bull. 2017. Order in disorder: Audience responses and political rhetoric in speeches from the second round of the 2012 French presidential election. *Pragmatics and Society* 8(4): 520–541. https://doi.org/10.1075/ps.8.4.03led.

Lee, Seung-Hee and Hiroko Tanaka. 2016. Affiliation and alignment in responding actions. *Journal of Pragmatics* 100: 1–7. https://doi.org/10.1016/j.pragma.2016.05.008.

Lee-Wong, Song Mei. 2009. Discourse as communicative action: Validation of China's new socio-cultural paradigm Qiye wenhua 'enterprise culture'. *Pragmatics* 19(2): 223–239. https://doi.org/10.1075/prag.19.2.04lee.

Leech, Geoffrey. 2007. Politeness: Is there an East–West divide? *Journal of Politeness Research* 3(2): 167–206. https://doi.org/10.1515/PR.2007.009.

Leech, Geoffrey. 2008. *Language in Literature: Style and Foregrounding*. London: Routledge.

Levenson, Joseph R. 1953. *Liang Ch'i-ch'ao and the Mind of Modern China*. Cambridge, MA: Harvard University Press.

Levinson, Stephen. 1983. *Pragmatics*. Cambridge: Cambridge University Press.

Levinson, Stephen. 2017. Speech acts. In Yan Huang (ed.), *Oxford Handbook of Pragmatics*. Oxford: Oxford University Press, 199–216.

Lewiński, Marcin. 2010. *Internet Political Discussion Forums as an Argumentative Activity Type: A Pragmadialectical Analysis of Online Forms of Strategic Manoeuvring in Reacting Critically*. Amsterdam: Rozenberg Publishers.

Liang, Zhiping. 2020. Civilization confronted with test: Discourse change of contemporary Chinese civilization. *Zhejiang Social Sciences* 4: 4–12 (in Chinese).

Lind, Jennifer. 2009. Apologies in international politics. *Security Studies* 18(3): 517–556.

Liu, Wenming. 2010. The concept of *wenming* in China and Europe before the middle of the 19th century. *Journal of Capital Normal University* 5: 130–137 (in Chinese).

Luke, Allan. 1997. The material effects of the word: Apologies, 'stolen children' and public discourse. *Discourse: Studies in the Cultural Politics of Education* 18(3): 343–368. https://doi.org/10.1080/0159630970180303.

Lyddon, Peter. 1996. *The Fall and Rise of Coercive Diplomacy in the Balkans*. Doctoral dissertation, United States Army Command and General Staff College, Kansas.

Ma, Laurence. 2005. Urban administrative restructuring, changing scale relations and local economic development in China. *Political Geography* 24(4): 477–497. https://doi.org/10.1016/j.polgeo.2004.10.005.

Maley, Yon. 1995. From adjudication to mediation: Third party discourse in conflict resolution. *Journal of Pragmatics* 23(1): 93–110. https://doi.org/10.1016/0378-2166(94)00030-I.

Malinowski, Bronislaw. 1935. *Coral Gardens and Their Magic*. London: Routledge.

Mao, Yansheng and Xin Zhao. 2020. A discursive approach to disagreements expressed by Chinese spokespersons during press conferences. *Discourse, Context and Media* 37, 100428. https://doi.org/10.1016/j.dcm.2020.100428.

Marinelli, Maurizio. 2008. How to build a 'Beautiful China' in the anthropocene: The political discourse and the intellectual debate on ecological civilization. *Journal of Chinese Politeness Science* 23: 365–386. https://doi.org/10.1007/s11366-018-9538-7.

Márquez-Reiter, Rosina. 2022. Translocalisation of values, relationality and offence. *Language & Communication* 84: 20–32. https://doi.org/10.1016/j.langcom.2022.02.003.

Márquez-Reiter, Rosina and Michael Haugh. 2019. Denunciation, blame and the moral turn in public life. *Discourse, Context & Media* 28: 35–43. https://doi.org/10.1016/j.dcm.2018.09.001.

Marrus, Michael R. 2007. Official apologies and the quest for historical justice. *Journal of Human Rights* 6(1): 75–105. https://doi.org/10.1080/14754830601098402.

McCullough, Michael E., Frank D. Fincham and Jo-Ann Tsang. 2003. Forgiveness, forbearance, and time: The temporal unfolding of transgression-related interpersonal motivations. *Journal of Personality and Social Psychology* 84(3): 540–557. https://doi.org/10.1037//0022-3514.84.3.540.

McIlvenny, Paul. 1996. Heckling in Hyde Park: Verbal audience participation in popular discourse. *Language in Society* 27: 27–60. https://doi.org/10.1017/S004740450002042X.

Meyer, Michael. 2001. Between theory, method, and politics: Positioning of approaches to CDA. In Ruth Wodak and Michael Meyer (eds.), *Methods of Critical Discourse Analysis*. London: Sage, 14–31.

Mills, Sara and Dániel Z. Kádár. 2011. Politeness and culture. In Dániel Z. Kádár and Sara Mills (eds.), *Politeness in East Asia*. Cambridge: Cambridge University Press, 21–44.

Molek-Kozakowska, Katarzyna. 2013. Towards a pragma-linguistic framework for the study of sensationalism in news headlines. *Discourse & Communication* 7(2): 173–197. https://doi.org/10.1177/1750481312471668.

Mufwene, Salikoko. 2002. Colonisation, globalisation, and the future of languages in the twenty-first century. *International Journal on Multicultural Societies* 4(2): 162–193.

Munday, Jeremy. 2012. A translation studies perspective on the translation of political concepts. In Martin Burke and Melvin Richter (eds.), *Why Concepts Matter:*

Translating Social and Political Thought. Leiden: Brill, 41–58. https://doi.org/10.1163/9789004194908_003.

Munro, Lyle. 2012. The animal rights movement in theory and practice: A review of the sociological literature. *Sociology Compass* 6(2): 166–181. https://doi.org/10.1111/j.1751-9020.2011.00440.x.

Murau, Daniela. 2012. Strategic maneuvering in diplomatic mediation. *Journal of Argumentation in Context* 1(3): 331–377. https://doi.org/10.1075/jaic.1.3.04mur.

Murphy, James. 2015. Revisiting the apology as a speech act: The case of parliamentary apologies. *Journal of Language and Politics* 14(2): 175–204. https://doi.org/10.1075/jlp.14.2.01mur.

Musolff, Andreas. 2011. Metaphor in political dialogue. *Language and Dialogue* 1(2): 191–206. https://doi.org/10.1075/ld.1.2.02mus.

Musolff, Andreas. 2021. Researching political metaphor cross-culturally: English, Hungarian, Greek and Turkish L1-based interpretations of the Nation as Body metaphor. *Journal of Pragmatics* 183: 121–131. https://doi.org/10.1016/j.pragma.2021.07.011.

Nakajima, Keiko. 2002. The Key to Intercultural Communication: A Comparative Study of Speech Act Realization of Sympathy/Empathy. PhD thesis, University of Mississippi.

Natsheh, Bayan and Ahmad Atawneh. 2021. Image polishing in Trump's digital campaign: The case of speech act of persuasion. *Hebron University Research Journal* 16(1): 292–322.

Nelson, Lisa. 2002. Protecting the common good: Technology, objectivity, and privacy. *Public Administration Review* 62(1): 69–73. https://doi.org/10.1111/1540-6210.62.s1.12.

Nguyen, Tao Thi Phuong. 2012. *The Discourse of Wenming ('Civilisation'): Moral Authority and Social Change in Contemporary Shanghai*. Doctoral dissertation, University of Western Australia.

Nida, Eugene A. 1964. *Toward a Science of Translating: With Special Reference to Principles and Procedures Involved in Bible Translating*. Leiden: Brill.

Nida, Eugene A. and Charles Taber. 1969. *The Theory and Practice of Translation*. Leiden: Brill.

Nobles, Melissa. (ed.) 2008. *The Politics of Official Apologies*. Cambridge: Cambridge University Press.

Norrick, Neal. 1987. Functions of repetition in conversation. *Text* 7(3): 245–267. https://doi.org/10.1515/text.1.1987.7.3.245.

Obeng, Samuel G. 1997. Language and politics: Indirectness in political discourse. *Discourse & Society* 8(1): 49–83. https://doi.org/10.1177/0957926597008001004.

Ochs, Elinor. 1979. Introduction: What child language can contribute to pragmatics. In Elinor Ochs and Bambi Schieffelin (eds.), *Developmental Pragmatics*. New York: Academic Press, 1–20.

Osojnik, Janez. 2022. Predlog Socialistične stranke Slovenije oktobra 1990 za izvedbo plebiscita o samostojnosti Republike Slovenije in odzivi nanj v Sloveniji. *Studia Historica Slovenica* 22(2): 463–502.

Páez, Darío. 2010. Peticiones de perdón públicas o disculpas políticas y mejora de relaciones intergrupo: Un marco de análisis neo-Durkheimiano a las disculpas oficiales en tanto rituales. *Revista de Psicología Social* 25(1): 101–115. https://doi.org/10.1174/021347410790193504.

Pan, Yuling and Dániel Z. Kádár. 2011. *Politeness in Historical and Contemporary Chinese*. London: Bloomsbury.

Partington, Alan. 2012. Corpus analysis of political language. In The Encyclopedia of Applied Linguistics. https://doi.org/10.1002/9781405198431.wbeal0250.

Parvaresh, Vahid. 2018. 'We are going to do a lot of things for college tuition': Vague language in the 2016 U.S. presidential debates. *Corpus Pragmatics* 2: 167–192. https://doi.org/10.1007/s41701-017-0029-4.

Parvaresh, Vahid. 2022. On the morality of taking offence. *Language & Communication* 87: 60–71. https://doi.org/10.1016/j.langcom.2022.07.004.

Parvaresh, Vahid and Tamineh Tayebi. 2018. Impoliteness, aggression and the moral order. *Journal of Pragmatics* 132: 91–107. https://doi.org/10.1016/j.pragma.2018.05.010.

Pask-Hughes, Alexander. 2013. A critical discourse analysis approach to media framing of activists use of Twitter. In Twitter and Microblogging: Political, Professional and Personal Practices. https://eprints.lancs.ac.uk/id/eprint/68570.

Pérez-González, Luis. 2012. Translation, interpreting and the genealogy of conflict. *Journal of Language and Politics* 11(2): 169–184. https://doi.org/10.1075/jlp.11.2.

Planken, Brigitte. 2005. Managing rapport in lingua franca sales negotiations: A comparison of professional and aspiring negotiators. *English for Specific Purposes* 24(4): 381–400. https://doi.org/10.1016/j.esp.2005.02.002.

Popper, Karl. 1954. *The Logic of Scientific Discovery*. London and New York: Routledge.

Pym, Anthony. 2006. Globalization and the politics of translation studies. *Meta* 51(4): 744–757. https://doi.org/10.7202/014339ar.

Qu, Wensheng. 2017. 'Wangxia Tiaoyue' dingli qinghou Zhong-Mei wanglai zhaohui ji fanyi huodong yanjiu 《望廈條約》訂立前後中美往來照會及翻譯活動研究 (Research of communications between China and US and the translation activities of Caleb Cushing's mission to China in 1844). *Fudan Journal (Social Sciences Edition)* 1: 113–126.

Rahmani, Hossein. 2022. Avoiding sincere apologies among Iranian politicians and its cultural justification: A pragmatic study. *Language Related Research* 13(2): 285–319. https://doi.org/10.52547/LRR.13.2.10.

Ran, Yongping and Linsen Zhao. 2018. Building mutual affection-based face in conflict mediation: A Chinese relationship management model. *Journal of Pragmatics* 129: 185–198. https://doi.org/10.1016/j.pragma.2018.01.013.

Rao, Sameer. 2011. 'Joke's on You!' Stand-Up Comedy Performance and the Management of Hecklers. Master's thesis. https://bit.ly/4dO4hjP.

Reisigl, Martin and Ruth Wodak. 2001. The discourse historical approach. In Ruth Wodak and Michael Meyer (eds.), *Methods of Critical Discourse Analysis*. New York: Sage, 87–121.

Renner, Judith. 2015. Germany–Czech Republic. In Christopher Daase, Stefan Engert, Michel-André Horelt, Judith Renner and Renate Strassner (eds.), *Apology and Reconciliation in International Relations: The Importance of Being Sorry*. London: Routledge, 87–105.

Repe, Bozo. 2002. *Jutri je nov dan: Slovenci in razpad Jugoslavije*. Ljubljana: Mladinska knjiga.

Repe, Bozo. 2004. *Viri o demokratizaciji in osamosvojitvi Slovenije (III. del: osamosvojitev in mednarodno priznanje)*. Viri 19. Ljubljana: Arhivsko društvo Slovenije.
Richley, Sean. 2009. Hierarchy in political discussion. *Political Communication* 26(2): 137–152. https://doi.org/10.1080/10584600902851419.
Roberts, Craige. 2018. Speech acts in discourse context. In Daniel Fogal, Daniel Harris and Dan Moss (eds.), *New Work on Speech Acts*. Oxford: Oxford University Press, 317–359. https://doi.org/10.1093/oso/9780198738831.003.0012.
Rosenfeld, Cynthia. 2021. Do you hear the people sign? A critical discourse analysis of comments on a 2015 online petition opposing North Carolina's ag-gag law. *Journal of Applied Communication Research* 49(5): 515–531. https://doi.org/10.1080/00909882.2021.1965185.
Rosoux, Valérie. 2022. How not to mediate conflict. *International Affairs* 98(5): 1717–1735. https://doi.org/10.1093/ia/iiac058.
Said, Edward W. 1978. *Orientalism*. New York: Pantheon Books.
Saito, Hiro. 2015. The cultural pragmatics of political apology. Cultural Sociology 1–18. https://doi.org/10.1177/1749975515590243.
Santora, Kimberley. 2013. *Exploring Self-Orientation in Personal Narratives of Mental Health among a Latino Clinical Sample*. PhD thesis, Northeastern University, Massachusetts.
Šaric, Liljana. 2010. Domestic and foreign media images of the Balkans. In Ljiljana Šarić, Andreas Musolff, Stefan Manz and Ingrid Hudabiunigg (eds.), *Contesting Europe's Eastern Rim: Cultural Identities in Public Discourse*. Bristol: Multilingual Matters, 51–72.
Schaffer, Frederic. 1997. Political concepts and the study of democracy: The case of Demokaraasi in Senegal. *Political and Legal Anthropology Review* 20(1): 40–49. www.jstor.org/stable/24497983.
Schaffer, Frederic. 2000. *Democracy in Translation: Understanding Politics in an Unfamiliar Culture*. Ithaca: Cornell University Press.
Schaffer, Frederic. 2012. The boundaries of transnational democracy: Alternatives to the all-affected principle. *Review of International Studies* 38(2): 321–342. https://doi.org/10.1017/S0260210510001749.
Schaffer, Frederic and Jean-Paul Gagnon. 2023. Democracies across cultures: The hegemonic concept of democracy has dissolved, what happens now? *Democratic Theory* 10(1): 91–104. https://doi.org/10.3167/dt.2023.100107.
Schäffner, Christina. 2002. Political discourse analysis from the point of view of translation studies. *Journal of Language and Politics* 3(1): 117–150. https://doi.org/10.1075/jlp.3.1.09sch.
Schäffner, Christina. 2004. Metaphor and translation: Some implications of a cognitive approach. *Journal of Pragmatics* 36(7): 1253–1269. https://doi.org/10.1016/j.pragma.2003.10.012.
Schäffner, Christina. 2012. Unknown agents in translated political discourse. *Target* 24(1): 103–125. https://doi.org/10.1075/target.24.1.07sch.
Schank, Roger and Robert Abelson. 1977. *Scripts, Plans, Goals and Understanding*. Hillsdale, NJ: Erlbaum.
Schettino, Ilario. 2011. Is coercive diplomacy a viable means to achieve political objectives? www.e-ir.info/pdf/1693.

Schiffrin, Amanda. 2005. *Modelling Speech Acts in Conversational Discourse*. PhD thesis, University of Leeds.

Sclafani, Jennifer. 2017. *Talking Donald Trump: A Sociolinguistic Study of Style, Metadiscourse, and Political Identity*. London: Routledge.

Scott, Kate. 2021. The pragmatics of rebroadcasting content on Twitter: How is retweeting relevant? *Journal of Pragmatics* 184: 52–60. https://doi.org/10.1016/j.pragma.2021.07.022.

Searle, John. 1969. *Speech Acts: An Essay in the Philosophy of Language*. Cambridge: Cambridge University Press.

Searle, John. 1975. *A Taxonomy of Illocutionary Acts*. Minneapolis: University of Minnesota Press.

Searle, John. 1979. *Expression and Meaning: Studies in the Theory of Speech Acts*. Cambridge: Cambridge University Press. https://doi.org/10.1017/CBO9780511609213.

Setiyadi, Desi, Hersulastuti Hersulastuti and Siti Widayanti. 2018. The Second Workshop on Language, Literature and Society for Education. https://doi.org/10.4108/eai.21-12-2018.2282790.

Sharoff, Serge, Reinhard Rapp, Pierre Zweigenbaum and Pascale Fung. 2013. *Building and Using Comparable Corpora*. New York: Springer.

Shire, Mohammed. 2020. Dialoguing and negotiating with Al-Shabaab: The role of clan elders as insider-partial mediators. *Journal of Eastern African Studies* 15(1): 1–22. https://doi.org/10.1080/17531055.2020.1863099.

Shi-Xu. 2012. Why do cultural discourse studies? Towards a culturally conscious and critical approach to human discourses. *Critical Arts* 26(4): 484–503. https://doi.org/10.1080/02560046.2012.723814.

Sidnell, Jack. 2009. *Conversation Analysis: Comparative Perspectives*. Cambridge: Cambridge University Press.

Sifianou, Maria. 2013. The impact of globalisation on politeness and impoliteness. *Journal of Pragmatics* 55: 86–102. https://doi.org/10.1016/j.pragma.2013.05.016.

Silva, Daniel N. 2019. The pragmatics of chaos: Parsing Bolsarano's undemocratic language. *Trabalhos em Linguística Aplicada* 59(1). https://doi.org/10.1590/010318136852914202000409.

Silverthorne, Collin P. and Lee Mazmanian. 1975. The effects of heckling and media of presentation on the impact of a persuasive communication. *Journal of Social Psychology* 96(2): 229–236.

Siniver, Asaf. 2006. Power, impartiality and timing: Three hypotheses on third party mediation in the Middle East. *Political Studies* 54(4): 806–826. https://doi.org/10.1111/j.1467-9248.2006.00635.x.

Siniver, Asaf. 2022. The power to blame as a source of leverage: International mediation and 'Dead Cat Diplomacy'. *The Hague Journal of Diplomacy* 17: 1–32.

Smith, Dan. 2012. Language and discourse in conflict and conflict resolution. *Current Issues in Language and Society* 4(3): 190–214. https://doi.org/10.1080/13520529709615498.

Smith, Graham, Peter John and Patrick Sturgis. 2013. Taking political engagement online: An experimental analysis of asynchronous discussion forums. *Political Studies* 61(4): 709–730. https://doi.org/10.1111/j.1467-9248.2012.00989.x.

Smith, Nick. 2013. An overview of challenges facing public apologies. In Daniël Cuypers, Daniel Janssen, Jacques Haers and Barbara Segaert (eds.), *Public Apology between Ritual and Regret*. Leiden: Brill, 27–43.

Smith, Sonia. 2006. Where do hecklers come from? The origins of booing (online). https://bit.ly/3XhbkdT.

Sotirova, Nadezhda. 2021. 'Good job, but Bulgarian': Identifying 'Bulgarian-ness' through cultural discourse analysis. *Journal of International and Intercultural Communication* 14(2): 128–145. https://doi.org/10.1080/17513057.2020.1760919.

Spencer-Oatey, Helen. 2000. Rapport management: A framework for analysis. In Helen Spencer-Oatey (ed.), *Culturally Speaking: Managing Rapport through Talk across Cultures*. London: Continuum, 11–46.

Spencer-Oatey, Helen and Dániel Z. Kádár. 2015. The bases of (im)politeness evaluations: Culture, the moral order and the East–West debate. *East Asian Pragmatics* 1(1): 73–106. http://dx.doi.org/10.1558/eap.v1i1.29084.

Spencer-Oatey, Helen and Jianyu Xing. 2019. Interdisciplinary perspectives on interpersonal relations and the evaluation process: Culture, norms, and the moral order. *Journal of Pragmatics* 151: 141–154. https://doi.org/10.1016/j.pragma.2019.02.015.

Stalnaker, Robert. 1999. *Context and Content*. Oxford: Oxford University Press.

Stein, Ernesto. 2005. Preface. In Ernesto Stein (ed.), *The Politics of Policies*. Cambridge, MA: Harvard University Press, v–viii.

Stivers, Tanya. 2006. 'No no no' and other types of multiple sayings in social interaction. *Human Communication Research* 30(2): 260–293. https://doi.org/10.1111/j.1468-2958.2004.tb00733.x.

Stopfner, Maria. 2013. *Streitkultur im Parlament: Linguistische Analyse der Zwischenrufe im österreichischen Nationalrat*. Tübingen: Narr.

Sugiyama Lebra, Takie. 1983. Shame and guilt: A psychocultural view of the Japanese self. *Ethos* 11(3): 192–209. www.jstor.org/stable/639973.

Sun, Qiuyun. 2006. Civilization: Connotation and changes – an analysis of an important concept in humanities and social sciences research. *Journal of Huazhong University of Science and Technology* 2: 48–53 (in Chinese).

Svensson, Isak and Mathilda Lindgen. 2013. Peace from the inside: Exploring the role of the insider-partial mediator. *International Interactions: Empirical and Theoretical Research in International Relations* 39(5): 698–722. https://doi.org/10.1080/03050629.2013.834261.

Swain, Elizabeth Anne. 2015. Language, (Impoliteness) and Diplomacy: The Zinoviev Letter Affair. PhD thesis, University of Trieste.

Tagar, Michal R., Scott Morgan, Eran Halperin and Lida J. Skitka. 2014. When ideology matters: Moral conviction and the association between ideology and policy preferences in the Israeli–Palestinian conflict. *European Journal of Social Psychology* 44: 117–125. https://doi.org/10.1002/ejsp.1993.

Tannen, Deborah. 1979. What's in a frame? Service evidence for underlying expectations. In Roy Friedl (ed.), *New Directions in Discourse Processing*. Norwood, NJ: Ablex.

Tavuchis, Nicholas. 1991. *Mea Culpa: A Sociology of Apology and Reconciliation*. Stanford, CA: Stanford University Press.

Thornborrow, Johanna. 2002. *Power Talk: Language and Interaction in Institutional Discourse*. London: Routledge.

Tome, Vicente. 1992. Maintaining credibility as a partial mediator: United States mediation in Southern Africa, 1981–1988. *Negotiation Journal* 8: 273–289. https://doi.org/10.1007/BF01000468.

Turner, Victor. 1969. *The Ritual Process: Structure and Anti-structure.* New Brunswick and London: Transactions.

Turner, Victor. 1979. Frame, flow and reflection: Ritual and drama as public liminality. *Japanese Journal of Religious Studies* 6(4): 465–499.

Turner, Victor. 1982. *From Ritual to Theatre: The Human Seriousness of Play.* New York: PAJ Publications.

van Dijk, Teun A. 1988. Opinions and ideologies in the press. In Allan Bell and Peter Garrett (eds.), *Approaches to Media Discourse*. Oxford: Blackwell, 21–63.

van Dijk, Teun A. 1998. *Ideology: A Multidisciplonary Approach.* Thousand Oaks, CA: Sage.

van Dijk, Teun A. 2008. News, discourse, and ideology. In Karin Wahl-Jorgensen and Thomas Hanitzsch (eds.), *The Handbook of Journalism Studies*. New York: Taylor & Francis, 191–204.

van Dijk, Teun A. 2017. What is political discourse analysis? *Belgian Journal of Linguistics* 11: 11–52. https://doi.org/10.1075/bjl.11.03dij.

van Gelder, Maartje and Tijana Krstić. 2015. Introduction: Cross-confessional diplomacy and diplomatic intermediaries in the early modern Mediterranean. *Journal of Early Modern History* 19(2–3): 93–105. https://doi.org/10.1163/15700658-12342452.

van Leeuwen, Theo. 2009. Critical discourse analysis. In Jan Renkema (ed.), *Discourse, of Course: An Overview of Research in Discourse Studies*. Amsterdam: John Benjamins, 277–291.

Vanderveken, Daniel. 1990. *Meaning and Speech Acts.* Cambridge: Cambridge University Press.

Vasquez, Camila. 2011. Complaints online: The case of TripAdvisor. *Journal of Pragmatics* 43(6): 1707–1717. https://doi.org/10.1016/j.pragma.2010.11.007.

Verschueren, Jef. 2012. *Ideology in Language Use: Pragmatic Guidelines for Empirical Research.* Cambridge: Cambridge University Press. https://doi.org/10.1017/CBO9781139026277.

Vessey, Rachelle. 2016. Language ideologies in social media: The case of Pastagate. *Journal of Language and Politics* 15(1): 1–24. https://doi.org/10.1075/jlp.15.1.01ves.

Vladimirou, Dimitra, Juliane House and Dániel Z. Kádár. 2021. Aggressive complaining on social media: The case of #MuckyMerton. *Journal of Pragmatics* 177: 51–64. https://doi.org/10.1016/j.pragma.2021.01.017.

Vollmer, Helmut and Elite Olsthain. 1989. Apologies in German. In Shoshana Blum-Kulka, Juliane House and Gabriele Kasper (eds.), *Cross-cultural Pragmatics: Requests and Apologies*. Norwood, NJ: Ablex, 197–220.

Wahlström, Jarl. 2016. Constructing the moral order of a relationship in couples therapy. In Maria Borcsa and Peter Rober (eds.), *Research Perspectives in Couple Therapy.* New York: Springer. https://doi.org/10.1007/978-3-319-23306-2_10.

Wallensteen, Peter and Isak Svensson. 2014. Talking peace: International mediation in armed conflicts. *Journal of Peace Research* 51(2): 315–327. https://doi.org/10.1007/978-3-030-62848-2_10.

Wang, Georgette and Yi-Ning Katherine Chen. 2010. Collectivism, relations, and Chinese communication. *Chinese Journal of Communication* 3(1): 1–9. https://doi.org/10.1080/17544750903528708.

Ware, Dale P. and Raymond K. Tucker. 1974. Heckling as distraction: An experimental study of its effect on source credibility. *Speech Monographs* 41(2): 185–188. https://doi.org/10.1080/03637757409375834.

Watts, Richard. 1999. Language and politeness in early eighteenth-century Britain. *Pragmatics* 9(1): 5–20. https://doi.org/10.1075/prag.9.1.02wat.

Wehr, Paul and John Lederach. 1991. Mediating conflict in Central America. *Journal of Peace Research* 21(1): 85–98. https://doi.org/10.1177/0022343391028001009.

Weizman, Elda and Gonen Dori-Hacohen. 2017. On-line commenting on opinion editorials: A cross-cultural examination of face work in the *Washington Post* (USA) and *NRG* (Israel). *Discourse, Context & Media* 19: 39–48. https://doi.org/10.1016/j.dcm.2017.02.001.

Weisser, Martin. 2014. Speech act annotation. In Karin Aijmer and Cristoph Rühlemann (eds.), *Corpus Pragmatics: A Handbook*. Cambridge: Cambridge University Press, 84–114.

Widdowson, Henry. 1995. Discourse analysis: A critical view. *Language and Literature* 4(3): 157–172. https://doi.org/10.1177/096394709500400030.

Winfield, Betty H., Takeya Mizuno and Christopher E. Beaudoin. 2000. Confucianism and constitutions: Press systems in China and Japan. *Communication Law and Society* 5(3): 323–347. https://doi.org/10.1207/S15326926CLP0503_2.

Wodak, Ruth. 2007. Pragmatics and critical discourse analysis: A cross-disciplinary inquiry. *Pragmatics & Cognition* 15(1): 203–225. https://doi.org/10.1075/pc.15.1.13wod.

Wodak, Ruth. 2011. Critical linguistics and critical discourse analysis. In Jan Zienkowski, Jan-Ola Östman and Jef Verschueren (eds.), *Discursive Pragmatics*. Amsterdam: John Benjamins, 50–70. https://doi.org/10.1075/hoph.8.04wod.

Wodak, Ruth. 2017. Discourse about nationalism. In John Flowerdew and John E. Richardson (eds.), *The Routledge Handbook of Critical Discourse Studies*. Routledge, London, 403–420.

Wodak, Ruth and Salomi Boukala. 2015. European identities and the revival of nationalism in the European Union: A discourse historical approach. *Journal of Language and Politics* 14(1): 87–109. https://doi.org/10.1075/jlp.14.1.05wod.

Wodak, Ruth, Michal Krzyżanowski and Bernhard Forchtner. 2012. The interplay of language ideologies and contextual cues in multilingual interactions: Language choice and code-switching in European Union institutions. *Language in Society* 41, 157–186. https://doi.org/10.1017/S0047404512000036.

Wood, Linda A. and Rolf O. Kroger. 2000. *Doing Discourse Analysis: Methods for Studying Action in Talk and Text*. Thousand Oaks, CA: Sage.

Woolard, Katharyn A. 2020. Language ideologies. In James M. Stanlaw (ed.), *The International Encyclopedia of Linguistic Anthropology*. London: Wiley. https://doi.org/10.1002/9781118786093.ie.

Wuthnow, Robert. 1987. *Meaning and Moral Order: Explorations in Cultural Analysis*. Berkeley: University of California Press.

Xu, Hongwu. 2003. Further discussion on the concept of wenming. *Red Flag Manuscripts* 20: 5–7 (in Chinese).

Yamazaki, Jane. 2006. *Japanese Apologies for World War II: A Rhetorical Study.* London: Routledge.

Yang, Mayfair. 1997. Mass media and transnational subjectivity in Shanghai: Notes on (re)cosmopolitanism in a Chinese metropolis. In Aihwa Ong and Donald Nonini (eds.), *Ungrounded Empires: The Cultural Politics of Modern Chinese Transnationalism.* New York: Routledge, 287–321.

Yusupova, Guzel. 2019. Exploring sensitive topics in an authoritarian context: An insider perspective. Social Science Quarterly. https://doi:10.1111/ssqu.12642.

Zeman, Zbyněk. 1984. *Heckling Hitler: Caricatures of the Third Reich.* London: Tauris.

Zimmer, Oliver. 2003. *Nationalism in Europe, 1890–1940 (Studies in European History).* New York: Palgrave Macmillan.

Zoodsma, Marieke, Juliette Schaafsma, Thia Sagherian-Dickey and Jasper Friedrich. 2021. These are not just words: A cross-national comparative study of the content of political apologies. *International Review of Social Psychology* 34(1): 1–13. https://doi.org/10.5334/irsp.503.

Glossary

alignment: In its original Goffmanian sense, this concept refers to the attitude of acting as expected. In single-source discourse, triggering alignment involves the strategy of prompting the readers of the discourse to align themselves with actors prioritised by the author.

altered speech act realisation: Cases when a speech act is not used according to its default function.

ancillary methodology: A methodology which precedes or follows the basic contrastive analysis as a form of pilot or additional study.

animator: A person or a media product who or which actually produces an utterance or larger discourse units without being responsible for it.

bottom-up approach: Pragmatics as we interpret it in the present book follows a typically Popperian bottom-up view of language use; the philosopher Karl Popper argued that in any respectable empirical research one should aim to disprove rather than confirm one's hypothesis.

case study: A small-scale study investigating an individual case, as the name suggests. Case studies are often used as pilot studies, preceding larger-scale investigations, and they can also be used to further investigate what was initially observed in a corpus.

colonial conceptualisation: In language and politics, this concept refers to mostly Western conceptualisations which subordinate non-Western understandings of political notions to Western understandings.

colonisation: The process through which more powerful countries take control over less powerful countries to exploit them.

communicative strategy: Strategies which create a sense of alignment and rapport between, on the one hand, the writer/speaker and the political entities she represents and, on the other, the readers/recipients of what is being said. In other contexts, communicative strategies include means–ends behaviour in a broader sense.

complex participation: A type of participation which integrates both those who directly interact with one another and others such as bystanders and overhearers.

context: The surroundings in which expressions, speech acts and discourse are embedded (see also contextual embeddedness).

contextual embeddedness: In pragmatics, utterances and discourse are examined as phenomena embedded in the context where they occur. Thus context always needs to be considered in pragmatic analysis.

Contra: If an utterance is turned down entirely it is 'contra-ed' in our terminology.

conventionalised ritual features: Features of diplomatic correspondence and other genres where the pragmatic rights and obligations of the participants are preset.

corpora: Collections of machine-readable oral or written texts of varying size and character.

Counter: Countering points to speech acts through which an initiation is countered; that is, objected to but not entirely rejected.

covert aggression: Instances of language use which have an aggressive overtone but which are not explicitly aggressive and rude, and which do not allow the other to make the speaker accountable.

covert translation: A type of translation in which the function of the original text is maintained.

critical discourse analysis (CDA): An approach to the study of discourse, which views language as a form of social practice and which conducts analysis in order to resolve social issues.

cross-cultural pragmatics: The contrastive study of language use drawn from different linguacultures, data types, dialects and so on.

cultural discourse analysis: An area of study where scholars take a typically top-down view of data, assuming that cultures define the behaviour of their members.

cultural filtering: A procedure used in covert translation by the translator in order to make the translation compatible with target culture, discourse norms and preferences.

difficulty of translation: When it comes to the study of politically relevant notions, one is recommended to consider the problem that many notions which are often used in a universalistic way mean different things across linguacultures and can be difficult to translate.

diplomatic mediation: A process whereby a mediator or group of mediators are involved in resolving a conflict between two countries.

diplomatic notes: Documents through which diplomats communicate the demands or complaints of their country to representatives of another country.

discourse: The highest unit of analysis in our framework.

disorder: In political institutions, disorder is often kept regulated by the ritual frame of the institution.

escalation: In language and politics, escalation includes both cases when an event is out of control and others which involve verbal escalation in the form of increasing aggression.

ethnocentrism: Interpreting data drawn from other linguacultures according to the researcher's preconceptions originating in the researcher's own prioritised linguaculture.

expressions: The smallest unit of analysis in our analytic framework.

footing: The alignment of communication between the participants in an interaction.

foregrounding: The practice of emphasising (politically relevant) information, which is important for the author, and structuring discourse accordingly.

formulae: Set phrases which can be plugged unchanged into many different contexts.

frame: Due to the institutionalised and ritual nature of many scenes of politics, the pragmatic dynamics of politically relevant language use are often influenced or even determined by an invisible frame.

gambits: Expressions which lubricate the flow of an interaction and support both the speaker and his addressee.

heckling: The disruption of a public speech or performance which can be described systematically with the aid of a pragmatic typology outlined in the present book.

honorifics: Expressions which, by default, have a deferential meaning.

ideological convictions: Personal beliefs which may motivate the behaviour of social members and may lead to conflicts. Ideological convictions may also influence researchers and lead to top-down takes on political language use.

Illocutionary Force Indicating Devices (IFIDs): Expressions which convey the illocutionary force of an utterance.

initiate: Initiating refers to speech acts through which an exchange is started.

institutionalised: We interpret the institutionalised nature of a political situation on a scale; that is, politically relevant contexts tend to be institutionalised to some degree, but this degree may significantly vary across data types.

intertextuality: A relationship between texts through which a text is influenced by another text.

intertwined speech acts: Cases when various speech acts support one another to achieve a stronger pragmatic effect.

linguaculture: Culture manifested through patterns of language use.

linguistic anchor: Cross-cultural pragmatics as we interpret the field operates ideally with linguistically based concepts and methodologies, reflecting an endeavour to avoid using cultural and psychological concepts such as 'values', 'attitudes' and 'identity'.

mimesis: A phenomenon which includes repeating what the other says. In other situations, mimesis refers to talking according to a script, as in ritual scenarios where the speaker needs to follow strict rights and obligations.

moral order: The expected order of interactional and related social behaviour in a standard (often ritual) situation.

moral oughts: Feelings of what is morally compulsory in a particular setting. Moral oughts are often pitted against social oughts.

nationalism: A strong sense of identification with one's own nation. As we point out in this book, while nationalism has problematic overtones in many Western liberal linguacultures, it cannot be assumed that it has the same negative overtones in every linguaculture.

orientalism: A patronising Western academic attitude towards the study of data drawn from supposedly 'exotic' (non-Western) linguacultures.

overt translation: A type of translation in which the original text is, as far as possible, preserved, such that the linguistic forms and structures of the original text often 'shine through' the target text.

participation framework: Goffman's notion which describes the various interactional roles played by different participants in an interaction.

policy expressions: Expressions which communicate social policies and as such are widely used, often beyond the realm of politics in the strict sense of the word. Policy expressions tend to be politically relevant.

political language: The language use of both professional politicians and activists and other social members inside and outside institutions, mediated descriptions of political language use such as news articles, and language use in sociopolitically relevant situations centring on sociopolitically burning issues.

political negotiation: Negotiation conducted by political actors, often taking place in diplomatic settings under the ritual constraints of diplomatic language use and the etiquette it enforces.

politically relevant data: Any form of discourse which is potentially relevant for politics, such as social media.

postcolonial conceptualisations: In language and politics, postcolonial conceptualisations encompass mostly Western accounts which describe how language is used in former colonies. Such conceptualisations are often seemingly 'neutral' and, unlike colonial conceptualisations (see above), they do not compare postcolonial countries with Western ones.

pragmatics: The field of studying language in use in different contexts.

public announcements (*gong'gao*): A Chinese genre of public communication which is frequent in times of crisis and other important events.

public ritual apology: Painful historical events often trigger public apologies which have many ritual features such as the intensive display of remorse.

ratified role: Having a ritual right to fulfil a certain role in political settings.

re-contextualisation: A concept that refers to the fact that a text in a source-language context is inserted into a new context in the target language.

replicability: In pragmatic analysis one is advised to exclude idiosyncratic behaviour from the scope of one's inquiry, considering that one can only capture conventionalised patterns of language use by looking at replicable pragmatic patterns.

rites of anti-structure: Ritual scenarios in which the rights and obligations of the participants are turned upside down. In political institutions, rites of anti-structure often encourage the participants to act aggressively, but only within the norms set by the institution.

ritual: Politically relevant language use often emerges in ritual scenarios where the rights and obligations of the participants are strictly determined by a political institution.

ritual frame indicating expressions (RFIEs): Expressions indicating that the speaker is aware of who and where he is; awareness of the rights and obligations and related conventions holding for a particular standard situation.

Satisfy: Satisfying includes speech acts through which an Initiating speech act is satisfied.

sensitivity in language and politics: There are various topics in politics which are painful or difficult to talk about for certain social members or social groups, and as such are delicate for the researcher to study. There are various sensitivity types, as we point out in this book.

single-source and multiple-source discourse: A categorisation of discourse, by means of which a manifestation of discourse is categorised according to whether it was produced by a single author or multiple authors.

social injustices: In CDA, in particular, the goal of many researchers is to address and improve social injustices such as racism, issues relating to gender and sexual orientation and so on. Due to our radically pragmatic focus on language use, in this book we concentrate on patterns through which an injustice is talked into being and whether these patterns are recurrent in other linguacultures as well, instead of considering whether linguistic pragmatics can help resolve this injustice.

speech acts: An utterance considered an action and a key unit of analysis.

speech act–anchored approach: Using speech acts as a central category in the study of politically relevant data.

spontaneous data: In language and politics, many data types tend to be prepared, even though spontaneous data exist and their study is relevant whenever possible.

stance: The way in which speakers position themselves in relation to the ongoing interaction.

standard situation: A situation qualifies as 'standard' for language users if the speaker assumes, with a fair amount of certainty, that the partner is able and willing to perform a certain act.

strictly linguistic approach: Through studying the language of politics we are looking at our data without any previously held political conviction at the outset of our investigation.

Glossary

top-down: An analytic approach where scholars aim to prove what they already know at the very outset of their research.

types of discourse: A categorisation through which one can reflect on the nature of any politically relevant data under investigation.

units of analysis: The three units of pragmatics analysis which we propose include expressions, speech acts and discourse.

veiled threats: Aggressive behaviour hidden behind conventional diplomatic civility with the goal of coercing representatives of the other state to do what the aggressor wants.

veneer of a 'neutral' style: In diplomatic negotiations, the mediator often engages in conflicts under a veneer of being neutral.

war apology: Public ritual speech centring on the speech act category of Apologise, delivered by a ratified person – usually a representative of the state or a state minister – following crimes which have been perpetrated during a wartime situation.

Index

activism, 134, 135, 137, 199
aggression, 10, 70, 90, 151, 172
alignment, 9, 10, 21, 121, 122, 130, 137
ancillary methodology, 32
Austin, John, 2

Blum-Kulka, Shoshana, 59
bottom-up approach, 2
Breeze, Ruth, 23
Brown, Penelope, 57, 97, 121, 139

Chafe, Wallace, 27
Chilton, Paul, 7, 77, 136
Chomsky, Noam, 29
colonialism, 16
complex participation, 22
context, 2
convention, 10
corpus, 28
critical discourse analysis (CDA), 5, 7, 136, 137, 152, 175, 199
Cross-Cultural Speech Act Realisation Project (CCSARP), 83
cultural filtering, 11

deference, 75
diplomacy, 53, 54, 75
diplomatic mediation, 21, 52
diplomatic note, 74

East–West dichotomy, 16
Edmondson, Willis, 19, 21, 45, 58, 78, 122
escalation, 81, 144, 146
ethnocentrism, 4, 6, 7, 8, 10, 15, 48, 50, 98, 175

Fairclough, Norman, 5, 6, 7, 12, 22, 26, 73
Fetzer, Anita, 7, 122, 153, 157

Gambit, 122
Goffman, Erving, 56, 75, 129, 130, 131, 136, 137, 156, 167, 191

Haidt, Jonathan, 10, 134, 147, 151
Harris, Sandra, 77, 101, 123

heckling, 10, 155
House, Juliane, 3, 11, 16, 17, 19, 20, 23, 24, 33, 36, 45, 56, 57, 75, 78, 87, 111, 122, 123, 136, 144, 155, 175, 176, 179, 180, 183

ideology, 5, 6, 72, 133, 134, 137, 151, 176
'individualistic' and 'collectivistic' cultures, 4
intertextuality, 26

Joseph, John, 3, 5

Kádár, Dániel Z., 2, 3, 16, 17, 19, 20, 26, 33, 36, 56, 75, 76, 102, 105, 106, 111, 114, 115, 122, 123, 134, 135, 136, 139, 144, 153, 154, 157, 175, 178, 183, 187, 196
Kampf, Zohar, 55, 77, 101, 118
Krzyżanowski, Michal, 6, 29

Levinson, Stephen C., 20, 25, 57, 97, 121, 139
linguaculture, 4

mimesis, 140, 141
moral order, 106, 111, 134, 135
Mufwene, Salikoko, 73

participation framework, 4
political discourse analysis (PDA), 5
Popper, Karl, 2, 17, 77, 90
power, 5, 49, 53, 75, 78, 79, 90, 129, 155
pre-held conviction, 7

re-contextualisation, 179
replicability, 2
rights and obligations, 8
ritual, 8, 10, 15, 19, 21, 23, 25, 26, 27, 53, 54, 55, 56, 58, 75, 77, 78, 96, 97, 98, 130, 151, 153, 154, 155, 159, 161, 172

Said, Edward, 16
Schäffner, Christina, 7, 120, 176
Searle, John, 2
social media, 1

Index

speech acts, 2, 8, 18–22, 45, 53, 57, 58, 59, 69, 74, 77, 78, 96, 98, 102, 106, 120, 134–141, 146

standard situation, 10, 155, 156, 157, 164, 172

Thornborrow, Johanna, 32

translation, 11, 34, 43, 54, 76, 79, 87, 97, 102, 105, 175

Turner, Victor, 154, 164, 172

typology of speech acts, 11, 19, 60, 77

van Dijk, Teun, 49, 134, 152

veiled threat, 75

war apology, 98

Wodak, Ruth, 5, 22, 26, 34, 133

For EU product safety concerns, contact us at Calle de José Abascal, 56–1°, 28003 Madrid, Spain or eugpsr@cambridge.org.

www.ingramcontent.com/pod-product-compliance
Ingram Content Group UK Ltd.
Pitfield, Milton Keynes, MK11 3LW, UK
UKHW022246220326
469255UK00019B/388